Structured Programming with COBOL and JSP
VOLUME 1

John Barrie Thompson

D1212589

Chartwell-Bratt   **Studentlitteratur**

British Library Cataloguing in Publication Data
Thompson, John Barrie
    Structured Programming with COBOL and JSP.
    - (Polytechnic computing series).
    1. Computer systems. Programming. Techniques: Jackson
    Structured Programming
    I. Title II. Series
    005.1'13

ISBN 0-86238-154-1

© John Barrie Thompson and Chartwell-Bratt Ltd, 1989

Chartwell-Bratt (Publishing and Training) Ltd
ISBN 0-86238-154-1

Printed in Sweden,
Studentlitteratur, Lund
ISBN 91-44-30531-1

1 2 3 4 5 6 7 8 9 10 | 1993 92 91 90 89

PREFACE

This text presents a highly integrated approach to commercial software production using the well known design method JSP (Jackson Structured Programming) and the COBOL language. It is intended for students and practitioners who need to be able to design and implement well structured software to support commercial data processing applications. The text includes many detailed solutions to commonly encountered real world data processing problems and to reinforce the topics as they are presented, each chapter concludes with a set of practical tasks, the majority of which are machined-based.

Unlike many other programming books this text is concerned both with program design and implementation and the learning of these two important topics in an integrated fashion. Most design text books tend to approach problems in a general manner without regard to a particular programming language or implementation environment. To produce designs in such a way is attractive in theory but in practically all real world cases a programmer will be told or will know very well, before he starts his design, which programming language and implementation environment is to be used. Similarly, many COBOL language texts promise in their titles structured programming. However, frequently they do little more than present some structured coding and often very little of that. To imply that it is possible to produce an implemented well structured program without having first spent time on the design is simply misleading. Thus this text presents an integrated approach: that we will design our programs using JSP and that these designs will then be implemented in COBOL.

The text is divided into two volumes. Volume 1 covers all the basics of COBOL and JSP while volume 2 covers more advanced features. Each volume is divided into a number of parts, each of which comprises two to four chapters. Volume 1 consists of four parts. Part 1 is concerned with some general aspects of program production, diagrammatic and narrative aids which help program design, an overview of the COBOL language and details of the structure and handling of data files and the types of processing activities which commercial programs support. This part should be quickly read at first and then the relevant sections, for example those concerning files held on direct access devices, should be read again when the topics are encountered again later in the text. Part 2 covers the basic features of the JSP method. Part 3 provides sufficient information on the COBOL language to enable the implementation of straightforward COBOL applications. Part 4 is concerned with the design and implementation of typical data processing programs - report programs, analysis programs and programs which involve the matching of sequentially organised files.

Volume 2 consists of three further parts and follows directly on from volume 1. Part 5 covers further data and file handling including the use of tables and directly accessed files. Part 6 explains how large complex programs can be subdivided into simpler and more comprehensible parts each of which can then be designed and implemented in a straightforward manner. Finally in part 7 the design and implementation of more complex programs involving data validation, abnormal and exception error handling and interactive I/O is covered.

Each volume contains appendices which list the reserved words in COBOL 74 and COBOL 85 and give the formats for the COBOL statements. Also to aid the reader who does not have volume 1 to hand volume 2 contains an additional appendix which provides an overview of the JSP method and the standards introduced in volume 1 for the documentation and implementation of JSP designs. Indexes are included in both volumes: that given in volume 1 relates only to that volume but that given in volume 2 is cumulative.

In both volumes each topic is supported by numerous examples. In the earlier chapters these tend to be of a general nature, but the later chapters concentrate on examples relating to the data processing activities of an imaginary Mail Order Company (MOCO). The reader is strongly recommended to undertake the tasks detailed at the end of each chapter which will culminate in the design and implementation of a large suite of programs for MOCO. In the case of some topics, for example table handling and the processing of directly accessed files the reader will probably find it easier to work part of the way through a chapter, then carry out the relevant tasks before completing the remainder of the chapter. The main point is that the reader should ensure that some practical work is carried out on each topic. To understand program design and the use of a language it is necessary to design and implement programs. Only by doing this can confidence and expertise be acquired.

ACKNOWLEDGEMENTS

Acknowledgements are due to:

Michael Jackson for the JSP method.

Past and present colleagues at Sunderland Polytechnic who have helped with my understanding of the JSP method and its teaching. Thanks are especially due to Mike Wyvill, Helen Edwards, Marilyn Ramshaw and Alan Robson (now of Birmingham Polytechnic) who have read and commented on my drafts for this text.

My students who over the years have suffered my attempts to try to integrate my JSP and COBOL teaching. Special thanks to Doris Edema for her excellent transcription of my lectures without which this book would not have been possible and to Alan Staves (now of Micro Focus) for the development of the JSP Quality Assurance Tool which was used to check implementation of the programs given in this text against the standards promoted in it.

Avril Silk for wordprocessing the text.

Philip Yorke and the staff at Chartwell-Bratt for their help in the production of the text and the generation of the figures and diagrams.

Margaret Thompson for her constant support and painstaking checking of my drafts and the text and her assistance in the production of the index.

The National Computing Centre Ltd. for permission to reproduce their copyright S34 flowchart sheet and S44 record sheet.

Micro Focus for their Personal COBOL and COBOL/2 Workbench development environments which were used in the production of the example programs in the text.

The originators and developers of the COBOL language at whose request the following is reproduced:

COBOL is an industry language and is not the property of any company or group of companies, or of any organisation or group of organisations.

No warranty, expressed or implied, is made by any contributor or by the CODASYL Programming Lanugage Committee as to the accuracy and functioning of the programming system and language. Moreover, no responsibility is assumed by any contributor, or by the committee, in connection herewith.

The authors and copyright holders of the copyrighted material used herein

FLOW-MATIC (trademark of Sperry Rand Corporation), Programming for the UNIVAC I and II, Data Automation Systems copyrighted 1958, 1959, by Sperry Rand Corporation; IBM Commercial Translator Form No. F28-8013, copyrighted 1959 by IBM; FACT, DSI 27A5260-2760, copyrighted 1960 by Minneapolis-Honeywell

have specially authorised the use of this material in whole or in part in the COBOL specifications. Such authorisation extends to the reproduction and use of COBOL specifications in programming manuals or similar publications.

To Margaret Victoria and Richard John

CONTENTS

Volume 1

Volume 2

XV

PART 1
INTRODUCTION

This part of the text covers the basic knowledge needed before you can commence the design and implementation of programs using the Jackson Structured Programming method and the COBOL language. Chapter 1 provides overviews of the programming task and approaches to the design of programs, while chapter 2 details some of the diagramatic and narrative aids that are used in the design of programs. Chapter 3 provides an overview of the COBOL language so that you can appreciate how it has developed and the facilities it offers the programmer. Finally chapter 4 provides information on the structure and handling of data files and on the types of processing activities which commercial programs support.

CHAPTER 1

Program Production

1.1 Computer Programming Today

The computer systems, which now play such a major part in our world, consist of two highly integrated parts:

(i) the physical equipment itself - the hardware, and

(ii) the programs and routines - the software, which controls and instructs the various hardware sub-systems.

Each program or routine within a software system is a logically ordered set of instructions and associated data areas which enable the machine to perform a specific task. As the hardware and software systems have become more and more sophisticated these programs have become more complex and the process of producing them more difficult. Thus the task of computer programming may no longer be regarded as a craft but as a highly skilled technical process which must be carried out in a professional manner.

Today it is no longer sufficient for a programmer to be simply taught a high level language, such as COBOL, and then be expected to produce correct and reliable software using his own intuitive powers. The programmer must understand much more about the process of producing quality software (i.e. that which will truly satisfy its requirements) and he must be equipped with the necessary knowledge, skills and abilities which will enable him to carry out his work in an effective and efficient manner. Also, it must be realised that the software systems

3

which are produced today will often be used for many years, even outliving the original hardware on which they were intended to run, and that during this time they will be liable to many modifications and revisions to match changing user requirements. Currently such maintenance of software systems devours a massive proportion of the budget of many data processing departments and figures of up to 70% or even more are quoted. Because of this the programmer of today must ensure that the programs which he produces are well designed and are capable of being understood by other programming staff who may have to maintain them in the future.

This text therefore is not simply concerned with teaching the COBOL language but also covers the design of programs using the widely accepted method known as Jackson Structured Programming (JSP). This is because I believe that it is only by taking an integrated approach to the learning of a language and a design method that we can produce programmers with the abilities we need today. To learn a programming language you need to write programs but to be able to write programs you need to design them correctly and to design programs you must have a knowledge of your intended target language, thus an integrated approach is needed.

1.2 Software Systems and Data Streams

The types of software systems which support commercial applications are often extremely large and complex. They may be considered to consist of two main types of software: application software which has been developed to support particular commercial applications and system software which provides the run-time environment in which the application programs operate. For example, running a simple program which you have implemented on a personal computer will normally not only involve the execution of the application code that you have written, but also system code which forms part of the operating system for the machine you are using plus run-time system code written by the supplier of the programming language you have been using. Furthermore, running an application program in a mainframe/minicomputer environment could additionally involve the execution of system software provided by the supplier of a database system and/or an on-line transaction processing system.

4

In large systems several individual application programs may have to be grouped together to perform a particular task in its entirety. For example, a system which supports the handling of electricity meter readings, the updating of customer accounts and the issuing of bills would normally consist of several interlinked programs. Such a group of programs is referred to as a program suite. The programs within the suite are linked together via intermediate data files - the output from one program providing the input to the next and so on.

Application programs typically involve the handling of some input data, carrying out specified operations or processes on that data and producing output. The input and output may flow from or to files held on magnetic disk or tape or the interface may be with user-orientated peripheral devices such as terminals or printers. Each type of input or output may be regarded as a stream of data to or from the relevant device and it is the form of these data streams that will provide the base for our program designs. For software systems are simply a means to an end - the processing of data. It is the data itself that actually represents the core of our applications.

You should note that a data stream can take a variety of forms and is not always simply a stream of records to or from a storage device such as a magnetic disk or tape. For example, it could be messages from an operator console, print lines to a hard copy device or even data from a reference table held within the program itself.

1.3 Software Development

In the development of software systems seven distinct types of programming activity can be identified. These are:-

(i) Task analysis and specification of user requirements

This activity is not wholly the preserve of the Systems Analyst/Designer as often the initial program specification is very brief and incomplete. In many cases the programmer may simply receive an initial verbal specification of the form "can you write a 'little' program to ... ". In such cases it is necessary for the programmer to carry out a detailed analysis of the task and produce a specification of what is really required by the user. Even if a detailed specification has been produced by a system designer or by a senior programmer it is extremely unlikely that every question has been answered and all details fully specified - the programmer should therefore never assume that he will not be concerned with analysis and the specification of user requirements.

(ii) Software Design

Depending upon the size of the system to be developed a number of successively more detailed design phases will usually be carried out. For example we could start with the division of a system into program suites and then break down each suite into its constituent programs. The programs themselves could be further subdivided into their constituent parts and finally a detailed design for each software item would have to be developed.

The task of producing detailed software designs is probably the most important and difficult which a professional programmer has to carry out. Thus much of the activity in programming today is concerned with the use of methods which will ease the task of software design and ensure that it is carried out in a systematic and correct manner.

(iii) Implementation

This activity involves converting the detailed software designs produced during activity (ii) into the code for the relevant target programming language and then implementing the code on the computer. If the design work has been carried out correctly and the programmer is fully conversant with the programming language used this activity can be very straightforward.

(iv) Certification

The purpose of this activity is to ensure that the implemented software meets the users requirements. Certification is usually achieved by testing the system against the design specifications. It is usually assumed by the programmer that the design specifications do accurately represent the user's requirements. However, for a system to be considered fully certified these too should be demonstrated to be correct.

The testing of a software system may proceed through several stages for example, individual routine or module testing, then linked module testing, building up to complete program testing. This could be then followed by linked program testing, suite testing and finally complete system testing. The process can prove very difficult and time consuming because relevant tests have to be identified, test data generated, the test carried out and the results examined. In the case of many systems sufficient time is never available to fully exercise the software and their complete certification remains in doubt.

(v) Installation and "Go Live"

This activity involves making the software available to its users, ensuring that it operates correctly in its final environment and that the "Go Live", i.e. the first running of the software under real conditions, is successful.

(vi) Maintenance

Following the delivery of a software system, amendments and modifications become inevitable because of changes in user requirements or because errors have been detected that were not removed during certification. Due to the desire of users to add new capabilities, improve old ones or remove outdated procedures software normally exists in a volatile environment where change is the norm. Thus maintenance becomes a very necessary and time consuming task in most data processing departments.

When a programmer carries out maintenance work he must first understand the program he is about to modify. It is very unlikely that it will be a program he has written himself; so unless the program has been designed and implemented in a standard manner this first task may prove very time consuming and in some cases may actually prove impossible due to the complexity of the existing code. Having managed to understand the program he must then understand the modification that is required, decide how to undertake the modification, check that his changes have had no detrimental effects on the program, implement his planned changes, re-test the program, amend the relevant program documentation and put the program back into live use. The time that must be devoted to these tasks can be out of all proportion to the actual changes made. For example maintenance which may involve the addition of only a few lines of code may actually take a programmer several days or weeks to accomplish.

7

The problems associated with software maintenance are compounded because requests for amendments occur over and over again. As more and more changes are made to a program it becomes easy to destroy its original structure and logic so that eventually the only solution is to completely redesign and implement it all over again. Thus there is a clear case for adopting methods and procedures that will reduce the costs of maintenance.

(vii) Documentation

A professional approach to the task of software development should ensure that good and complete documentation is produced while undertaking activities (i)-(iv). Unfortunately this is often not the case and documentation is left until the system has become live, the staff concerned are then often moved to new tasks, or simply have little motivation to document what they have just completed. The resulting poor documentation that is produced becomes another problem for the unfortunate maintenance programmer in the years to come.

The remainder of this text is concerned with activities (ii), (iii) and (vii) for if we get these right then the problems associated with activities (iv) and (v) will be greatly reduced.

1.4 Approaches to the Design of Programs

Since we need to produce high quality programs which can be easily certified and maintained it is necessary that their design is undertaken in a systematic and logical fashion. Many different ways of designing programs have been developed by individuals and organisations which suit particular problem environments, calibre of staff and organisational and management structures. Details of many of these different approaches and the concepts underlying them can be found in texts such as those by Bleazard [1], Fairley [2], Longworth [3] and Yourdon [4].

In this text we are concerned primarily with the systematic design method known as JSP. However, it will be useful for you to have an appreciation of more informal approaches such as modular programming and top-down design and an understanding of the general concepts associated with structured programming.

8

1.4.1 Modular Programming

Programs which are large and/or complex need to be subdivided into parts so that each part can be easily understood, designed and implemented. This subdivision of programs also means that the work can be allocated between different programmers within a team and thus overall software delivery times can be reduced. Within the world of commercial data processing this process of program subdivision is usually referred to as modular programming. The result of this approach is the definition of a hierarchy of modules which represent the overall structure of the program. Such a modular structure for a simple payroll program is shown in figure 1.1. Ideally, each module corresponds to a particular program function and can be treated as a separate logical entity which can then be implemented and tested independently. Common modules can be specified which can then be shared between a number of different programs, for example, a module which provides the interface with a particular file type. Also changing requirements should be more easily met by simply changing existing modules or by adding new modules to the system.

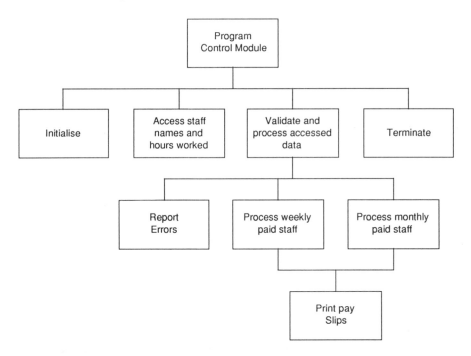

Figure 1.1 Modular Structure for a Payroll Program.

9

In producing a modular design there are two main approaches: top-down and bottom-up. The top-down approach is essentially an analytical process in that the program is considered as a whole and is then subdivided in progressively increasing levels of detail until the lowest level modules are identified. With the bottom-up approach the lower level modules are identified first. They are then combined at successively higher levels until the complete program is formed. The problem with this second approach is that it assumes that not only will it be possible to build up a final program structure which meets the specification but also that those initially specified lowest level modules will really represent the detailed solution to the problem. Thus a top-down approach or a combination of top-down and bottom-up is usually undertaken.

Although there are several recognised "rules" regarding modular programming such as:

(i)   The top level control module makes all major decisions regarding the flow of data through the process.

(ii) Each module must have one entry point and one exit point.

(iii) A module can only be entered from a higher level module i.e. no module can direct data flow to another processing routine at the same or at a higher level.

There is no clear concensus as to what actually constitutes a module. Some installations equate modules to simply a number of separately developed lines of code (typically 50/100) while others would place more weight on the separation of logical functions. However, the main problem with modular programming is that little is said about how each module itself should be structured.

1.4.2 Structured Programming

Following from work carried out in academic institutions the ideas of top-down development have been further formalised into a number of systematic approaches which are classed together under the general term structured programming. Again no consensus definition of structured programming exists but the main principles are those that were laid down by Professor E. W. Dijkstra [5] in 1972 viz:

(i) Successive refinement of design (essentially a top down approach).

(ii) The use of the three logical constructs of sequence, selection and iteration which are used in the design phase and are carried out into the target language coding.

(iii) Decomposition of the programs into partitions (essentially modules) which will assist in achieving more correct and more easily maintainable programs.

Particular structured programming approaches differ in the degree of emphasis placed upon particular principles and to the extent that concepts and embellishments have been added to them. However, what distinguishes them from modular approaches is the discipline of their application and the use of the three basic logical structures which had first been identified by Bohm and Jacopini [6].

These three logical structures are -

(i) Sequence - components follow one another in order

(ii) Selection - components are dependent upon conditions

(iii) Iteration - components are repeated while a condition is true

where in a program a component may be single instruction, or a group of instructions or an occurrence of a lower level component.

Many of the older and the more superficial accounts of structured programming equate it with the elimination of the GOTO statement in the implemented code. This view of structured programming followed from the controversy which raged between academics in the late 1960s and early 1970s. However, the total avoidance of the GOTO, particularly when using high level languages such as COBOL, can lead to awkward constructs which are difficult to understand. Therefore, it is now recognised that the implementation of well structured designs via controlled GOTOs is perfectly acceptable. In fact this concern with the final code has in many texts been overemphasised as it is the development of correct designs that should be the primary aim. (For the interested reader many of the original papers concerned with the GOTO controversy have been collected into convenient texts by Yourdon [7,8].)

1.4.3 Jackson Structured Programming (JSP)

Structured programming methods may be classed as function-driven, event-driven or data-driven. The best known example of this latter approach is JSP which was originally developed by Michael Jackson [9], during the period 1972 to 1974 and since then has been promoted by his company Michael Jackson Systems Ltd. (MJSL).

In Jackson's method the data streams on which the program operates are represented hierarchically using the three logical constructs of sequence, selection and iteration. The program structure is then derived from the composite structure produced by fusing together the individual data structures. The method consists of a number of distinct stages, each of which can be checked before the next stage is commenced. As each stage is carried out documentation of the design process is generated.

The main benefits which users of JSP recognise are:

(i)   that it generates non-inspirational designs, i.e. the solutions do not depend on the whims of the individual programmer,

(ii) the method is straightforward to teach and learn,

(iii) it leads to standard solutions for common data processing tasks,

(iv) the method is machine and programming language independent,

(v)   its self checking and documenting features lead to more reliable and maintainable software.

A further indication as to the success of JSP is that it has formed the core of the UK governments' mandatory standard method for all new programming projects started since 1982. This government approved method known as Structured Design Method (SDM) [10] has been developed by the Central Computer and Telecommunications Agency in collaboration with major government departments and it incorporates, in addition to the JSP method, techniques for assuring software quality and for formally testing the structure of the implemented programs.

1.5 Program Implementation

To produce a working program the design must be converted into code in the relevant target programming language. This code, once it is set up in a computer file must be translated by computer software into a machine processible form which can then be executed in a test environment. Thus, to produce a working program we must have a knowledge of: the target programming language, the creation of computer files, the translation system for the language and the run-time environment for the computer system which we are using.

1.5.1 Programming Languages

Just as there are many human languages there are many computer programming languages. Some of these are oriented towards a particular machine or range of machines, while others are machine independent and are usually designed for particular types of task. These machine independent languages are usually referred to as high-level languages as their features are far removed from the architecture of any particular manufacturer's computer.

Examples of high-level programming languages and their application areas are:

COBOL - commercial data processing applications
FORTRAN - scientific applications
ADA   - real time control applications
BASIC   - primarily developed as teaching language, this has a
          wide range of application areas.

Analysis of different high level languages and their technical strengths and weaknesses can be found in texts such as those by Pratt [11] and Ghezzi and Jazayeri [12]. As these latter authors emphasise, programming languages do not exist in a vacuum: they are simply tools which programmers use for producing software and hence should aid us in the implementation of our designs and not constrain us. Unfortunately, many of the most frequently used programming languages such as COBOL were developed long before the advent of structured programming and lack some of the features which can facilitate the straightforward implementation of structured designs. In cases such as these a set of implementation coding rules, such as those drawn up by the Central Computer and Telecommunications Agency for SDM [13], have to be employed. These often produce code which at first sight appears inelegant to some data processing practitioners. However, on closer inspection such code will be found to exactly mirror the structured design from which it was derived. It is more important that we preserve the good structure of our designs than we produce superficially elegant code because it is the design that must be the primary item that is referenced when maintenance has to be undertaken.

When learning a programming language it must be understood that to become really proficient in the use of that language you must at the earliest opportunity become familiar with the languages' reference manual for the machine you are to work on. A text such as this can guide and help you during the learning process but eventually you will have to use your skills on real applications and you will have to reference technicalities far beyond the scope of an introductory text, hence throughout the learning process after each new language feature is encountered, reference should be made to the relevant part of the language manual so that you become familiar with the manual's use.

1.5.2 Setting up a Program

The first stage of converting our design into an executable program is to produce code in our chosen programming language. The code is usually written out on special coding sheets, those for COBOL are detailed in Chapter 7. Having produced our code it should then be carefully checked to ensure no errors have been inadvertently introduced into it. The next stage is to set up our program code in a file, called a source file, on the computer. This is normally done in one of two ways. The first is by typing the program line by line directly into our source file via a terminal. To do this we normally use a program called an editor which will receive each line typed at the terminal and store it in our named source file. The editor can be used again later to amend the file should you discover any errors in it. The second way of entering the program is to use off-line data preparation facilities. Here the program is entered at a keyboard onto either punched cards, magnetic tape or disk. The file produced must then be transferred to the computer via a peripheral device which will interface with one of the computer's operating system routines to create a source file with the code for our program in it.

1.5.3 Translating Source Code

Once our code has been created in a source file on the computer it can be translated into machine processible form, i.e. it can be converted from text which we can understand to machine instructions which the hardware can execute. Depending on the way in which the translation is carried out the task is referred to as compiling or interpreting. With a compiled language such as COBOL programs are translated completely and then executed, with interpreted languages such as BASIC programs are translated and executed a statement at a time. Compiling and interpreting are carried out by programs known as compilers and interpreters. Since each programming language is different and since many languages have different dialects a different language translator is needed for each. So to be able to use a particular programming language or a dialect of it you must ensure that the relevant translator is available on the computer you wish to use.

To compile our COBOL source file we must run the relevant compiler against it. This will access our code, translate it, and produce an output

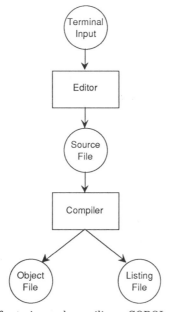

Figure 1.2 The process of entering and compiling a COBOL program.

15

file, called an object file, which contains the translated program code. The compiler will also normally produce a listing file which is a print out of your program plus details of any errors which the compiler has detected. If any of these errors are of a serious nature the compiler will not usually produce an object file as the program would not run correctly.

The process of entering a program on-line and compiling it is depicted by the system network diagram shown in figure 1.2.

1.5.4 Executing the Program

Having created an object file the program can finally be executed. To do this will require a knowledge of the COBOL run time environment provided on the computer system you are using. On some systems all you will have to do is type the name of the object file, however, on other systems additional commands will have to be given. This is illustrated by the following examples for different run time environments.

(a) Microsoft COBOL environment within MS-DOS operating system on an IBM PC compatible microcomputer.

(i) Compiling a COBOL program held in a file

```
PROG1.COB
```

will result in a object file being created named

```
PROG1.INT
```

(ii) The object file can then be executed using the command

```
RUNCOB PROG1
```

(b) Micro Focus WORKBENCH environment within MS-DOS operating system on an IBM PC compatible microcomputer.

Here the user is provided with a comprehensive development environment to create, edit, compile, run and test his COBOL programs. The package is designed around a hierarchy of menus which support and guide the user during the various stages.

(i) Pre-compiling (Checking) a COBOL program held in a file

```
PROG1.CBL
```

will result in the generation of the files:

```
PROG1.INT and PROG1.IDY
```

these are then used in the Animation phase of the package which supports program execution and debugging.

(ii) However, the program can be executed, once checked, without further user intervention from a DOS command line with

```
WB ZOOM PROG1
```

(c)   VAX COBOL environment within a VMS operating system environment on a Digital Equipment VAX minicomputer.

(i) Compiling a COBOL program held in a file

```
PROG1.COB
```

will result in a object file being created named

```
PROG1.OBJ
```

(ii) The object file must then be link loaded with system files using the command

```
LINK PROG1
```

which produces an executable program image in the file

```
PROG1.EXE
```

(iii) The executable program image is then run using the command

```
RUN PROG1
```

(d) ICL COBOL environment within a VME operating system environment on an ICL 2900 or 3900 series mainframe.

(i) Here compilation of a COBOL source file generates an object file whose name is determined by the PROGRAM-ID clause within the program (see chapter 7). Thus compilation of a COBOL program with the ID PROG1 will result in a file being created in the users object file library with the name

```
user-id STDOMF.PROG1
```

where user-id is the users identifier.

(ii) The object file can then be executed simply by giving the name as given with the PROGRAM-ID i.e.:

```
PROG1
```

In addition to the above commands on some systems files which are used by the program may have to be assigned to it before the command to execute it is given. Details of this will normally be found in a user manual for your COBOL run time system.

TASKS - CHAPTER 1

1. Find out how programs are entered onto the computer you are going to use.

2. If you intend to use an on-line editor to enter and amend your programs find out how to use it and practice editing a simple text file, e.g. a file containing a letter to a friend.

3. Find out if there are any example COBOL programs on your computer system, if there are, then practice compiling and running them.

CHAPTER 2

Diagrammatic Aids to Program Design

2.1 Flowcharts

Traditionally program designs have been produced with the aid of flowcharting symbols. Here a rectangular box is used to represent a process, a diamond shaped box is used to represent a decision and links between parts of the flowchart are represented by circles; an example is shown in figure 2.1.

Unfortunately often the programs produced with the aid of flowcharts have an extremely complex structure and are difficult to test and maintain. The main reason for this is that flowcharts do not really aid the constructive process of design, they simply allow the programmer to document his inspirational thoughts.

In fact one could say that the academic GOTO controversy of the 60s and 70s was misdirected by considering language features rather than design approaches and that Professor Dijkstra instead of publishing his paper [14] "Go To Statement Considered Harmful" should have written on "The Diamond Shape Considered Harmful"! Because it is the use of that unconstrained decision box that leads to so much tangled logic.

2.2 Structure Diagrams

To aid in the design of well structured programs a number of different notations have been developed. The diagrammatic notation for JSP

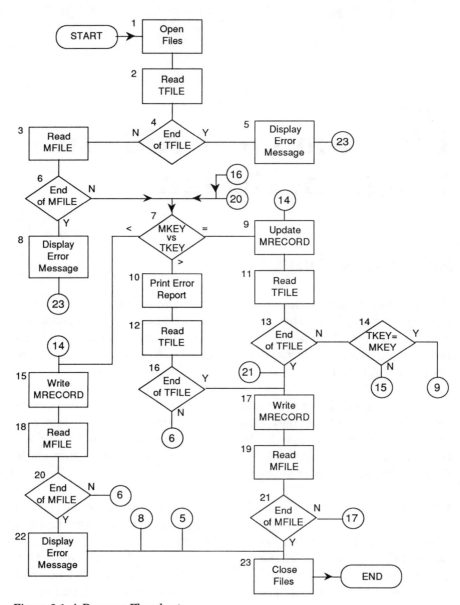

Figure 2.1 A Program Flowchart.

employs a straightforward system of three types of process box to represent hierarchic structures comprised of sequenced, selected, iterated and elementary components. A simple example of such a hierarchic structure is shown in figure 2.2. Those components labelled B, D, G, H, I and J are classed as elementary because they are not developed further.

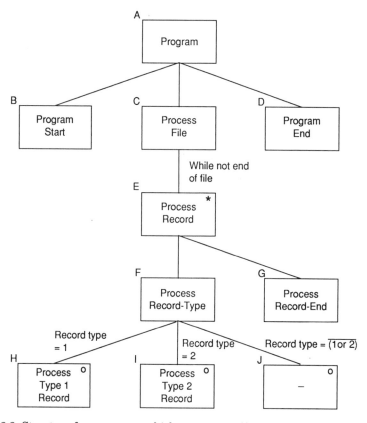

Figure 2.2 Structure for a program which processes a file counting occurrences of type 1 and type 2 records.

The basic forms and associated rules for these diagrams which depict sequence, selection and iteration structures within JSP are as follows:-

2.2.1 Sequence

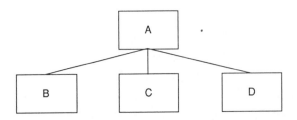

Component A is a sequence of the lower level components B, C and D i.e. component A can be subdivided into these other parts. The term sequence refers to the highest level component i.e. A; the lower level components are the elements of the sequence.

An example of a sequence is the days of the week, i.e. a week may be viewed as a sequence of the individual days: Monday, Tuesday, Wednesday and so on.

2.2.2 Selection

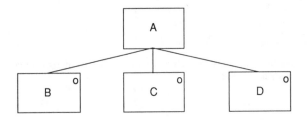

Component A on examination is found to be either B, C or D. The term selection refers to the higher level component, i.e. A; the lower level components are the selected components and are denoted by a circle in the top right hand corner of each box.

Examples of selections are:-

(i)   An integer number which can be odd or even,

(ii) A weather forecast which could be for sunshine, fog, snow or rain.

2.2.3 Iteration

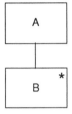

Component A consists of zero, one or many occurrences of component B. The term iteration refers to the higher level component, i.e. A, the lower level component is the iterated component and is denoted by an asterisk in the top left hand corner of the box. The name of the iterated component is always written as singular in the diagram as it represents one instance of the iteration, but when read out it is made plural, i.e. the asterisk represents the 's'.

Examples of iterations are:-

(i)   A class consists of an iteration of students.

(ii) The weather for a forecasted rainy day could consists of an iteration of showers i.e. lots of showers of rain, or one shower of rain or none at all - the forecaster got it wrong!

2.2.4 Rules and Conventions

(i) As is illustrated in figure 2.2, all the components which originate from one component at the level immediately above must be of the same type. Thus combinations such as

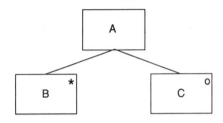

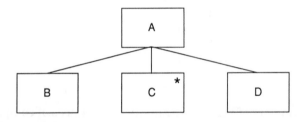

are incorrect.

(ii) There is only one path from the highest level component to each lower level component i.e. there is no cross linking of components as with component F below.

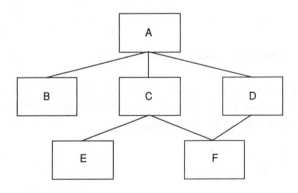

(iii) Negation of conditions, such as not type 1 record, can be represented by placing a bar over the positive condition i.e. type 1 is equivalent to not type 1. Also the final else leg of a condition where no action is to be taken can be represented by a null box, a box with a dash in it, as in figure 2.2.

2.3 Pseudocode

An additional aid to program design, which then provides an ideal base for coding is pseudocode. This is a narrative equivalent of a hierarchic program structure and it represents the program logic in the form of a set of structured English statements which describe the operations which the program has to perform. The pseudocode used within JSP is called Schematic Logic. It takes the form of an indented block structured language where the block names provide a direct link with the corresponding program structure.

The following examples illustrate the form of JSP schematic logic for the three program constructs of sequence, selection and iteration. Since the diagrams represent program components, controlling conditions have been added to the structures relating to selection and iteration. These conditions are represented here as simply C1, C2, C3 and are shown on the structure diagram beside the relevant lines joining the higher and lower level components.

(a) Sequence

Structure:

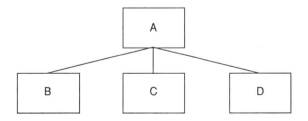

Schematic Logic:

```
A-SEQ
  B
    operations associated with component B
  C
    operations associated with component C
  D
    operations associated with component D
A-SEQ-END.
```

The suffixes -SEQ and -SEQ-END are added to the name of the sequenced component and these are then used to delimit the start and end of the sequence.

(b) Selection

Structure:

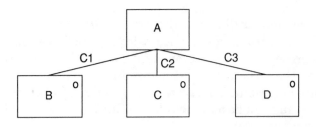

Schematic Logic:

```
A-SEL if C1
  B
    operations associated with component B
A-OR1 if C2
  C
    operations associated with component C
A-OR2 if C3
  D
    operations associated with component D
A-SEL-END.
```

Here the start and end of the selection are delimited by the suffixes -SEL and -SEL-END and the second and subsequent branches of the selection each commence with the name of the selected (top level) component followed by the suffix -OR1, -OR2 etc. It should also be noted that the condition shown on the legs of the structure diagram are repeated in the schematic logic following the relevant suffixed name.

The operational blocks (A-SEL to A-OR1, A-OR1 to A-OR2 and A-OR2 to A-SEL-END) show the control flow within the program. For example if condition C1 is true the lower level components following A-SEL are executed until the end of the block (A-OR1) is encountered when control will pass to the end of the selection (A-SEL-END). Similarly if condition C2 is true the lower level components following A-OR1 are executed until the end of the block (A-OR2) is encountered when control will again pass to the end of selection (A-SEL-END).

(c) Iteration

Structure:

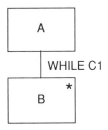

Schematic Logic:

```
A-ITER while C1
   B
      operations associated with component B
A-ITER-END.
```

The start and end of the iteration are delimited by the suffixes -ITER and -ITER-END and the controlling condition for the iteration is repeated in the schematic logic following the -ITER suffix. Again the block A-ITER to A-ITER-END represents the operational control within the program. While condition C1 is true the lower level components

27

within the block are repeatedly executed. Only when condition C1 is not true will control pass to the end of the iteration.

A more comprehensive example of schematic logic which relates to the program structure shown in figure 2.2, where the number of Type 1 and Type 2 records held on a file are counted, is given in figure 2.3. Remember that the schematic logic blocks show the operational control within the program, for example the operations within the block PROCESS-FILE-ITER to PROCESS-FILE-ITER-END will be repeated while there are records to process. Only when the end of file condition is satisfied will execution proceed to the component PROGRAM-END.

```
PROGRAM-SEQ
    PROGRAM-START
        Open File
        Zero Count-1, Count-2
        Read record from file
    PROCESS-FILE-ITER          While not end of file
        PROCESS-RECORD-SEQ
            PROCESS-RECORD-TYPE-SEL      If type1 record
                PROCESS-TYPE1-RECORD
                Add 1 to Count-1
            PROCESS-RECORD-TYPE-OR1      If type2 record
                PROCESS-TYPE2-RECORD
                Add 1 to Count-2
            PROCESS-RECORD-TYPE-OR2      Else
                no action
            PROCESS-RECORD-TYPE-SEL-END
            PROCESS-RECORD-END
                Read record from file
        PROCESS-RECORD-SEQ-END
    PROCESS-FILE-ITER-END
    PROGRAM-END
        Output details of the number of records counted
        Close files
        Stop program run.
PROGRAM-SEQ-END.
```

Figure 2.3 Schematic logic for the program depicted in figure 2.2

2.4 System Network Diagrams

The relationship between a program or a process and the data streams which it handles needs to be clearly understood and documented. This can be achieved using Systems Network Diagrams (SNDs) the notation for which is given in figure 2.4 along with an example. The example represents a simple task of handling a set of student marks and producing, for each student, an average. Here the input data stream comprises the students' names and their associated marks. The process involves accessing each name and associated marks, computing the average and outputting along with each name the original marks plus the calculated average. The output stream comprises the names, the original marks and the averages.

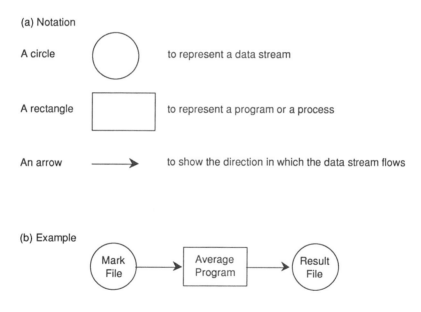

(a) Notation

A circle ⬭ to represent a data stream

A rectangle ▭ to represent a program or a process

An arrow → to show the direction in which the data stream flows

(b) Example

Mark File → Average Program → Result File

Figure 2.4 System Network Diagrams.

A more complex SND is shown in figure 2.5 for a system where the marks from individual subject files are merged together before being averaged and then finally being printed out in ascending order.

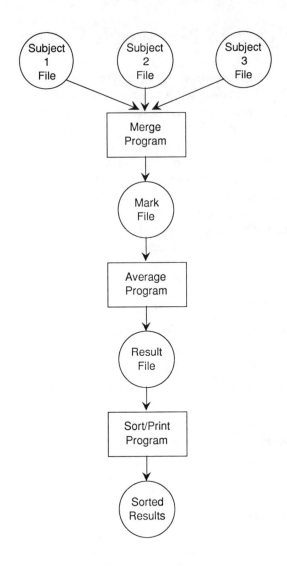

Figure 2.5 SND for a Suite of Programs.

TASKS - CHAPTER 2

1. Attempt to produce a structure diagram for the activities you carried out yesterday.

2. Draw a structure diagram to represent the order of a child's train which is made of an engine plus some wagons and carriages - do a sketch first of what you imagine the train to look like, then draw the structure diagram.

3. Consider the changes that would have to be made to the program depicted in figure 2.2 if a third type of record were to be counted.

4. Following task 3 what changes would be made to the schematic logic shown in section 2.3?

CHAPTER 3

An Introduction to the COBOL Language

3.1 COBOL

COBOL (COmmon Business Oriented Language) is an English based machine independent high level language which supports the implementation of business data processing systems. Such systems are typified by high volume input-output, extensive data manipulation, validation and formatting, and relatively straightforward arithmetic procedures. However, they often have extremely complex processing requirements.

COBOL has enormous use world-wide. In the U.K. it is the major programming language on both mainframe and mini based computer systems as has been shown by successive Datapro surveys [15]. It is a language that has constantly developed during its lifetime to keep up with changing technology and user needs. Hence it is certain that it will remain in wide use for the foreseeable future not only because of its continuing evolution but also because of the large investment there is in existing programs and trained personnel.

This chapter provides information relating to the origins and development of COBOL, its state in the late 1980s, the general structure of a COBOL program and an overview of the data types and operations which COBOL supports.

3.2 The Origins and Development of COBOL

3.2.1 Origins

During the 1950s computer systems to support business and administrative tasks were being developed by many organisations using a wide range of computer hardware from different manufacturers. Some of the major problems with these systems were that they were difficult to produce and maintain and they had very poor, if any, portability as they were developed using relatively low level languages which related to one model or range of machines. These problems were particularly acute for very large organisations such as the United States Department of Defense where independent branches of the armed services were developing very similar applications but in different languages on different machines.

On April 8th 1959 a meeting of computer professionals interested in the development of a common business language was held at the University of Pennsylvania Computing Centre. Those attending included representatives from users, manufacturers and academia. The positive outcome of this meeting led to the creation, under the sponsorship of the Department of Defense (DOD) of a voluntary organisation comprised of users and manufacturers known as CODASYL (the acronym originally came from the "COmmittee on Data Systems Languages" but subsequently "COnference on Data Data Systems Languages" has also been used). This organisation undertook to design a common business language whose main characteristics were to be:

(a) it was to make maximum use of simple English language,

(b) it would be machine independent and problem oriented,

(c) it should be easy to use, thus allowing more people to become involved in programming,

(d) it would not be biased by current compiler problems,

(e) it would be open-ended and capable of accepting change and modification.

A subgroup known as the Short Range Committee was set to work examining three existing language specifications (FLOW-MATIC from Remington-Rand Univac, AIMACO from the United States Air Material Command and Commercial Translator from IBM) in order to produce a short term composite solution. In fact the committee worked on the initial development of the language, which they named COBOL, and by December 1959 the members had defined what they understood to be an interim language with a lifetime of only one to two years. However, their work turned out to be the basis of COBOL as it is today and led to the first formal specification of the language. This specification entitled "COBOL Initial Specifications for a COmmon Business Oriented Language" was published for CODASYL by the DOD in April 1960 and become known as COBOL 60.

3.2.2 Language Development

The members of CODASYL recognised that there were major problems and deficiencies in their 1960 specification and therefore set up a maintenance committee to work on the further development of COBOL. New specifications were produced in 1961 (COBOL 61 the first version of the language to be widely implemented), 1962 (COBOL 61 Extended) and in 1965 (COBOL 65). Each of these was published by the DOD and were recognised as the current specification for the language. Since 1968 internationally recognised standard specifications for COBOL have been produced by both American and international standards organisations. However, the responsibility for the development and maintenance of the language still resides with CODASYL which through its various committees has ensured that the language has evolved and been kept up to date. The specifications produced for COBOL by CODASYL are published on a regular basis in the COBOL Journal of Development (JoD).

The work to produce an American Standard for COBOL was commenced in 1962 by a committee of the then United States of America Standards Institute, now called the American National Standard Institute (ANSI). This work culminated in the first American National Standard (ANS) for COBOL in 1968 which is usually referred to as ANS COBOL 68. This was followed by the 1974 COBOL standard and later by the current 1985 COBOL standard. Due to close co-operation between ANSI and the International Organisation for Standardisation (ISO) in each case the ANSI standard has been adopted as the ISO COBOL standard.

3.2.3 Standardisation

When producing a new COBOL standard the procedure adopted by ANSI's COBOL technical committee, which is known as X3J4, is to start with the specifications contained in CODASYL's Journal of Development as they stand at a particular time and also the previous COBOL standard. This is to ensure that not only are new language developments considered but also that the new standard will have forward compatibility with its predecessor. A draft standard is then produced for public review and comment. Members of X3J4 deal with submitted comments and the draft standard is amended, if necessary. It is then submitted to a parent ANSI committee for approval and once this is obtained, again after any required amendments, it is submitted to ANSI for final approval and publication.

A major innovation by ANSI has been in the formatting of its COBOL specifications. Each ANSI standard defines COBOL in terms of a Nucleus (those elements of the language necessary for the internal definition and processing data) and a number of functional modules (such as Sequential I-O). The 65 standard comprised eight functional modules, the 74 standard twelve and the 85 standard comprises eleven. Each module (including the nucleus) in a standard can be defined at two levels of complexity - high or low. Also several modules have a null level meaning that the module need not be implemented. In the 1968 and 1974 standards a module could have up to 3 levels, including the null, associated with it; but in the 1985 standard this is limited to two.

The structure of modules and levels gives COBOL implementors (i.e. the compiler suppliers) the means to plan and easily describe the particular implementation of COBOL they intend to produce. But it has also produced problems - the 1968 and 1974 standards placed very few restrictions on the combination of modules and levels which meant that in theory there could be an enormous number of different compilers all of which were implementations within the standard! For example, there are 104,976 different ways in which the 1974 standard could be implemented. In practice things have not been as bad as this due to the fact that the United States Government has its own Federal version of the 1974 standard which permits only four combinations of modules and levels. And since the US Government is the world's largest purchaser of data processing equipment most compilers for the 1974 standard are very close to one of the four Federal approved combinations.

The state of affairs is much better with the 1985 standard where ANSI has itself limited the maximum number of approved combinations to 162. However, four of the modules, which were rarely included in COBOL 74 implementations, are declared as optional and if these are left out the number of approved combinations is reduced to three.

In addition to the problems caused by having the possibility of compilers which relate to different permitted versions of ANS COBOL there are those caused by language extensions. Various implementors have added their own "enhancements" to the COBOL language in order to make their compilers more attractive to potential users. This practice, which is not prohibited by ANSI's standards, has given rise to a wide range of COBOL dialects. Obviously having such enhancements reduces language portability but their presence must not be regarded as totally detrimental as it often provides a means of testing potential improvements before they are incorporated into the next standard.

Facilities exist within the United States, Britain, France and Germany to validate COBOL compilers against the current ANSI standard. Certificates are issued stating the results of the tests and these are the means employed by the US Government to ensure that compilers do conform to the ANSI standard as they will only buy compilers that have been certified. However, the validation tests make no checks on implementors' extensions to the language which means that even a certified compiler may contain many elements which are not in the current COBOL standard.

For those readers who are interested in the development of COBOL further details can be found in references 16-17.

3.3 COBOL Today

Once a new standard has been published by ANSI that becomes 'The COBOL Standard'. But that does not mean that all existing COBOL compilers become instantly obsolete and disappear overnight. It normally takes several years for the use of compilers written to the new standard to become the norm and therefore in the late 1980s and early 1990s there will be COBOL compilers relating to both ANS 74 and ANS 85 in existence. Nevertheless, as time goes on more and more new programs will be written with ANS 85 features in mind and there will be a gradual conversion to the new standard as programs are modified during maintenance. However, it should be noted that one of the major features of ANSI's 1985 standard is its forward compatibility with that of 1974 and in fact, it was the public pressure [19] for this compatibility that delayed the finalisation of the standard for five years. This means that the majority of programs written to the 1974 standard will need minimal changes to be usable with compilers produced to the 1985 standard.

The overall modular structure for ANSI's 1974 standard and 1985 standard is very similar as can be seen in table 3.1. The major changes that have been introduced with the 1985 standard are:

(i) There has been a general tightening up throughout the specification to remove ambiguities and reduce the number of implementation decisions which were previously left to the compiler producer. These changes should mean that programs written to the COBOL 85 standard are much more portable between different manufacturers compilers.

Table 3.1   Structure of COBOL 74 and COBOL 85

COBOL 74	COBOL 85
Nucleus	
Table Handling	Nucleus
Sequential I-O	Sequential I-O
Relative I-O	Relative I-O
Indexed I-O	Indexed I-O
Sort-Merge	Sort-Merge
Library	Source Text Manipulation
Interprogram Communication	Interprogram Communication

Report Writer	Report Writer	⎤
Communication	Communication	⎬ Optional Modules
Debug	Debug *	
Segmentation	Segmentation *	⎦

* modules defined as obsolete which are due for deletion from the next ANSI COBOL standard.

(ii) The inclusion of new features which will support structured programming such as statement deliminators which control the scope of conditionals and allow nesting, an improved case statement and the facility to 'perform' routines in-line as well as out-of-line.

(iii) Improved facilities for defining, manipulating and initialising data items.

(iv) The facilities of the Library module which permits the inclusion of source code held in libraries into the user program at compile time has been extended and it has been renamed as Source-Text Manipulation.

(v) The Interprogram Communication module which aids modularity by providing a means for a program to transfer control to one or more separately compiled subprograms has been extended to provide the nested type procedure mechanisms that are found in languages such as Pascal and Algol.

(vi) The standard has been divided into required and optional modules each with two implementation levels. An implementation of the standard must include one of three subsets of the required modules and may include any combination of levels of the optional modules or none at all. The optional modules, which are those that were most often omitted from implementations of the 1974 standard, are: Report Writer which supports the semi-automatic production of printed reports; Communication, which provides on-line transaction processing facilities; Debug which provides a capability for interrupting normal program flow and executing diagnostic routines; Segmentation which allows the object code to be segmented into separate files so that on limited main store machines overlaying of code can take place at run time.

(vii) The introduction of a new category within the standard known as Obsolete Elements. These are features which have become outdated and do not meet the needs of current COBOL users. It is intended that these features are to be deleted from the next COBOL standard but are included in the current standard to give users time to deal with possible conversion problems. Obsolete elements are scattered throughout the standard and include the whole of the Debug and Segmentation modules.

Readers who wish to gain further technical details relating to COBOL 85 should consult one of the two recent texts published by the UK National Computing Centre [20,21].

3.4 The COBOL Used in this Text

Currently COBOL is in a state of transition between standards and some installations will have moved to the new 1985 standard while others will remain with the old 1974 standard for some time. It is even reported [19] that some installations have been concerned about the costs that would be involved in changing from their existing 1968 standard compilers! The situation at the author's own Polytechnic is probably typical of many academic institutions which operate a variety of machines. In the current academic year (1988/89) there are eight different COBOL compilers available to students and staff. Of these six relate to the 1974 standard and two relate to the 1985 standard. Because of this current transitional situation and since this is an introductory text which is likely to be used by students whose access may be to a compiler which relates to either the 1985 or 1974 COBOL standard, it will cover a basic subset of the language which is common to both standards. Where there is the possibility of implementation differences these will be pointed out. For it is important that a beginner becomes familiar with the basics of the language which underpin both standards.

Descriptions of those elements of the language, including the Debug and Segmentation modules, which have been designated as obsolete in the 1985 standard will generally be omitted. Also the length of the text precludes details of the Report Writer and Communication facilities both of which are rarely implemented and have optional status in the 1985 standard.

3.5 The General Structure of a COBOL Program

3.5.1 An Example Program

Many of the later chapters in this text are concerned with describing the technical aspects of COBOL in detail. However, it is useful at this point to look at a simple COBOL program. Figures 3.1 and 3.2 show the code and an outline structure for a program which processes student marks. The input to the program is a file of student records where each record consists of a students' name and three marks. The layout of the input file is that each record is 26 characters long with 20 characters for the name and two digits for each percentage mark. The output from the program is a file of result records where each record on this file contains the original data for the student plus his average mark. The program simply reads each input record in turn, calculates the average mark, writes out the resulting output record and terminates once the end of the input file is detected. Some sample input and output is shown in figure 3.3. Although you are not yet familiar with the details of the COBOL language it should be possible for you to understand the program, due to COBOL's English form and relate its operation to the structure diagram of figure 3.2. You should note that each line commencing with an asterisk is treated as a comment by the compiler and is ignored by it. They are simply there to improve the layout of the program and explain its operation.

```
        IDENTIFICATION DIVISION.
        *************************

        PROGRAM-ID. PROGRAM1.

        * A PROGRAM TO COMPUTE AVERAGE MARKS: READS EACH INPUT RECORD
        * FROM THE FILE SMARKS.DAT THEN COMPUTES THE AVERAGE OF THE
        * THREE MARKS ON THE RECORD AND WRITES THE RESULT WITH THE
        * ORIGINAL DATA TO THE OUTPUT FILE SRESULTS.DAT
```

41

```
      ENVIRONMENT DIVISION.
      **********************


      CONFIGURATION SECTION.
      *----------------------


      SOURCE-COMPUTER. A-PC.
      OBJECT-COMPUTER. A-PC.


      INPUT-OUTPUT SECTION.
      *--------------------


      FILE-CONTROL.
      *------------


          SELECT INPUT-FILE ASSIGN TO "SMARKS.DAT".
          SELECT OUTPUT-FILE ASSIGN TO "SRESULTS.DAT".


      DATA DIVISION.
      **************


      FILE SECTION.
      *------------


      FD  INPUT-FILE.
          01  INPUT-RECORD.
              03  IR-NAME          PIC X(20).
              03  IR-MARK-1        PIC 99.
              03  IR-MARK-2        PIC 99.
              03  IR-MARK-3        PIC 99.


      FD  OUTPUT-FILE.
          01  OUTPUT-RECORD.
              03  OR-ORIGINAL-DATA.
                  05  OR-NAME      PIC X(20).
                  05  OR-MARK-1    PIC 99.
                  05  OR-MARK-2    PIC 99.
                  05  OR-MARK-3    PIC 99.
              03  OR-AVE-MARK      PIC 99.



      WORKING-STORAGE SECTION.
      *-----------------------


          01  EOF-INPUT-FILE       PIC 9.
```

```
PROCEDURE DIVISION.
********************

PROGRAM1-SEQ.
PROGRAM-INITIALISATION.
     MOVE 0 TO EOF-INPUT-FILE.
     OPEN INPUT INPUT-FILE.
     OPEN OUTPUT OUTPUT-FILE.
     READ INPUT-FILE AT END MOVE 1 TO EOF-INPUT-FILE.
PROCESS-FILE-ITER.
     IF EOF-INPUT-FILE = 0 NEXT SENTENCE
                           ELSE GO TO PROCESS-FILE-ITER-END.
PROCESS-STUDENT-RECORD.
     COMPUTE OR-AVE-MARK ROUNDED
             = (IR-MARK-1 + IR-MARK-2 + IR-MARK-3) / 3.
     MOVE INPUT-RECORD TO OR-ORIGINAL-DATA.
     WRITE OUTPUT-RECORD.
     READ INPUT-FILE AT END MOVE 1 TO EOF-INPUT-FILE.
     GO TO PROCESS-FILE-ITER.
PROCESS-FILE-ITER-END.
PROGRAM-TERMINATION.
     CLOSE INPUT-FILE , OUTPUT-FILE.
     STOP RUN.
PROGRAM1-SEQ-END.
```

Figure 3.1 PROGRAM1 a simple program processing student marks.

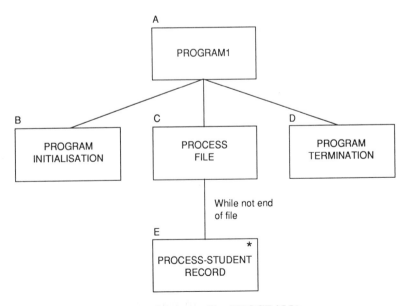

Figure 3.2 Outline Program Structure For PROGRAM1.

```
Input data

AHMAD J            605055
BELL R             656050
BLOOR C            657050
BROWN A            504545
CLARK I            456565
CLIFFE W           503560
CLIFFORD J         455060
DUNNE P            757555
FLETCHER E         558055
FOSTER R           456555
            :
            :
            :


Output results

AHMAD J            60505555
BELL R             65605058
BLOOR C            65705062
BROWN A            50454547
CLARK I            45656558
CLIFFE W           50356048
CLIFFORD J         45506052
DUNNE P            75755568
FLETCHER E         55805563
FOSTER R           45655555
            :
            :
            :
```

Figure 3.3 Sample input and output for program PROGRAM1.

3.5.2   The Four COBOL Divisions

COBOL programs are divided into 4 divisions, IDENTIFICATION, ENVIRONMENT, DATA and PROCEDURE. For ease of reference the names of each of these divisions is highlighted in figure 3.1 by following it with a comment line consisting of a row of asterisks. The purpose of each of the divisions is as follows:-

IDENTIFICATION DIVISION

This gives the program a name and provides a convenient place to include documentary information about the program. The example program is given the name PROGRAM1.

ENVIRONMENT DIVISION

This describes the external environment for the program. It consists of two sections: the CONFIGURATION SECTION where the type of computer(s) being used to compile and execute the program is given and the INPUT-OUTPUT SECTION which identifies the files which the program handles. In the example two files are detailed: their internal names, i.e. the names by which they are referenced in the Data and Procedure Divisions, are INPUT-FILE and OUTPUT-FILE while their external names, the names by which the computer's operating system knows them, are SMARKS.DAT and SRESULTS.DAT.

DATA DIVISION

Here the storage that is to be reserved for data is defined. It normally consists of two parts: the FILE SECTION which defines the layout of the records for each file named in the Environment Division; and the WORKING-STORAGE SECTION where internal data items are defined. In the example the format of the records on INPUT-FILE and OUTPUT-FILE are given and a single Working-Storage data item EOF-INPUT-FILE, which is used to signal when the end of the input file has been detected, is also defined. (The formats of data records and items are explained further in section 3.5.2).

PROCEDURE DIVISION

Here the actual operations which are to be executed are specified. The English nature of the COBOL language is reflected in the structure of the Procedure Division which is divided into named paragraphs each of which can contain a number of sentences all terminated by full stops.

In the example program execution commences at paragraph PROGRAM1-SEQ. The operations specified within paragraph PROGRAM-INITIALISATION are then carried out. The value of the data item EOF-INPUT-FILE is set equal to zero and after the two files have been made ready for processing an attempt is made to access the first record from the input file. If this is successful the record will be transferred from the input file into the data area INPUT-RECORD. If

45

the file contains no records then the AT END phrase will be actioned and the value of the data item EOF-INPUT-FILE will be changed from zero to 1. It is unlikely that the program would be run against an empty file but this situation should be catered for. The iterative routine PROCESS-FILE-ITER is then executed repeatedly while the value of EOF-INPUT-FILE is zero (i.e. while the end of the input file has not been reached).

In routine PROCESS-STUDENT-RECORD the average mark is calculated, the output record is set up and it is written to the output file. Then the input file is accessed again for the next student record and control returns to the start of the iteration. Once the end of the file is reached (i.e. there are no more records to read) the value of EOF-INPUT-FILE will become 1 and control will then be transferred to paragraph PROCESS-FILE-ITER-END. Finally the operations within paragraph PROGRAM-TERMINATION will be executed causing the files to be closed and the processing brought to an end. You should note that in the example program some paragraphs, for example PROGRAM1-SEQ contain no operations. This is allowed in COBOL and the reason I have coded such documentary paragraphs is to provide compatibility with the program structure shown in figure 3.2.

Also the use of punctuation in the example program should be carefully noted. All the division, section and paragraph headings must be followed by a full stop. The full stop also delimits entries in the Identification, Environment and Data Divisions and sentences in the Procedure Division.

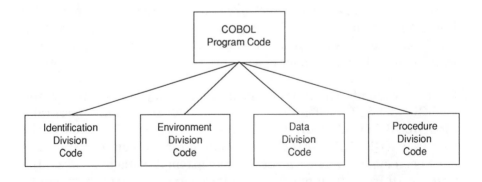

Figure 3.4 The structure of the source code for a COBOL program.

In summary: a COBOL program consists of four distinct major parts or divisions each of which performs a specific function. These divisions must be written in a strict sequence and thus the source code for any COBOL program will have the overall structure shown in figure 3.4.

3.6 An Overview of COBOL Operations and Data Types

To understand COBOL's sphere of application and hence be able to design programs for implementation in COBOL, it is necessary to appreciate the basic operations which the language supports and the data types which it can handle.

3.6.1 Basic Operations

Executable operations in COBOL are coded in the Procedure Division as statements. A number of statements make up a COBOL sentence which is terminated by a full stop. Each COBOL statement commences with a verb and most of these are self explanatory because of their English language form. The basic types of operations in COBOL and the verbs that support them are as follows:

(a) File handling operations which initialise and terminate the processing of a file and cause records to be transferred from and to the file (OPEN, CLOSE, READ, WRITE).

(b) Low volume input-output operations which support transfers between a program and a terminal or visual display unit (ACCEPT, DISPLAY).

(c) Data manipulation operations which will transfer a copy of data values from a sending data item to a receiving data item (MOVE) and analyse and manipulate strings of characters (INSPECT, STRING, UNSTRING).

(d) Arithmetic operations which perform addition, subtraction, multiplication, division and compound calculations (ADD, SUBTRACT, MULTIPLY, DIVISION, COMPUTE).

(e) Conditional operations whereby subsequent actions are dependent upon the evaluation of a condition (IF, IF ... ELSE).

(f) Procedural control operations which cause program control to be transferred to a specific paragraph name (GO TO), which cause the instructions within a paragraph or group of consecutive paragraphs to be executed before proceeding to the next instruction in-line (PERFORM) and which cause execution to be terminated (STOP RUN).

The technicalities associated with the use of each of the verbs listed above are detailed in the later chapters of the text.

3.6.2 Data Types

The data types which COBOL supports are:

> elementary items
> group items
> records
> tables (arrays)
> files

An elementary data item is one whose subdivision is not necessary, for example, a numeric value which represents an examination mark or a string of characters which represent a person's surname. Such elementary items form the base of all the other COBOL data types. Records are composed of elementary items which can be grouped together at different levels to form a hierarchic structure. Composite group items form the intermediate levels of the hierarchy. The structure of the hierarchy is defined by the allocation of a number for each level within it starting with 01 for the topmost level.

For example

```
01   STUDENT-RECORD.
   03   STUDENT-NAME.
      05   STUDENT-SURNAME            PIC A(20).
      05   STUDENT-FORENAMES          PIC A(30).
   03   STUDENT-ADDRESS.
      05   STUDENT-HOME-ADDRESS       PIC X(100).
      05   STUDENT-COLLEGE-ADDRESS    PIC X(100).
```

The 01 level is the record itself and the substructure of the record is determined by the lower level number (03, 05 etc.). It is common practice to use odd numbers for the levels, to allow for possible future insertions, and to indent each level to reflect its place in the hierarchy. These lower levels of the record are often referred to as the fields of the record. Thus the record may be described as consisting of the fields STUDENT-NAME and STUDENT-ADDRESS both of which are group items, and these in turn may be described as consisting of the fields STUDENT-SURNAME, STUDENT-FORENAMES, STUDENT-HOME-ADDRESS and STUDENT-COLLEGE-ADDRESS all of which are elementary items.

The format of all elementary items must be defined by a PICTURE clause which can be abbreviated to PIC. This describes the size of the item, the category (alphabetic PIC A, numeric PIC 9 or alphanumeric PIC X), any presence of a sign and the location of any assumed decimal point. The size of the item is given by repeating the picture character or by following the picture character by the relevant number in brackets. Thus a numeric item which is two digits long could be described as PIC 99 or PIC 9(2).

Tables may be composed of a repeated record or may exist within a record as a repeated group item or elementary item.

For example it may be that we wish to record the different addresses that a student could have while he attends college (up to a maximum of 5) this can be achieved by specifying that the item STUDENT-COLLEGE-ADDRESS-FIELD in our previous example OCCURS the relevant number of times viz

```
03  STUDENT-COLLEGE-ADDRESS    PIC X(100) OCCURS 5 TIMES.
```

Files are composed of records and are defined in the File Section of the Data Division by means of a File Description (FD) entry followed by a record description for each type of record held on the file. This is illustrated in figure 3.5 by the FD for our file of student records which we will assume also contains a second type of record for Sandwich Course students who are on work experience. Figure 3.6 gives the corresponding structure diagram for the file. Note that we can use the same names for items within the two records so long as there is a higher level name, in this case the record name, which is unique. This is because we can qualify the non-unique name with the unique one to give a unique identifier for example -

```
STUDENT-NAME OF STUDENT-RECORD
STUDENT-NAME OF WORK-RECORD
```

give unique identifiers for the two name fields.

As is illustrated in figure 3.5 a File Description entry can contain several different record descriptions. In fact these are simply different ways of interpreting the same piece of store - in this case that reserved for input records. Each alternative description in the FD implicitly redefines the previous description(s). Where it is required to provide alternative views of parts of a record or complete records defined in Working-Storage an explicit REDEFINES clause is used.

Further details of files and the roles they play in COBOL based applications will be found in the next chapter.

```
FD   STUDENT-FILE.
*        student details while at college
   01   STUDENT-RECORD.
      03   STUDENT-NAME.
         05   STUDENT-SURNAME           PIC A(20).
         05   STUDENT-FORENAMES         PIC A(30).
      03   STUDENT-ADDRESS.
         05   STUDENT-HOME-ADDRESS      PIC X(100).
         05   STUDENT-COLLEGE-ADDRESS   PIC X(100) OCCURS 5 TIMES.
*        student details during work experience
   01   WORK-RECORD.
      03   STUDENT-NAME.
         05   STUDENT-SURNAME           PIC A(20).
         05   STUDENT-FORENAMES         PIC A(30).
      03   STUDENT-ADDRESS.
         05   STUDENT-HOME-ADDRESS      PIC X(100).
         05   STUDENT-WORK-ADDRESS      PIC X(100).
```

Figure 3.5   File description for student name and address file

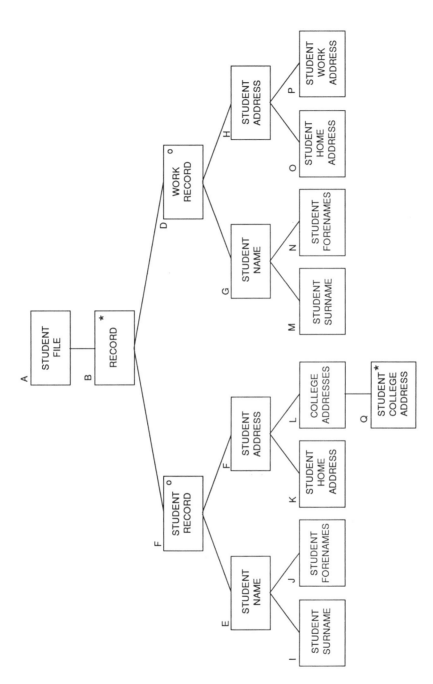

Figure 3.6 Structure Diagram for Student Name and Address File.

TASKS - CHAPTER 3

1. Find out where you can consult a copy of the COBOL reference manual for the computer system you are going to use.

2. Check your COBOL reference manual for the following information:

    (a) Which ANSI standard does it relate to?

    (b) Which COBOL modules are implemented (check with Table 3.1)?

    (c) Are any language extensions clearly identified? Are language extensions even mentioned?

3. Ask someone who is familiar with the compiler you are going to use whether the program listed in figure 3.1 is compatible with the compiler, or whether any amendments, say to the Environment Division, are needed. Once you have checked the program out try setting it up on your computer system and then compile it. If you have compilation errors check very carefully what you have typed in, if you still have problems again consult someone who is familiar with the system. Once your program is error free set up a test input file according to the data descriptions for INPUT-FILE and try running the program.

    You need to note that most COBOL compilers expect the code to be strictly formatted. In the example program, the text commencing with an asterisk should start in column 7 and the rest of the code should be aligned relative to this as shown in figure 3.1. The layout of some of this program on a COBOL coding sheet is shown in figure 7.1 and reference to this may be helpful.

4. (a) Redraw the structure diagram shown in figure 3.4 to show that the Environment Division is subdivided into a Configuration Section and an Input-Output Section and the Data Division is subdivided into a File Section and a Working-Storage Section.

    (b) The Procedure Division may be regarded as an iteration of

52

lines of text each of which may be a paragraph heading or an executable line of code or a comment. Redraw your structure diagram to reflect this.

(c) Can you think of a different structure for the Procedure Division to that given in part (b)? Can you draw a structure diagram to represent your view?

CHAPTER 4
Data Processing Programs and Data Files

4.1 Introduction

This chapter is concerned with ensuring that you are familiar with and understand the terminology and concepts that you may meet when you have to design and implement COBOL based applications.

In commercial data processing the systems are usually too complex to be implemented using single stand-alone programs. They have therefore to be implemented using suites of programs each of which consists of a number of interlinked programs. Thus the output from a program may not be information directly useful to a user but data for input to another program within a suite. This is illustrated in the SND shown in figure 4.1 for a suite of programs which perform a sequence of data validation, master file interrogation and report production. The basic unit of input, output and transfer between programs is a data record and these in turn are grouped together into files.

4.2 Data Files

A file is simply a collection of related records and its main purpose is to hold data in a form that enables it to be easily processed yet is compact and secure. Examples of everyday files are:

(i) A telephone directory

(ii) A library catalogue

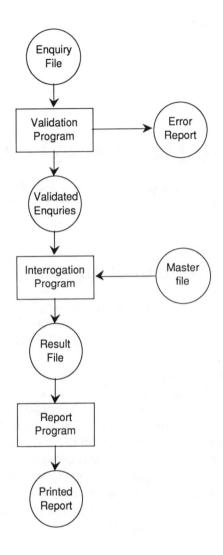

Figure 4.1 SND for a validation/interrogation/report suite of programs.

(iii)   A folder containing paid bills (electricity, gas, telephone, credit cards etc.).

Similarly within a business environment data will be organised into relevant files holding information on areas such as: payroll, customers, customer orders, sales, stock, inventory, personnel details etc.

4.2.1 Record Structure

Each record within a file is normally a collection of data items or fields. For example, each entry in a telephone directory may be regarded as a record consisting of:

Name of subscriber
Address of subscriber
Telephone number

As was detailed in section 3.6.2 each data item within a record may be a group item or an elementary item. An elementary item is one whose further subdivision is not necessary and a group item is one which is composed of other items. A group item is normally an item that one would wish to view either in its composite form or in terms of its constituent parts, for example:

Group Item	Parts
name	surname, initials
address	house number, street, town, county, post code
post code	prefix, suffix
telephone number	exchange code, exchange number
date	day, month, year

Files may be composed of fixed or variable length records. Fixed length records are those where the same set of fields (items) are present in each record and each field has a fixed size. Variable length records are those where there are optional fields or alternative fields within a record or where individual fields can vary in size. For example, a file of names and addresses could be held as fixed length records by allocating a fixed number of characters to each field as shown in figure 4.2(a). However, this would be very wasteful of space as each field would have to be large enough to hold the maximum sized data item. A much more satisfactory arrangement is shown in figure 4.2(b) where variable length fields, each delimited by a special terminating character, are used. Here the size of each record will be simply the number of characters in the relevant name and address plus the two terminators. The fields can be separated within a COBOL program when needed using the Unstring statement.

57

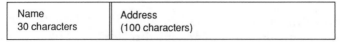

(a) Fixed Length

Name 30 characters	Address (100 characters)

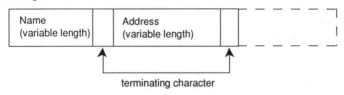

(b) Variable Length

terminating character

Figure 4.2 Fixed and Variable Name and Address Records.

4.2.2 Key Fields

Records often need to be identified and accessed individually or sorted into specific orders. Thus one or more fields within a record may be used as a key which will enable such identification and processing. Examples of the key fields for our everyday files listed above are:

```
      File                    record key field(s)

Telephone Directory      subscriber's surname and initials

Library Catalogue        author's name or book title or
                                 accession number

Folder of paid bills     date and name of organisation
```

4.3 File Organisation and Access Methods

This section is concerned with providing an overview of the file organisation and access methods which are supported by COBOL. If you need more technical details of methods of storing data on magnetic media and the ways of accessing it you should consult texts relating to file structure and design such as those by Cunningham [22] and Hanson [23].

4.3.1   File Organisation Methods

A problem which students often encounter when learning about file organisation is that of terminology. Unfortunately many alternative terms are used by systems designers and even the terms employed by the UK National Computing Centre [24] are somewhat different to the terms used within the COBOL language. Hence it is important that any COBOL programmer recognises the equivalences and differences. In this section in order to distinguish between the two sets of terminology, the more general terms will be printed normally while the COBOL terms as used in the ORGANIZATION clause in a COBOL program's File-Control entry will be printed in block capitals.

There are basically five different forms of file organisation which can be supported by COBOL programs, the general terms which are used to describe them are:-

> serial
> sequential
> random
> indexed
> inverted

Serial and sequential organisations can be supported on both magnetic tape and disk. However, the remaining three organisations can only be supported on disk or some other direct access device.

(a) Serial and Sequential Organisations

In a serially organised file records are stored one after another on the medium and there is no relationship between a record's key and its position on the file. Input data files are normally serially organised. In a sequentially organised file the records are again stored one after another but they are held in key sequence order, i.e. a sequential file will be produced after sorting a serial file on its key field. These differences are illustrated in figure 4.3.

In COBOL both these file organisations are classed as SEQUENTIAL for in both the records are stored one after another. SEQUENTIAL is the default organisation for a COBOL file and need not be specified explicitly.

(a) Serial

117	120	210	118	113	200

(b) Sequential

113	117	118	120	200	210

Each box reprecents a record and the figure inside it represents the value held in its key field.

Figure 4.3 Serial and Sequential File Organisations.

(b) Random Organisation

In a randomly organised file the records are stored throughout the file in an apparently random manner, their actual physical positions being determined by applying an addressing algorithm or formulae to the keys. Unless the formulae used to calculate the record position is known it will appear that the records are held completely randomly. Alternative names for randomly organised files are algorithmic, hashed and direct. Also the addressing mechanism is sometimes referred to as randomising, hashing or address generation. One problem with random file organisations is that more than one key may be converted to the same address and hence overflow mechanisms have to be set up to deal with these synonyms. Another problem is that there may be under-used areas in the file to which few records have been directed.

To provide such random processing COBOL supports a file organisation known as RELATIVE. Here records are placed in positions relative to the start of the file according to a relative record number which the programmer has to compute from the records key value using an appropriate algorithm.

(c) Indexed and Inverted Organisations

With an indexed file organisation a cross reference index of record key vs physical position is maintained. Thus the file consists of two parts, the index and the data records as is illustrated in figure 4.4. To access a record the index is searched for the required key and once this is found the corresponding address is used to directly retrieve the record.

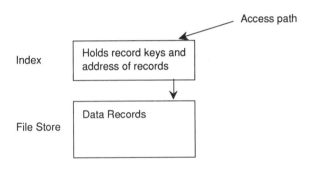

Figure 4.4 Indexed File Organisation.

One of the commonest forms of indexed file organisation is Indexed Sequential. Here the index is maintained to support direct access but in addition the data records are held in sequential order. This form of file organisation is very popular as it can support fast access to individual records via the index and efficient sequential processing for times when the record "hit rate" is very high i.e. when the majority of the records in the file have to be accessed.

An inverted file organisation is one where several different key fields may be used to access a record. Simply this means that more than one index (one for each different key field) is used to cross reference the data records.

COBOL supports Indexed Sequential and Inverted files via its INDEXED organisation. The organisation demands that each record has a unique primary key but an inverted file may be defined by specifying additional unique or non unique secondary keys.

4.3.2 File Access Methods

Here again there are some problems regarding terminology so the same convention will be adopted of using normal type for general terms and block capitals for the COBOL terms which are used in the ACCESS MODE clause of a File Control entry. There are basically three different ways in which files may be accessed -

Serially
Sequentially
Directly (also referred to as Randomly or Selectively)

When using serial access records are retrieved one after another in the physical order they lie in the file starting with the first record in the file. To retrieve a particular record all the records before it must be accessed first. When using sequential access records are retrieved in logical key sequence. To retrieve a record with a given key all the records with lower keys may have to be accessed first. When using direct (random or selective) access records are retrieved directly without the need to access all previous records.

COBOL supports two main access mechanisms namely SEQUENTIAL and RANDOM. The type of retrieval achieved by them depends on the way in which the file is organised. The viable possibilities are:-

(a) Access SEQUENTIAL organisation SEQUENTIAL

Records are retrieved in physical order. If the file was sorted into sequential order the access is actually sequential if it was not sorted the access is serial.

(b) Access SEQUENTIAL organisation INDEXED

Records are retrieved in specified key order i.e. access is sequential.

(c) Access SEQUENTIAL organisation RELATIVE

Records are returned in the physical order they lie in the file. Since this order is unlikely to be their key order, as an addressing algorithm will have been used to place them, the access is serial.

(d) Access RANDOM organisation INDEXED

Records are retrieved directly using the specified key value.

(e) Access RANDOM organisation RELATIVE

The record at the specified relative record position is accessed directly.

4.4 Classification of Computer Files

Files may be classed according to their technical aspects as detailed above or as in this section they may be classified according to use. The classes we shall consider are: master files, transaction files, transition files, reference files, report files, spool files and dump files. Examples of several of these file types appear in the electricity billing system depicted in figure 4.5.

(a) Master Files

These contain current information about one particular aspect of an operation. These are permanent files which must be maintained in an up-to-date state so that they can provide accurate information for use in processing runs. They are usually organised in whatever way provides the most efficient processing for the major applications that access them.

In the electricity billing application the Accounts Master File could hold the following information:

    Account Reference Number (Primary key)
    Name of Customer
    Details of Previous Consumption
    Details of Payment

a) Main Update System

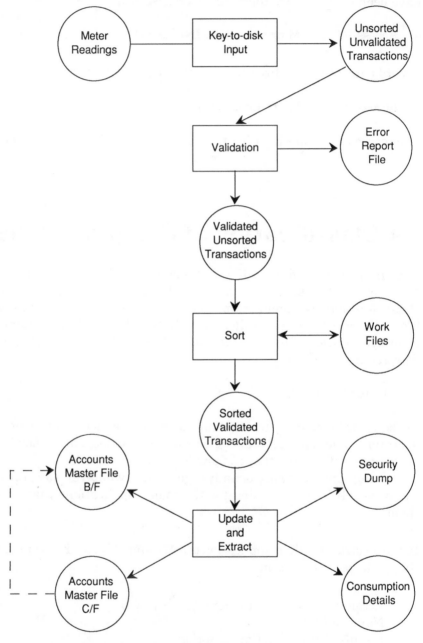

Figure 4.5 SND for Electricity Billing Operation.

64

b) Billing System

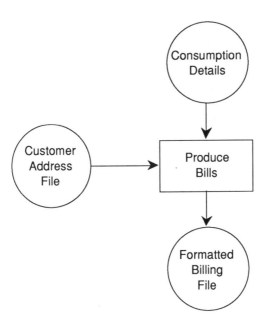

c) Print Sub-Systems

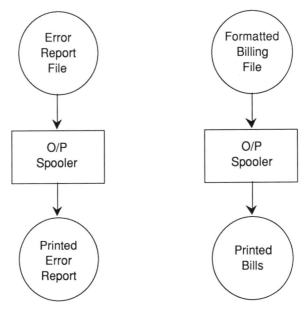

Figure 4.5 continued.

A suitable organisation for this file would be index sequential as this would support efficient processing of bulk transactions (meter readings, as illustrated, and payments) and also occasional on-line enquiries.

(b) Transaction Files

These contain data that relate to specific events or activities for example:

Event/Activity	Data
Meter Read	Account reference number, meter reading
Payment Made	Account reference number, payment

Transaction files are often serially organised when they are first created and are then reorganised (e.g. sorted on a specific key field) for more efficient processing against master files. Sometimes on a transaction file there may be more than one record with the same key, for example two payments relating to the same account. Transaction files are usually kept for a specified time after processing in case a master file has to be recreated and the updates on it repeated.

(c) Transition Files

These are intermediate or work files which are created for the organisation's operational convenience. They are normally used to hold temporary data during a process (e.g. while sorting) or to pass data from one process to another.

(d) Reference Files

These are really a form of master file but one where the data tends to remain relatively static. Examples of such files are:

In an electricity billing application - the addresses of dwellings and premises.

In a payroll application - employee's names and addresses

In a library - the subject index.

(e) Report Files (Printer Files)

These are known as "hard copy" files and contain the results of the processing, many of which will be produced on special preprinted stationery. For example:

Electricity bills
Wage slips
Validation and error reports

(f) Spool Files

These are temporary files normally maintained by the computer's operating system. They hold records read from slow input devices (e.g. keystations, cardreaders) or awaiting output to slow devices (e.g. printers, plotters).

(g) Dump Files

These are often also referred to as Backup or Logging Files. Their purpose is to ensure the integrity of the data in the system. For example, in our Electricity Billing Application during the running of the update program dumps of the state of the program could be taken at regular intervals. If the system then "crashed" during a run it would be unnecessary to repeat the whole update process, as the files could simply be recreated from the latest security dump and reprocessing could commence from that point.

4.5 File Processing Activities

The principal types of process that can be carried out on files are described in this section. Those we shall consider are: validation, matching, main file referencing and updating, sorting, merging, summarising, searching, weeding, report production and spooling. Again several of these activities are depicted in the Electricity Billing Application shown in figure 4.5.

(a) Validation

Ideally all the data presented to a system should be correct and complete. However, in practical situations, this is seldom the case. It is therefore essential to validate all transaction data which enters a system if we wish to avoid corrupting our master files and producing garbage output.

Errors in data can be introduced before it reaches the DP department or within the DP department itself. There may be errors in the original accession and recording of the data or in its manual handling prior to computer processing. Errors are frequently introduced when the data is transcribed onto a computer-processible medium (e.g. during key-punching) and there is also the possibility of misreading by input devices such as card and bar code readers. To overcome these problems several checking procedures can be introduced.

Checking procedures include the introduction of manual activities to oversee the handling of the data and often this is performed by a section of the DP department known as data control. Input to the computer may be transcribed and then re-entered verifying the original values and 'parity' checks can be included on all input devices. However, despite all these precautions it is still highly likely that errors will remain and hence the validation of data by software routines is of paramount importance in any computer system.

The types of validation which a programmer may be asked to provide are:-

(i)   batch total checks - the number of records or a total cash value agrees with a supplied total,

(ii) format (picture) checks - the data must match a prescribed format or formats e.g. UDA 167G and E448 BPT are both valid car registration numbers,

(iii) limit checks - a data value must be within a specified range,

(iv) value checks - a quantity must match prescribed rules e.g. orders are only accepted for items in multiples of ten,

(v) combination checks - two or more values must produce a meaningful result e.g. value of goods ordered multiplied by cost must be less
than £500,

(vi) compatibility checks - separate fields must agree with each other
e.g. age < 18 and status = minor would be acceptable,

(vii) presence checks - does a master file record exist for this key.

Also validation may be performed on codes such as check digits and
there may even be probability checks which involve counting the total
number of individual errors and if this is too high, rejecting the whole
of the input data.

(b) Sequential Matching

This file activity is also referred to as collation. It involves the
processing of two or more input files which are in the same key sequence
to determine which key values match and which do not. The files are
compared record by record; those records whose key values match may
be processed further and those whose keys fail to match may be reported
for further investigation or manual action. Examples of collation
processes are:-

(i) the matching of a file of purchase orders against a file of goods
received notes to determine which orders had been received and
which are still outstanding,

(ii) the matching of a transaction file against a master file to update the
information on the master file - matched transactions would be
processed and those that failed to match would be reported.

(c) Master File Referencing and Updating

Referencing merely implies that information will be copied from the
master file records during the processing run, while updating will

involve changing the information that is held on the master file. Updating often involves three types of processes:

(i)   the amendment of existing records to bring them into an up-to-date condition,

(ii)   the insertion of new records to the file,

(iii) the deletion of old records from the file.

Examples of referencing and updating are both present in the Electricity Billing System depicted in figure 4.5 The Customer Address File would be referenced for addresses and the Accounts Master File would be updated with the latest energy consumption figures.

The actual mode of accessing the mainfile records obviously depends upon the mainfile organisation. However, if it is indexed sequential then bulk transactions which involve a high main file hit rate are probably best sorted and then processed using a collation process. Conversely transactions with a low hit rate can be processed individually with the main file being accessed directly via its index.

(d) Sorting

This is the process of bringing a file of keyed records into a particular sequence or sequences depending upon the values held in one or more key fields within the records. Sorting is usually carried out on transaction files so that the records will be in the same order as a master file and can then be efficiently sequentially processed. In the Electricity Billing Application the transaction file of meter readings would be sorted into account reference number order for processing against the Accounts Master File.

With the introduction of on-line transaction processing systems over the last few years there has been a reduction in the number of sorts carried out in most DP systems. However, many applications, often due to the size of files involved, are unsuitable for totally on-line processing and for these sorts are still an essential feature.

(e) Merging

Here two or more files in the same key sequence are combined into one file. Basically these are types of collation processes which can be classed as:

(i)   a file merge where separate files of similar records are merged into one file of the same sequence. Here the total number of records in the output file is equal to the sum of the records in the input files.

(ii) a record merge where the corresponding records from two or more input files are combined into one record on the output file. For example, the merging of individual subject files holding student marks for each subject into one composite results file.

(f) Summarising

Information from records with the same key value is gathered together to form one output record. For example a summary of payments made into a company pension scheme which were originally recorded on separate yearly files.

(g) Searching/Extracting

This process involves looking for a record or a set of records which contain specific data values. Data may be extracted from the records or a count of occurrences may simply be accumulated. For example we could search through the Electricity Billing Application's Accounts Master File accumulating a count of the number of consumers who used more than 2000 units of electricity during a particular accounting period.

(h) Weeding

This involves the deletion of records with a certain characteristic from a file. It is often achieved in practice by copying all the records without that characteristic to a new file. For example, a mail order firm may wish to delete from its files details of all those customers who have not placed any orders during the last three years.

(i) Report Production

This activity is also referred to as output editing and it involves the formatting of information into a form suitable for use by either DP or non DP personnel. It may often involve the formatting of information so that it can be output onto special preprinted stationery. For example, the output from the Electricity Billing Application will be printed electricity bills which will normally be on specially preprinted forms which contain headings such as Tariff, Meter Readings, Units Used, Units Charged, Unit Price and Amount Charged plus details of how to make payments.

(j) Spooling

This process is normally under the control of the computer's operating system and it involves the transfer of data between fast and slow input/output devices. For example the formatted output for the electricity bills would normally be held in a disk or magnetic tape file; then when a printer is available the preprinted stationery would be loaded and the spooler program would be used to actually send the formatted text to the printer.

4.6 Documentation

A programmer needs to be given information on the program he has to produce, the files the program will use or create and the format of the individual records on each file. The UK National Computing Centre [25] have devised a comprehensive set of Data Processing Documentation Standards which have been adopted for use within many DP departments and academic institutions. These include specific forms (NCC numbers S32, S42 and S44) which are to be used for specifying programs, files and records.

An example of a completed S44 Record Specification is shown in figure 4.6 for a record from a personnel file. The COBOL description that would be generated from this is:

```
01  PERSONNEL-RECORD.
    03  PR-NAME                 PIC A(20).
    03  PR-ADDRESS.
        05  PR-ADDRESS-BODY.
            07  PR-STREET       PIC X(20).
            07  PR-TOWN         PIC X(15).
            07  PR-COUNTY       PIC X(15).
        05  PR-POST-CODE        PIC X(7).
    03  PR-TELEPHONE-NUMBER.
        05  PR-AREA-CODE        PIC 9(3).
        05  PR-NUMBER           PIC 9(7).
```

The equivalent structure diagram is shown in figure 4.7.

Having acquired an overview of the implementation language we are going to use and its application environment we can now proceed to consider the design of programs. This is covered in the next part of the text.

Record Specification N C C	Record description: PERSONNEL RECORD			System: PER	Document: 4.7	Name: PERSONNEL–REC	Sheet S44: 1

File specification refs. 4.4 PERSONNEL
Record size: 87
Record format: Fixed ☑ / Variable ☐
Record length: Fixed ☑ / Variable ☐
Medium: DISK

Ref.	Position From	Position To	Level	Name (In system design)	Data Type	Size	Picture
1	1	20	03	PR-NAME	C	20	A(20)
2	21	77	03	PR-ADDRESS			
3	21	70	05	PR-ADDRESS-BODY			
4	21	40	07	PR-STREET	C	20	X(20)
5	41	55	07	PR-TOWN	C	15	X(15)
6	56	70	07	PR-COUNTY	C	15	X(15)
7	71	77	05	PR-POST-CODE	C	7	X(7)
8	78	87	03	PR-TELEPHONE-NO			
9	78	80	05	PR-AREA-CODE	C	3	9(3)
10	81	87	05	PR-NUMBER	C	7	9(7)

S 44
Author | Issue | Date

Figure 4.6 Example Record Specification.
S44 record sheet is copyright of The National Computing Centre and is reproduced with their permission.

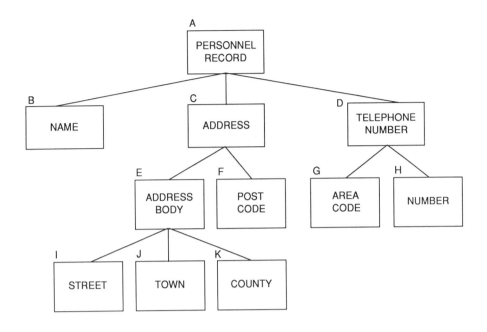

Figure 4.7 Structure Diagram of the Personnel Record Specified in Figure 4.6.

TASKS - CHAPTER 4

1. Draw structure diagrams of the files described in section 4.1.

2. Make sure you understand what is meant by serial, sequential, direct, index sequential and inverted file organisations. Where could each of these file types occur in the Electricity Billing System shown in figure 4.5?

3. Identify the COBOL equivalents to the above file organisations and detail in which way(s) each may be accessed from a COBOL program.

4. Distinguish between transaction and transition files.

5. Explain:

   (a) What is meant by the term "hit rate"?

   (b) Why an Indexed Sequential file organisation may be a good choice when there is the possibility of a high high rate for one type of enquiry and a low hit rate for another?

6. (a) Draw a structure diagram to represent national telephone numbers such as 091-232-8585 showing the subdivision into national code, exchange code and exchange number. Does your structure show you what you would dial if you were making a local call?

   (b) Decide how you would validate such a number.

PART 2

JACKSON STRUCTURED PROGRAMMING

The following two chapters describe the basics of the Jackson Structured Programming method. Chapter 6 gives an overview of the complete method and then proceeds to cover the stages which lead to the creation of the basic program structure that shows the overall logic of the program. Chapter 7 explains the remaining stages of the method, the determination of the detailed operations that the program has to carry out, the allocation of these functions to the program structure, the production of schematic logic and finally the implementation of the completed design in code. Details are also given of documentation standards which relate to structure diagrams and schematic logic.

CHAPTER 5
Fundamentals of JSP

5.1 The Method

Jackson Structured Programming is a data driven systematic program design method which leads to well structured solutions that do not depend on the inspirational whims of the designer. It is based on the premise that the structure of the program should reflect the structure of the underlying task and that this can be defined by deriving structures which represent the logical view of the data to be processed. Application of the method leads to standard design solutions for the types of programs which are commonly encountered in computer-based information systems. Also its staged approach to program production means that quality assurance and progress checks can be carried out as each task is completed.

The method itself is language and machine independent, but it should be realised that normally before a particular program design is commenced the target programming language and operational environment will be known. Therefore, the design for a particular program will obviously depend on the features of that chosen target language and the intended operational environment.

The stages in producing a program using the JSP method are:

0.   Understand what is required.

1.   Produce, according to the problem requirements, a logical data structure for each data stream on which the software is to operate.

2.   Fuse (combine) the logical data structures and create a basic program structure showing the controlling conditionals.

3. Determine from the problem requirements the processes which are to be carried out. Express these in terms of functions (executable operations) and produce a function list.

4. Finalise the program structure by allocating the functions to the appropriate elementary components of the basic program structure.

5. Produce schematic logic to support the final program structure.

6. Implement in the chosen target programming language from the schematic logic.

Stage 0 is not an explicit stage within Jackson's original method. However, this activity is implied in his text [9] and it is obviously necessary to carry it out before we can proceed to the following stages. Stage 6 is simply implementation, the design process being complete once the schematic logic has been produced.

JSP involves both analytical and compositional stages. Stages 0, 1 and 3 are essentially analytical in that they are concerned with developing a greater understanding of the problem and operations needed to solve it. Stages 2, 4 and 5 are compositional and involve the synthesis of two or more entities (e.g. a basic program structure and a function list) into one prescribed deliverable (e.g. a final program structure). These compositional stages provide a checking mechanism throughout the method. This is because, if their execution proves difficult or impossible, it indicates that previous stages have probably not been carried out fully. For example, if an appropriate elementary component cannot be found for the allocation of a specific function then it would appear that the basic program structure was developed insufficiently. Conversely if after allocating functions an elementary component remains with no functions allocated, the designer should consider carefully whether or not his function list is complete and whether his allocation of functions has been exhaustive.

In the remainder of this chapter and in the following we will consider each of the JSP stages in detail.

5.2 Stage 0 : Understand What Is Required

Before we can start to produce a solution we must fully understand what is required. If a detailed program specification has been produced this task may prove to be relatively straightforward. However, in too many instances programmers are supplied with only rudimentary specifications and it is often up to them to determine what is really wanted. Nevertheless for both types of situation some or all of the following activities can prove useful:

(i)   Ensure that you have identified the input data that is to be operated on, the outputs that are to be produced and the major processes that are to be carried out.

(ii) Ensure that the data streams on which the program operates and the intended operational environment are understood. This can be detailed by producing a System Network Diagram (SND) as described in section 2.4.

(iii) For each data stream that is to be handled ensure that the physical structure of the stream and the items in it are understood. The physical structure is simply a diagrammatic equivalent of a COBOL description or a NCC file/record specification such as that shown in figure 4.6. It is a view of the data stream or item in isolation i.e. it does not take into account the processing require ments. This activity is best accomplished by simply sketching out the structure of files and records as the specification for them is being studied. Doing this ensures that the basic structure of the data is understood and appreciated.

This stage and those following it are best understood by means of an example:-

Analysis of Orders Program

MOCO a mail order company deals with agents throughout the country. Each agent has his own identifying code comprising a two character area code and a four digit agent number which uniquely identifies him within an area. Orders from the agent detail the agent code, the catalogue reference number for the item ordered, the catalogue price, the number of items ordered and the type of payment: cash with order (coded 'M' for money) or credit (coded 'C').

Orders are recorded on a Monthly Orders File for sales analysis. The file is sorted on agent code so that the order of the file is agent within area. However, there may be many orders for each agent. Records on the file have the following COBOL description.

```
01   ORDER-RECORD.
    03   OR-AGENT-CODE.
        05   OR-AREA-CODE          PIC X(2).
        05   OR-AGENT-NUMBER       PIC 9(4).
    03   OR-CATALOGUE-REF          PIC X(6).
    03   OR-CATALOGUE-PRICE        PIC 9(3)V99.
    03   OR-NO-ORDERED             PIC 9(2).
    03   OR-PAYMENT-TYPE           PIC X.
```

Note that the field OR-CATALOGUE-PRICE is a five digit field with an assumed decimal point between the third and fourth digits (indicated by the V) and thus represents values in pounds and pence.

A program is required which will count the number of cash and credit orders and display the results on the user's terminal in the form:

NUMBER OF CASH ORDERS nnn   NUMBER OF CREDIT ORDERS nnn

where nnn represents the relevant numbers.

The results of the Stage 0 analysis for this program are shown in figure 5.1. The structure diagram for the file reflects the ordering of the file: zero, one or many orders for each agent, many agents within an area and many areas represented on the file. The structure for the output display shows it is a simple one line output consisting of two pieces of information.

(a) Inputs/Outputs/Processes

    Inputs: Monthly orders file

    Outputs: Counts of cash and credit orders

    Processes: Access records from montly orders file
                 Accumulate counts of cash and credit sales
                 Display accumulated counts

(b) SND

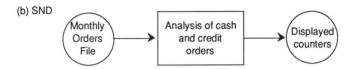

(c) Physical Structures

(i) Input File

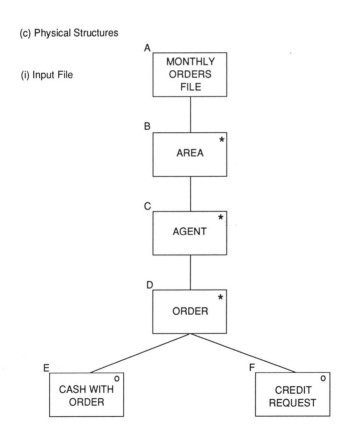

Figure 5.1

83

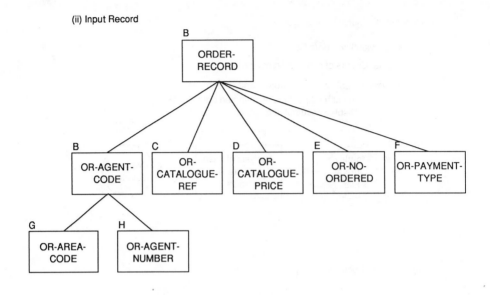

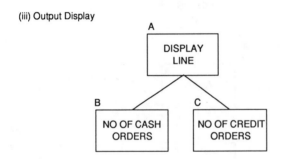

Figure 5.1 continued

5.3 Stage 1 : Produce Logical Data Structures

Once we have understood what the program requirements are we can proceed to the first formal stage of JSP. This is to produce a logical structure for each data stream i.e. a picture of the data from the point of view of the software that is going to process it. The physical structures which we have drawn up to now have represented data streams in isolation, i.e. data as it was specified with no allowances being made for the specific process that a particular program will carry out on it. A logical data structure on the other hand is totally dependent upon these specific processes.

The concept of logical data structures is best understood by means of a set of examples involving the Monthly Orders File detailed in the previous section:

Example 1

The program that was specified was required to count the number of cash and credit orders on the file. We are therefore concerned with the following entities:-

    the file
    the orders: cash and credit

but we are not concerned with:

    areas,
or agents

thus the logical structure for the file will be as shown in figure 5.2(a).

Example 2

Suppose all we wanted to do was count the numbers of orders on the file. Here we are concerned with:

    the file
    the orders

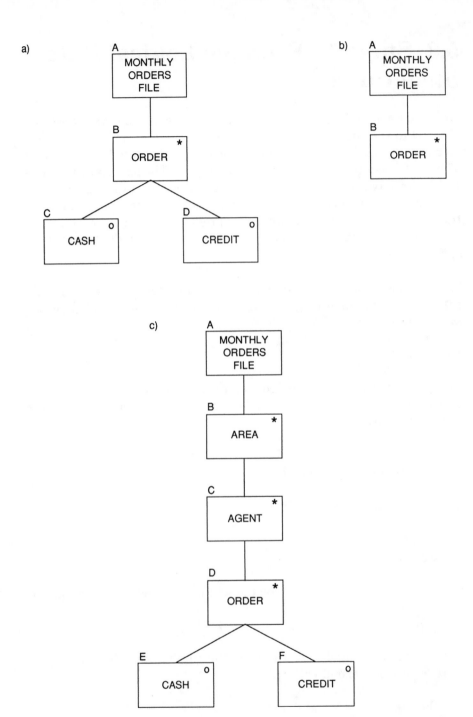

Figure 5.2 a-c Logical data structures for alternative views of Monthly Orders File.

and we are not concerned with

        cash,
        credit,
        areas,
or   agents

thus the logical structure will be as in figure 5.2(b).

Example 3

Suppose we now want to count the credit and cash orders by area and agent. Now we are concerned with

        the file
        the orders: cash and credit
        areas
and agents

thus the logical structure will be as in figure 5.2(c) i.e. it will be the same as the physical structure.

Example 4

Finally suppose we wish to count the credit and cash orders by area and agent but we wish to know how many of each type have a value of less than £100 and how many have a value of £100 or more (the value of an order is obtained by multiplying the catalogue price by the number ordered). Now we are concerned not only with all those entities detailed in example 3 but also with:

        credit orders of value less than £100
        credit orders of value of £100 or more
        cash orders of value of less than £100
        cash orders of value of £100 or more

thus the structure must be extended as shown in figure 5.2 (d).

It is normally sufficient when developing a logical data structure to decompose down to levels associated with the entity which is the unit of input/output e.g. data record, print line, VDU screen etc. This is

d)

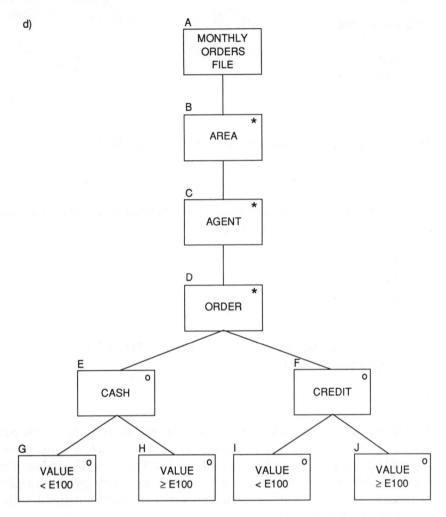

Figure 5.2 d Logical data structure for alternative view of Monthly Orders file.

illustrated in the diagrams shown in figure 5.2 where we are concerned at the lowest level with an order, a credit order, a cash order or an order of a particular value and type. Any elaboration of the structure below what is essential record level will depend upon the application but usually only occurs when iterated or selected fields are involved, for example, in a data validation program a field within a record may be valid or not. Also it should be noted that while in a physical record structure sub-record components should be shown in the order they physically occur, in a logical data structure this is not necessary. Here components should be shown in the logical order that they are processed. This reordering is perfectly acceptable, for once a record has been accessed by a program and brought into primary store all its constituent data fields may be referenced in any order and any number of times.

Basically the rules associated with producing data structures are -

(i) Develop the structure until there are no more levels which require decomposition i.e. will reference to the structure diagram provide the answers to all questions which relate to the program's requirements regarding that data stream?

(ii) Ensure that the structure is logically sound i.e. does it really represent the processing of the data stream.

Producing logical data structures is probably the most difficult stage of the JSP method. It requires patience and creativity as well as an insight into how programs actually process data coupled with the ability to produce abstract views of this data. It is an iterative process that can involve many revisions before a correct structure is derived. Often problems with logical data structures will not be detected until later stages of the method are attempted which will lead to further reconsiderations. However, with practice and the experience gained from considering different types of problems this stage does become much easier.

5.4 Stage 2 : Create a Basic Program Structure

This stage of the method involves three activities:

(i) Fusing (combining) the logical data structures into a composite fused data structure.

(ii) The transformation of the fused data structure into a basic program structure which may involve the insertion of additional components to aid the subsequent allocation of functions.

(iii) Attaching conditions to all the selections and iterations.

Each of these activities will be considered in turn and will be illustrated by applying them to the Analysis of Orders Program and similar simple processing examples.

5.4.1   Fusing the Data Structures

Here we wish to produce a single composite structure from the individual logical data structures that were produced in Stage 1. This is achieved by identifying "correspondences" between components within the data structures. Components which correspond are fused into a single component in the composite fused data structure. This activity of fusing data structures by identifying correspondences is of paramount importance in the JSP method and the whole of Chapter 11 is devoted to it. Therefore all we shall do here is to detail the results of fusing the data structures for the Analysis of Orders program.

The logical structures for the Monthly Orders File and the line of Displayed Counters are shown in figure 5.3 (a). The arrowed line between the two structures shows the correspondence: from the Monthly Orders File there is produced a Displayed Counters Line. These two components therefore fuse together, i.e. the two components labelled A merge into one, and we have the fused data structure shown in figure 5.3 (b). This is probably the simplest possible example of fusing there is. Those detailed in Chapter 11 become much more complex!

5.4.2   Transforming the Structure

When transforming our fused data structure into a basic program structure we make some changes to the text in each component box. The top component now represents the top most level of the program and hence is given the title PROGRAM. This may be followed by an

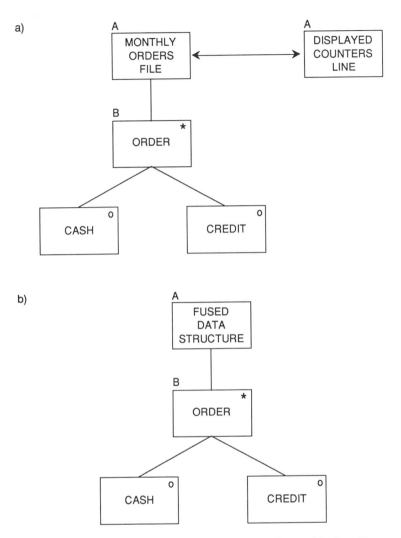

Figure 5.3 Logical and Fused Data Structures for Analysis of Orders Program.

identifying name. The prefix P- is added to all the other texts. For example a component entitled ORDER in the fused data structure becomes P-ORDER in the basic program structure. The P prefix is an abbreviation for process as in the program we are concerned with processes i.e. P-ORDER represents process order.

5.4.3 Additional Components

Stage 4 of the design method involves the allocation of functions to elementary components of the program structure. Sometimes the fused data structure will provide all the relevant elementary components and in such cases the fused data structure becomes the basic program structure. However, in most cases there are insufficient elementary boxes and some additions are necessary. These additions take the form of extra sequenced components or levels of sequenced components which are inserted into the program structure. Their main purpose is to provide for the positioning of initialisation and terminal functions before and after the actioning of a lower level component.

Two types of addition are common:-

(i) The insertion of a new level into the structure, consisting of a sequence of P-START, P-BODY and P-END components, immediately above an existing iterated or selected component. For example:

(a) extract from a fused   (b) resulting part of
data structure   program structure

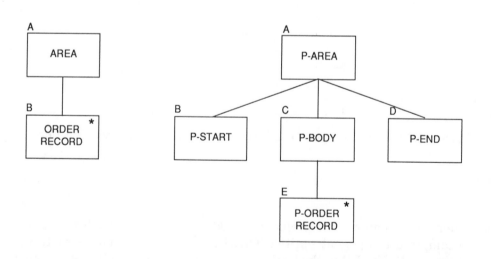

What we are doing here is providing two additional elementary components, P-START and P-END to which functions associated with start and end "housekeeping" processes can be allocated. The P-START, P-BODY and P-END components relate to the level immediately above them, i.e. in diagram (b) the three inserted components represent: process-area-start (initial processing associated with an area), process-area-body (the main processing associated with an area) and process-area-end (the terminal processing associated with an area).

(ii) The insertion of a new level into the structure consisting of a sequence of P-BODY and P-END components. This type of addition is normally made immediately below an iterated component which represents a unit of transfer from an input data stream, for example, immediately below a component which represents an input record. What we are providing here is an additional elementary component P-END to which will be allocated the function(s) associated with the accession of the next item from the input data stream. The need for such P-END components is detailed in the following section when we consider the principles of read ahead and read replace. As in (i) the new components relate to the iterative level immediately above them.

It should be noted that the insertion of either of these types of additional components has not distorted the basic logical structure of the program. All the original sequenced, selected and iterated structures still retain their former logical form. The additions which we have made are basically of a cosmetic nature and are needed simply because of the rule that functions should only be allocated to elementary components.

With experience the task of inserting additional components becomes almost second nature. For example, we could say that the top levels of any program should almost always include additional housekeeping components such as B, C and D as shown below.

To overcome the problem of deciding where additional levels have to be inserted some installations simply instruct their designers to insert an additional level above every iteration and selection. This simplifies the designers job but many additional levels can prove excessive especially in large programs and make the structure unnecessarily complicated.

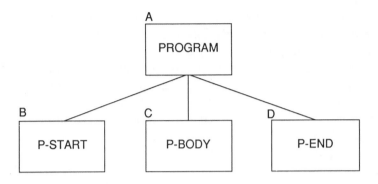

5.4.4 Principles of Read Ahead and Read Replace

Iterations occur zero, one or many times while a condition is true. This means that when handling a serial or sequential input data stream we will be processing items "while not end of data stream". The fact that iterations are implemented using WHILE constructs (i.e. constructs where the test is at the start of the iteration) means that we must attempt to access the item before the test can be performed. Thus we must use the principle of 'read ahead' or 'access ahead'. This means that before the iterative construct we must access the first item from the data stream. Then once the processing for that item is completed the last operation within the body of the iteration will be to access the next item. This latter operation is then a 'read replace' or 'access replace'.

The principles of read ahead and read replace can be best understood by a simple example. Suppose we have a copy program which reads records in turn from an input file and writes a copy of each record to an output file. The structure of each file is an iteration of records and since one is a perfect copy of the other the structures will be identical and will fuse together as shown in figure 5.4 (a). From this we can create a basic program structure as shown in figure 5.4 (b). Extra component levels have been added to cater for initial and terminal housekeeping on the file and for processing the current record and accessing the next. In the figure, for ease of understanding, the file handling operations necessary to carry out the task have simply been added below the relevant

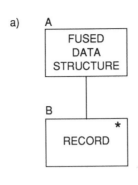

a)

A
FUSED DATA STRUCTURE

B
RECORD *

b)

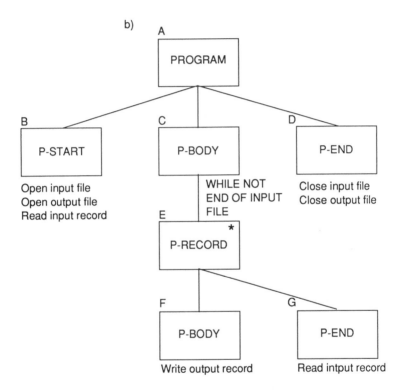

A
PROGRAM

B
P-START

Open input file
Open output file
Read input record

C
P-BODY

WHILE NOT
END OF INPUT
FILE

D
P-END

Close input file
Close output file

E
P-RECORD *

F
P-BODY

Write output record

G
P-END

Read intput record

Figure 5.4 Read ahead/Read replace structure.

components. At component B the first input record is accessed, the iterative test is then carried out and if we have not reached end of file a copy of the record is written at component F. The next input record is accessed at component G and the process is repeated while the condition is still true. Once the end of file is encountered the iteration is terminated and the files are closed at component D.

5.4.5 Attaching Conditions to the Program Structure

The final activity within this stage is to attach conditions to all the selections and iterations in the program structure. The condition(s) associated with an iteration should specify the circumstances under which the iterative structure will be executed. Similarly the condition(s) associated with a leg of a selection should specify the particular circumstances for that leg to be executed. Conditions may be written in full on the structure diagram alongside the relevant controlling paths as shown in figure 5.4(b). However, in many cases the size and complexity of the conditions will make annotation of the diagram very difficult. Thus it is much better in these cases to draw up a separate condition list and only allocate the condition numbers to the structure.

Conditions are usually listed as C1, C2, C3 ... The word 'IF' need not be written on the diagram before a condition which controls a selection, nevertheless the word 'WHILE' should always be written with the condition which controls an iteration to ensure there is no confusion with the non-zero based condition 'UNTIL' (logically the word until implies that something is to be done at least once, however, as we will see later the originators of the COBOL language did not view it in this way).

Conditions should be expressed clearly and unambiguously as English Language statements, for example:

C1 : Record type is credit
C2 : Same agent number
C3 : Not end of orders file

Conditions may be simple or compound and may be negated on the diagram by placing a bar over the condition, for example:

simple condition   C4 : Same area code

compound condition   C5 : Same area code and not end of
                              orders file

C5 is then equivalent to C4 and C3

negated condition: $\overline{C2}$ is equivalent to Not C2

Some installations prefer to avoid negative conditions such as "not end of orders file". In such instances the positive equivalent 'there is an order record to process' can be used instead.

Note - Conditions are only shown on program structures they are not shown on data structures. The text within the component boxes on data structures should be clear enough to identify what is being iterated or selected.

5.4.6   Analysis of Orders Example

In Figure 5.3 (b) the fused data structure for the Analysis of Orders Program was given. Application of the activities detailed in the two preceeding sections leads to the basic program structure shown in figure 5.5 with the controlling conditions listed below it. Additional components B, C and D have been added to provide process-program-start, process-program-body and process-program-end positions. The former and latter of these will be used for the allocation of file housekeeping functions and the first read function. Components F and G representing process-record-body and process-record-end are added to facilitate the placement of the read replace function. It should be noted that the addition of components F and G is not absolutely essential as the read replace function could be allocated to both of the selected components H and I. However, if we bear possible maintenance activities in mind it is much better to have the read replace function allocated only once in the correct logical position i.e. at the end of the iteration.

The operational flow through the basic program structure is depicted by the directed graph shown in figure 5.6. Components A, B, C are traversed first then the iterative structure is traversed while condition C1 (not end of orders file) is true. Once this condition becomes false the iteration is exited and component D is traversed. Within the iteration control flows via components E and F to component H or component I depending upon condition C1 or C2. The flows then rejoin at component G.

Program Structure

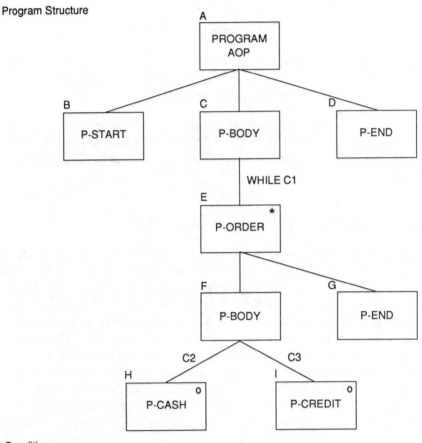

Conditions

       C1 not end of orders file

       C3 cash order (OR-PAYMENT-TYPE = M)

       C3 credit order (OR-PAYMENT-TYPE = C)

Figure 5.5 Basic structure for Analysis of Orders Program.

98

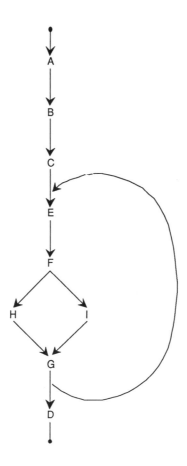

Figure 5.6 Directed graph for the Flow Though the Analysis of Orders Program.

5.5 Review

We have now reached the point where we have produced a basic structure for the Analysis of Orders Program. This has involved understanding the problem, producing logical data structures, fusing them together, adding additional components and detailing the controlling conditionals. The activities we have undertaken may at first sight have appeared excessive and prolonged for such a simple program.

However, you must bear in mind that the purpose of these sections has been to describe the method in detail so that it can be applied to any problem no matter how complex it is. As experience with the method is gained, application of the techniques associated with the various stages becomes easier and can often be performed almost subconsciously. For example, the explicit step of producing a fused data structure and then transforming it into a basic program structure, as described in section 5.4, can be omitted and it is perfectly acceptable to go straight from logical data structures to a basic program structure. Nevertheless, it is extremely useful for newcomers to the method to explicitly perform all the steps within each stage.

The remaining stages in completing the design are:- determine the detailed functions which the program carries out, allocate the functions to the program structure, and finally produce schematic logic. These stages are explained in the following chapter along with details of documentation standards for the structure diagrams, schematic logic and other items of documentation which application of the JSP method generates.

TASKS - CHAPTER 5

1. Produce physical data structure diagrams to represent the follow
    ing records and files:

```
(a)      01  A-RECORD.
           03  AR-PART-1.
             05  ARP1-FIELD1          PIC X(10).
             05  ARP1-FIELD2          PIC X(5).
           03  AR-PART-2.
             05  ARP2-FIELD1          PIC 9.
             05  ARP2-GROUP1.
               07  ARP2-FIELD2        PIC X(10).
               07  ARP2-FIELD3        PIC X(100).
           03  AR-PART3               PIC X(20).

(b)    FD  STOCK-TRANSACTIONS.
         01  ISSUE-RECORD.
```

```
            03   RECORD-TYPE               PIC X.
            03   PART-NUMBER               PIC X(6).
            03   NUMBER-ISSUED             PIC 9(3).
         01  RECEIPT-RECORD.
            03   RECORD-TYPE               PIC X.
            03   PART-NUMBER               PIC X(6).
            03   NUMBER-RECEIVED           PIC 9(3).
         01  STOCK-BALANCE.
            03   RECORD-TYPE               PIC X.
            03   PART-NUMBER               PIC X(6).
            03   NEW-STOCK-LEVEL           PIC 9(4).
```

(c)
```
         01  A-PAGE.
            03   A-LINE   OCCURS 60 TIMES.
               05   A-CHARACTER   OCCURS 80 TIMES   PIC X.
```

(d)
```
         01  A-REPORT.
            03   HEADING-LINE   OCCURS 3 TIMES     PIC X(60).
            03   REPORT-DETAIL.
               05   DISTRIBUTION-NAMES            PIC X(100).
               05   REPORT-LINE   OCCURS 50 TIMES  PIC X(80).
```

2. (a) A program only accesses, in order, data from fields ARP2-
         FIELD2 and ARP1-FIELD1 of the record defined in task
         1(a). Draw the logical record structure.

    (b) A program counts the number of issue records (RECORD-
         TYPE = 1) on the stock file defined in task 1(b). Draw the
         logical structure for the file.

    (c) Amend the structure to allow for separate counts to be
         maintained of issues of up to and including 10 items and
         issues of over 10 items.

3. (a) Explain why additional components may need to be added to
         a fused data structure when transforming it into a basic
         program structure.

    (b) Ensure you understand what is meant by the terms 'read
         ahead' and 'read replace'. Explain where the relevant func-
         tions would be placed on a basic program structure for

a program which accesses each record from the STOCK-
TRANSACTIONS file defined above.

4. Produce a basic program structure for a program which is to count
the number of persons called 'JOHN SMITH' whose details are held
on a file of personnel records as defined in section 4.6. Assume the
output from the program is a simple one line display on a VDU:

Number of people called JOHN SMITH = nnn

CHAPTER 6
Completing the Program

6.1 Stage 3 : Determine Functions and List Them

6.1.1 Functions

In stage 3 of the JSP method we have to determine from the problem requirements what operations the program has to carry out. These operations are expressed in terms of functions (executable operations) each of which has to be a clear unambiguous English language statement such as:

request and access student's name
clear the count of orders (NO-OF-ORDERS)
open sales file
read record from sales file
close sales file

When we identify functions we must ensure that they can eventually be implemented in our chosen target language - in our case COBOL. Thus the features of the language will obviously influence our choice of functions. Also where a specific program variable is to be used in the function this should be named (see section 6.1.2). But there does not need to be one to one mapping between functions and eventual coded statements. For example a function such as:

create heading line for output report

is perfectly acceptable so long as the format of this heading line has been clearly defined elsewhere, for example, in a NCC record specification. The general rule is that a function should normally map onto a sequence of source language statements that are concerned with one entity in the eventual program, for example, a heading line. Because of the English nature of COBOL many of the functions that we define will be identical or very similar to COBOL statements themselves. But we should avoid producing a function list that is simply a set of COBOL statements - the functions must be clear, unambiguous and written so that an inexperienced programmer could understand the intention of each.

6.1.2 Determination of Functions

Functions should be determined from the program requirements without reference to the program structure which we derived in stages 1 and 2 of the method. This is done so that when we allocate the functions to the structure in stage 4 there can be a double check on the completeness of both the function list and the program structure. Functions when identified should be entered in the function list and given a sequential reference number. It is important to try and ensure that the function list is exhaustive and that no program operations have been omitted. It is therefore wise to approach function identification in a logical and ordered manner. Any details of program input, outputs and processes plus a SND that may have been generated in stage 0 (see section 5.2) will prove helpful. A sensible approach is to:

(a) identify and list the functions associated with the handling of each input data stream,

(b) identify and list the functions associated with the handling of each output data stream,

(c) consider the processes that have to be carried out on each input stream to generate the relevant output - list the resultant functions,

(d) consider start of program housekeeping, for example, clearing counters, and end of program actions - list the resultant functions,

(e) similarly consider any housekeeping that needs to be done at the start and end of processing a group of records, for example,

saving a key value or group identifier value for subsequent checking
- list the functions,

(f) stand back from the problem and ask "have I omitted any operations?" - list any additional functions you have identified.

When drawing up a function list, internal data items will often also be
identified, for example, counters to hold accumulated totals. Each of
these should be named, their format (picture) determined and they
should be entered in a list of variables and constants along with a
relevant narrative description. These items will form the Working-
Storage entries for our program and hence need to be formally identified
and defined. Internal data items may also have been identified when the
condition list was drawn up and they too should be included in the list.

6.1.3 Detection of the End of Input Data Files

In COBOL the end of a file (eof) is detected when we attempt to read past
the last data record in the file. The AT END phrase of the relevant read
statement would then be executed which will allow us to set an end of
file indicator which can subsequently be tested at the start of an
iteration, for example the COBOL statement

```
READ ORDERS-FILE RECORD
    AT END MOVE 1 TO EOF-ORDERS-FILE.
```

will cause the value of the data item EOF-ORDERS-FILE to be set to 1
once the end of file is detected. Thus when drawing up our function list
we need to include with the relevant read functions the 'at end' option
and we need to define an end of file indicator for each of the relevant files.

6.1.4 Analysis of Orders Example

We can now proceed to draw up our function list for the Analysis of
Orders Program. The list of functions is given below in figure 6.1 and
the relevant internal data items that are needed are defined in the list
of variables given in figure 6.2

```
1   Open monthly orders file
2   Read record from monthly orders file, at end set the
          value of EOF-ORDERS-FILE equal to 1
3   Close monthly orders file
4   Display counts of cash and credit orders with explana-
          tory text
5   Add 1 to count of cash orders ( M-COUNT )
6   Add 1 to count of credit orders ( C-COUNT )
7   Set count of cash orders ( M-COUNT ) = 0
8   Set count of credit orders ( C-COUNT ) = 0
9   Set value of EOF-ORDERS-FILE = 0
10  Stop program run
```

Figure 6.1   Function list for Analysis of Orders Program

```
Variable            Picture      Description

EOF-ORDERS-FILE     9            defines state of monthly
                                 orders file
                                 value zero = not eof
                                 value  1   = eof

M-COUNT             9(3)         counter for accumulating the
                                 number of cash orders

C-COUNT             9(3)         counter for accumulating the
                                 number of credit orders
```

Figure 6.2   List of internal variables for Analysis of Orders Program

6.2 Stage 4 : Finalise the Program Structure

6.2.1 Allocation of Functions

To produce our final version of the program design we have to allocate the individual functions to the appropriate elementary components of the basic structure we developed in stage 2 of the method. To do this we work down the function list in order and allocate each function in turn to the elementary component(s) to which it relates by writing its reference number below the component(s). Function numbers should be written under a component in the order they are to be executed and should be separated by commas. Care must be taken to ensure that a

106

function is allocated to every component where it is to be actioned. You should not assume that since a function has been allocated to one component it does not have to be allocated to any others.

In deciding where to place a particular function the following considerations will prove helpful:

(i) How often should this function be carried out? Once in the whole program? Once for a file? Once for a group of records? Once for each record? Once for a particular data item? etc.

(ii) Where in the program should each of the occurrences for the function be carried out? At the start of the program? At the end of the program? At the start of processing a file? At the end of processing a file? etc.

(iii) If the function is a serial or sequential read remember the principle of read ahead and read replace when placing the function. The read ahead should preceed the relevant iteration and the read replace should normally be allocated to the last component within the iteration.

6.2.2 Checking Function Allocation

It should be remembered that functions must only be allocated to elementary components. The reason for this rule is simply that if the structure was not extended as described in section 5.4.3, and functions were added to both elementary and non-elementary components, the final diagram would become extremely complex and it would be very easy for mistakes to arise over the ordering of functions. If you find that there is no suitable elementary component to allocate a function to, although there is a suitable non-elementary component, this simply means that insufficient additional components were identified in stage 2 of the method. However, if no non-elementary component can be identified this means that either an error or an omission has occurred. In this case you should:

(i) Check if the function really exists or whether it needs to be expressed more clearly.

(ii) Check the logical data structure(s) that relate to the relevant part of the processing.

(iii) Check that the fusing of the logical data structures has been carried out correctly.

107

Similarly, if after the allocation of functions has been completed there remains elementary components in the structure which have had no functions allocated to them then further checks should be carried out. It

Program Structure

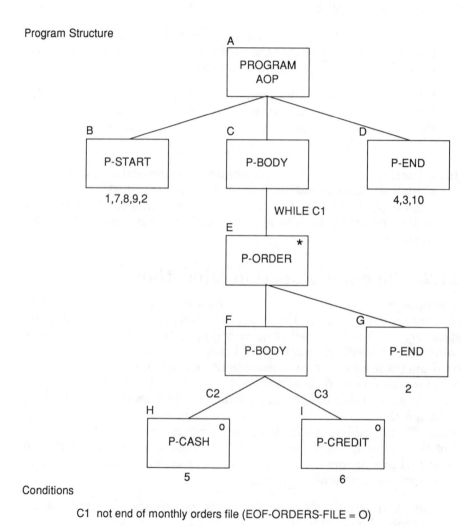

Conditions

C1 not end of monthly orders file (EOF-ORDERS-FILE = O)
C3 cash order (OR-PAYMENT-TYPE = M)
C3 credit order (OR-PAYMENT-TYPE = C)

Figure 6.3 Final Program Structure for Analysis of Orders Program.

may be that there are really no functions to be allocated and that the action associated with the component is 'do nothing'. On the other hand this situation may also indicate that the function list is incomplete and that functions still await identification.

Figure 6.3 shows the final program structure for the Analysis of Orders Program with the functions from figure 6.1 allocated. For ease of reference the conditions have been listed beneath the program structure. If there are few functions and they are reasonably concise it is acceptable to write the actual functions below the components instead of the numbers. Similarly the actual conditions may be used in place of the condition numbers.

6.3 Stage 5 : Produce Schematic Logic

6.3.1 Schematic Logic

The last formal stage of the JSP design method is to produce schematic logic from the final program structure diagram. As described in section 2.3 schematic logic is a form of pseudocode which provides a textual representation of the program logic. The hierarchic structure of the design is reproduced in the schematic logic by indenting the text at each level and by representing each component in the structure diagram by a clearly defined textual block. The names of these blocks provide a direct link with the program structure and where they are non-elementary their type and scope are defined by adding a suffix to the name of the block. The suffixes are:-

(i)	for sequences:	-SEQ
		-SEQ-END
(ii)	for selections:	-SEL
		-OR1, -OR2, -OR3 etc.
		-SEL-END
(iii)	for iterations:	-ITER
		-ITER-END

If the textual block represents a selected or iterated component the relevant controlling conditional is written in the schematic logic alongside the -SEL, -ORn or -ITER suffix. The name of the blocks within the schematic logic may be derived from the text within the component box on the structure diagram or may be generated from the box identifier. For example, from the structure diagram shown in figure 6.3 the first approach could generate for component E the name -

```
P-ORDER-SEQ
```

while the second method could generate a name such as

```
AOP1E-SEQ
```

where the first part of the name was generated from a program identifier (AOP), the page number of the diagram (1, as this diagram is contained on a single page) and the component identifier (E). The schematic logic for these two approaches are given in figures 6.4 and 6.5. Note that with the first approach some names have had to be extended to include information from the superior component to ensure the uniqueness of each name. These alternative approaches will be considered further in section 6.5.

```
PROGRAM-AOP-SEQ
    P-START
        Open monthly orders file
        Set count of cash orders (M-COUNT) = 0
        Set count of credit orders (C-COUNT) = 0
        Set value of EOF-ORDERS-FILE = 0
        Read record from monthly orders file at end set the
                            value of EOF-ORDERS-FILE = 1
    P-PROGRAM-BODY-ITER while not end of monthly orders file
                            (while EOF-ORDERS-FILE = 0)
        P-ORDER-SEQ
            P-ORDER-BODY-SEL if cash order (OR-PAYMENT-TYPE = M)
                P-CASH
                    Add 1 to count of cash orders (M-COUNT)
            P-ORDER-BODY-OR1 if credit order (OR-PAYMENT-TYPE = C)
                P-CREDIT
                    Add 1 to count of credit orders (C-COUNT)
            P-ORDER-BODY-SEL-END
            P-ORDER-END
                Read record from monthly orders file at end set the
                            value of EOF-ORDERS-FILE = 1
        P-ORDER-SEQ-END
    P-PROGRAM-BODY-ITER-END
```

```
P-PROGRAM-END
    Display counts of cash and credit orders with explanatory text
    Close monthly orders file
    Stop program run
PROGRAM-AOP-SEQ-END
```

Figure 6.4   Schematic Logic for Analysis of Orders Program Version 1

```
AOP1A-SEQ
  AOP1B
    Open monthly orders file
    Set count of cash orders (M-COUNT) = 0
    Set count of credit orders (C-COUNT) = 0
    Set value of EOF-ORDERS-FILE = 0
    Read record from monthly orders file at end set the
                    value of EOF-ORDERS-FILE = 1
    AOP1C-ITER while not end of monthly orders file
                    (while EOF-ORDERS-FILE = 0)
      AOP1E-SEQ
        AOP1F-SEL if cash order (OR-PAYMENT-TYPE = M)
          AOP1H
              Add 1 to count of cash orders (M-COUNT)
        AOP1F-OR1 if credit order (OR-PAYMENT-TYPE = C)
          AOP1I
              Add 1 to count of credit orders (C-COUNT)
        AOP1F-SEL-END
        AOP1G
            Read record from monthly orders file at end set the
                    value of EOF-ORDERS-FILE = 1
      AOP1E-SEQ-END
    AOP1C-ITER-END
    AOP1D
      Display counts of cash and credit orders with explanatory text
      Close monthly orders file
      Stop program run
AOP1A-SEQ-END.
```

Figure 6.5   Schematic Logic for Analysis of Orders Program Version 2

6.3.2   The Need for Schematic Logic

Schematic logic needs to be produced for three main reasons:-

(i)   It provides an easily understood, but detailed, description of the program logic and the operations which the program is to carry out. It hence supports program maintenance and aids communication between programmers themselves and also between programmers and other DP staff and users. Program structure diagrams are ideal for understanding the overall logic of a program. However, when trying to understand the detailed logic, for example, while undertaking the maintenance of the program, the use of program structures and separate functions and condition lists, which have to be constantly cross referred to, is less than ideal. In situations such as these schematic logic plus the structure diagram is much more satisfactory.

(ii) It provides a bridge between the final program design expressed by the structure diagram and our target programming language. If we are using a non block structured language such as COBOL for implementation, and we wish to produce code which mirrors the control flow through the program structure, then schematic logic provides an ideal base to code from. This aspect will be considered further in the next section.

(iii) It provides support for the JSP techniques of Backtracking and Program Inversion which are considered in part two of the text.

6.4 Stage 6 : Implement in Target Programming Language

Once the design has been completed the program must be implemented in the chosen target programming language; which in our case is COBOL. Since COBOL is not a block structured language, unlike say Pascal or ADA, it is necessary to use a set of coding rules when undertaking the implementation. There are two different approaches which are commonly used to convert JSP designs into COBOL code, these are classed as "hierarchic coding" and "in-line coding" (also known as "flat coding").

6.4.1 Hierarchic Coding

In pure hierarchic coding each component of the program structure is coded as a separate PERFORMed routine. The selective and iterative control structures are implemented using IF statements, which are frequently nested within one another, and controlled forms of the

PERFORM itself. The main problem with hierarchic COBOL code is that it is not totally compatable with two particular JSP techniques known as Backtracking and Program Inversion. However, even if these techniques are not being used it has two possible weaknesses when used to implement large programs:

(i)   The logic of the implemented code can prove difficult to follow. This is due to the fact that the control flow 'jumps' from one PERFORMed routine to another and placement of the routines in the code can be very disparate (i.e. they may be a significant distance from one another).

(ii) It has been recognised [27] that if this approach is taken to extremes the overheads of the multilevel PERFORMs may in some cases exceed the cost of the actual PERFORMed code.

Nested IF statements are considered in section 9.2.3 and some examples of hierarchic code are given in chapter 17 where the PERFORM statement is considered in detail.

6.4.2 In-Line Coding

In-line coding mirrors the schematic logic in layout and uses controlled GO TO statements to implement iterative and selected structures. The code is produced by a straightforward line by line conversion of the schematic logic. This leads to a COBOL Procedure Division which contains many paragraph names compared with hierarchic code; because a paragraph name is generated for each name in the schematic logic. However, these do not generate extra code in the object program and they do provide links with the design documents and emphasise the pseudo block structure of the code.

In-line code is compatible with the JSP techniques of Backtracking and Program Inversion and will generally produce programs that will run faster than hierarchically coded equivalents. However, many existing COBOL practitioners at first find its form inelegant and lacking in readability. Neverthless, once it is realised that the code simply serves as an implementation medium for the design, and it is the design documents that should be the primary reference material these objections lose their importance.

The implementation of the Analysis of Orders program using in-line code is detailed in Chapter 9 after we have devoted some time to the COBOL language itself.

6.5 Documentation Standards

Whilst undertaking a JSP design the following major items of documentation will have been generated.

(i)   a logical data structure for each data stream on which the program operates,

(ii) details of correspondences between the structures,

(iii) a program structure with allocated conditions and functions,

(iv) condition and function lists,

(v)   schematic logic.

In addition to the above further documents detailing SNDs, physical data structures, fused data structures and the like may also have been generated.

All these documents not only help in the creation of a program but they are also needed by those people who in the future are going to maintain it, for over the lifetime of a program there will probably be many people who have to understand it. Thus the documentation that we generate for real programs must itself be capable of being organised and referenced.

The JSP documentation standards outlined in this text are based on those that are in use at Sunderland Polytechnic [28]. These are themselves based on standards published by the UK National Computing Centre [25] and by what is now the UK Central Computer and Telecommunications Agency [29]. Lack of space prevents a detailed description of each document and therefore only the more important aspects will be covered.

6.5.1 Forms and Document Referencing

Two NCC forms are ideally suited for JSP documentation. These are the

114

S34 (A4 size) and S33 (A3 size) chart sheets which were originally produced by the NCC for recording flowcharts. Figure 6.6 shows a completed S34 for the structure of the Analysis of Orders Program. Along the top of each NCC form there are a set of reference boxes which allow each document to be uniquely identified plus there is space to give a brief description of the subject matter of the document. The references are:

(i) System - the name of the system of which the program is a part.

(ii) Document - a predefined code given to each document type to ease filing and enable logical groups of documents to be readily identified, for example, all the logical data structures for a program.

(iii) Name - a name or code that uniquely identifies the subject of the document, for example, the name of a program, the name of a file etc. The system used at Sunderland is to give each program within a system a unique alphabetic identifying code which will then be used for cross reference purposes.

(iv) Sheet number - sequential sheet number.

Unique reference to any document is then given by the values of these four boxes.

6.5.2 Labelling Components on Structure Charts

The components on each sheet of any structure chart are labelled in the sequence A to Z, left to right and top to bottom as illustrated in figure 6.6. The sequence recommences on each new sheet with the letter A. If more than 26 components lie on a sheet the sequence is continued with AA, AB, AC etc. Similar pairs of letters are used if during amendment additional component(s) are inserted. Existing components are not relabelled during amendment of a document. The combination of sheet number and component label thus allows unique identification of a single component within a named structure.

If we allocate to each program within a system a unique alphabetic code then the identifier formed by combining this code with the sheet number and component label provides a unique reference within a system. This identifier is used at Sunderland Polytechnic not only to reference the

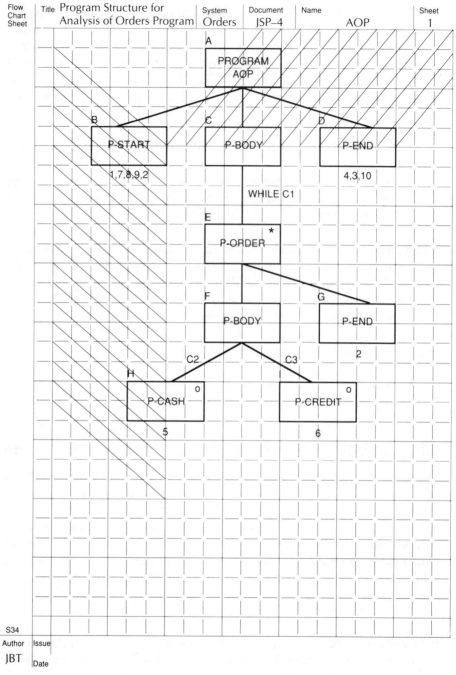

Figure 6.6 Completed S34 showing a program structure. (S34 flowchart sheet is copyright of The National Computing Centre and is reproduced with their permission).

116

relevant component in the program structure but it is also used in the schematic logic and it is carried over into the Procedure Division coding of the source program. We thus have a unique set of identifiers that link together the three primary items used in program maintenance. i.e. the program structure diagram, the schematic logic and the source code listing. For example, the identifier AOP1E uniquely identifies component E in the structure diagram shown in figure 6.6. The name of the corresponding textual block in the schematic logic is AOP1E-SEQ and this will also be the name of the corresponding paragraph in the Procedure Division of the program.

A code such as AOP1E-SEQ allows quick reference to be made to the three corresponding items in the Procedure Division, schematic logic and program structure. Such referencing would be much more difficult if we used the text within the program component as the identifier. This is illustrated by considering how do we locate items named P-ORDER and P-ORDER-SEQ? This task may appear straightforward in the given example but suppose the program structure stretched over many pages with say 15/20 components on each page?

6.5.3 Cross Referencing Large Program Structures

The program structure for the simple Analysis of Orders program could be written out on one sheet. However, this is exceptional and most real programs would have designs that occupy many pages. We therefore need a means of extending the diagrams over more than one page which allows the parts to be linked together. This is achieved as follows: where a structure has to be extended over a page the component to be continued has a stripe along the bottom giving the cross reference of the expanded structure. The component is then repeated at the top of the expanded structure with a stripe along the top giving the cross reference of the originating component.

For example suppose the structure shown in figure 6.6 had to be fitted on two smaller pages with a break at component E. The result is shown in figure 6.7. The original component E has a cross reference stripe added to the bottom of it quoting AOP/2A i.e. the top component on the continued page. A copy of component E with the remainder of the structure appears on the second page relabelled A-F. The cross reference AOP/1E is given in the stripe at the top of the new component A.

6.5.4 Schematic Logic For Large Program Structures

For each sheet of a program structure a schematic logic text will be generated. The name given in the name box at the top of the NCC form used for the schematic logic is the three character program code plus the sheet number of the relevant part of the program structure, for example, AOP1. This also forms the first part of the name of each textual block, the remainder being composed of the component identifier and its type. It should be noted that the schematic logic generated from one program structure sheet may fill more than one sheet and these should be given sequential sheet numbers.

Where, as detailed in section 6.5.3, a program structure is expanded on a subsequent sheet the linking reference is given in the schematic logic for the superior part of the structure preceded by the word DO. For example the schematic logic for components C and E in figure 6.7a would be

```
AOP1C-ITER while not end of monthly orders file
    AOP1E
        DO AOP2A
AOP1C-ITER-END
```

and the schematic logic for component A in figure 6.7(b) would be

```
AOP2A-SEQ
    :
    :
    :
    :
AOP2A-SEQ-END
```

Page 1

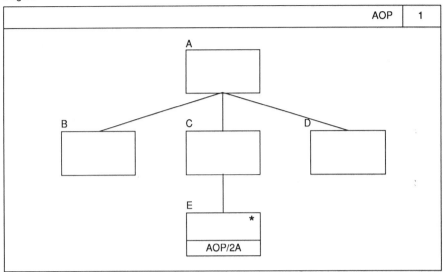

Page 2

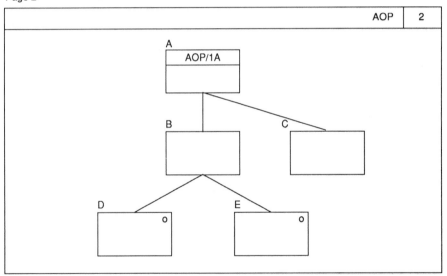

Figure 6.7 Illustration of cross component referencing in a large program.

119

TASKS - CHAPTER 6

1. Try to complete the design of the program that counts the number of persons called JOHN SMITH (task 4 in chapter 5).

2. Look at a friend's solution to the JOHN SMITH count problem. Can you understand his solution? Can he understand yours?

3. Obtain a copy of the NCC, Data Processing Documentation Standards (reference 25). Check for example in your college or public library. Read the introductory sections and browse through the text to get the feel of the importance of standards.

4. Check if you have access to a supply of S34/33 chart sheets; if so use them for your structure diagrams.

5. Talk to an experienced programmer about the task of program maintenance and its problems. Discuss how a set of properly completed program documents can help.

PART 3
THE COBOL LANGUAGE AND THE IMPLEMENTATION OF COBOL DESIGNS

Part 1 included an overview of the COBOL language, details of its facilities and descriptions of the types of applications which it is intended to support. This background knowledge, as has been shown in Part 2, can then be used in the analysis of problems and in the production of solutions. However, to be able to implement program designs in COBOL it is obviously necesssary to have a detailed knowledge of the language itself. The four chapters which comprise this part provide sufficient information to enable you to implement straightforward COBOL applications. They cover the basic elements of the language, the structure and form of each of the four divisions, the basic COBOL verbs, how control structures and JSP designs are implemented, how reports can be produced and how arithmetic operations are supported.

CHAPTER 7

COBOL Fundamentals and the First Three Divisions

7.1 Introduction

Before you can commence with the COBOL implementation of a program design you have to acquire a technical knowledge of the language itself. This entails understanding the language's structure and form, i.e. its syntax, and also the meaning of syntactically correct components within the language, i.e. its semantics. Thus we need to break the language down into its constituent parts and then consider each part in turn.

As we saw in chapter 3 a COBOL program is subdivided into four divisions:

```
IDENTIFICATION DIVISION.
ENVIRONMENT DIVISION.
DATA DIVISION.
PROCEDURE DIVISION.
```

The Environment Division consists of a CONFIGURATION SECTION and usually an INPUT-OUTPUT SECTION. The Data Division can contain a FILE SECTION, a WORKING-STORAGE SECTION and a LINKAGE SECTION. The Procedure Division, which specifies the operation of the program, consists of paragraphs each with its own paragraph heading. The paragraphs in the Procedure Division can also be grouped into sections each with its own section heading. Paragraphs are comprised of sentences, sentences are comprised of statements,

statements are comprised of words with separators between them, and finally words consists of characters. Thus just like the English Language, on which it is based, the COBOL language has a structure of paragraphs, sentences, statements, words and characters. However, unlike English speakers who can accept and understand poor grammar and imprecise meaning a COBOL compiler can only accept input which is both syntactically and semantically correct.

7.2 The Basic Elements of the COBOL Language

7.2.1 The COBOL Character Set

The most basic element of COBOL is its character set. This group of 51 characters which form all COBOL words and separators are:

the upper case alphabet A through to Z,
the digits 0 through to 9,

and the special characters:

	space
+	plus
-	minus
*	asterisk
/	solidus
=	equals sign
£ or $	currency sign
,	comma
;	semicolon
.	full stop and decimal point
"	quotation marks
(	left parenthesis
)	right parenthesis
>	greater than sign
<	less than sign

It must be remembered that the characters given above are those that are used for coding a COBOL program. However, the data on which the program operates can contain any character which the computer can handle. Also it should be noted that in some COBOL implementations the apostrophe (') is treated as equivalent to the quotation mark (") and the two can be used interchangeably.

7.2.2 Separators

Separators are those characters from the COBOL character set which are used to delimit COBOL words and literals. They are:

(i) one or more spaces,

(ii) comma (,), semicolon (;), or full stop (.) each of which must be followed by a space,

(iii) the left and right parenthesis (( )) appearing in balanced pairs,

(iv) quotation marks (" ") defining the beginning, continuation or end of a non-numeric literal. The opening quotation mark must be immediately preceded by a space or left parenthesis. The closing quotation mark must be immediately followed by a space, right parenthesis, comma, semicolon or period.

A space may precede and/or follow any of the above separators. However, if a space is within the quotation marks delimiting a literal it obviously becomes part of the literal.

7.2.3 The Full Stop

This needs special mention as it is probably the most important character in the COBOL character set and it is also the most troublesome to anyone learning COBOL! All division, section and paragraph headings must be followed by a full stop. So must individual entries in the first three divisions and sentences in the Procedure Division. If the necessary full stops are omitted or misplaced the result will either be compilation errors or code which probably does not execute as the programmer intended.

7.2.4 Words

A COBOL word is a string of not more than 30 characters which is formed from the reduced character set - A through to Z, 0 through to 9 and hyphen. These character strings form either a user-defined name, a reserved word or a level number which is used in data definitions.

(a) User-defined Names

These must contain at least one alphabetic character and if a hyphen is used it must not be the first or last character of the name. The types of names that can be defined by a COBOL user may be classed as:

data-names	paragraph names
record-names	section-names
file-names	condition-names
program-names	index-names
implementor-names	text-names
mnemonic-names	library-names

The use of most of these classes is self explanatory and the remainder will become clear as we look at each of the four COBOL divisions in detail. Wherever possible user-defined names should be meaningful and follow a predefined standard as this will make the program easier to understand and maintain.

When we manipulate a data entity, which may be a file, a record or a field within a record or an array, we need to make unique reference to it. Such a unique reference in COBOL is referred to as an identifier. It may be a unique data-name, a non-unique data name qualified by a unique higher level name, or it may be a reference to an item within a table. Examples of identifiers are:

```
EOF-ORDERS-FILE
M-COUNT
```

which are two of the internal data items needed for the Analysis of Orders program.

```
STUDENT-WORK-ADDRESS
STUDENT-NAME OF STUDENT-RECORD
STUDENT-COLLEGE-ADDRESS(1)
```

which are all fields from the definition for the Student Name and

Address File detailed in figure 3.5. The second of these examples illustrates qualification where the non unique data name STUDENT-NAME is qualified by the unique name STUDENT-RECORD. The third identifier references the first item in the table STUDENT-COLLEGE-ADDRESS, the reference number within the table being specified within the parenthesis.

(b) Reserved Words

These are words which are part of the COBOL language itself and must therefore not be used as user-defined names. Appendix A gives the reserved words for the 1974 standard and appendix B gives the extended list of reserved words for the 1985 standard. As can be seen the lists are extensive, and many words that a programmer may be tempted to choose as a data name are reserved words and would lead to probable compilation errors. For example:

```
COUNT
DATA
DATE
HEADING
```

To avoid having to remember all these reserved words simply ensure that at least one hyphen is included in every name that you define. This substantially reduces the number of reserved words you are likely to fall foul of. Also if part of your data name is a code rather than an English word, as in for example EOF-ORDERS-FILE, then there is very little chance of having chosen a reserved word in error

7.2.5 Literals

A literal is a string of characters that represent a value. There are three types of literals in COBOL: non-numeric, numeric and figurative constants.

(a) Non-numeric Literals

These consist of a string of any characters that the computer can handle enclosed by quotation marks. The value of the non-numeric literal is the actual characters in the string, for example,

```
"ERROR IN DATA"
"12345"
"non-numeric literals"
```

Within a non-numeric literal, a quotation mark is represented by two adjacent quotation marks, for example the literal

```
"HE SAID ""I AM A FREE MAN"""
```

has the value

```
HE SAID "I AM A FREE MAN"
```

The maximum length of non numeric literals is 120 characters in the 1974 standard and 160 characters in the 1985 standard. However, the limits set by some COBOL implementors may be different to these.

(b) Numeric Literals

A numeric literal is a string of one to eighteen digits which represent a decimal value that could be used in arithmetic calculations. It may have a sign (+ or -) as its leftmost character, however, if no sign is given the number is assumed to be positive. A decimal point may be included at any position except the rightmost. If no decimal point is specified then the literal is assumed to be an integer. Examples of numeric literals are:

```
3.162
-56
+87.3
0.0056
1
1.0
```

Any decimal point included in a numeric literal is treated as an assumed decimal point i.e. it simply indicates the boundary between the integer and fractional parts of the number.

(c) Figurative Constants

These are COBOL reserved words which represent particular literal values. The six figurative constants are:-

(i) ZERO, ZEROS, ZEROES - are all equivalent to the numeric value zero or a string of the character zero depending upon the context.

(ii) SPACE, SPACES - are both equivalent to a space character or a string of space characters.

(iii) LOW-VALUE, LOW-VALUES - represent one or more occurrences of the character in the computer's character set which has the lowest equivalent binary value.

(iv) HIGH-VALUE, HIGH-VALUES - represent one or more occurrences of the character in the computer's character set which has the highest equivalent binary value.

(v) QUOTE, QUOTES - represent one or more occurrences of the quotation mark character. These figurative constants must not be used as the delimiter of a non-numeric literal.

(vi) ALL non-numeric literal - represents one or more occurrences of the non-numeric literal specified, for example, ALL "B" represents one or more occurrences of the letter B.

7.3 Source Program Format

Due to COBOL's origins in the days of punched cards the format of source code statements is 80 column card image oriented and it is not free format. To assist in the accurate coding of programs specially laid out COBOL coding sheets should be completed before the program is keyed at whatever sort of input device is being used. An example of a completed coding sheet for part of the program described in section 3.5 is illustrated in figure 7.1.

7.3.1   Format of COBOL Statements

COBOL coding sheets are produced with specific delimited sets of columns which reflect the standard format for COBOL statements. The purpose of each of these sets of columns is as follows:

(i)   Columns 1-6 (Sequence Number)

These allow each source code line to be given a sequential sequence

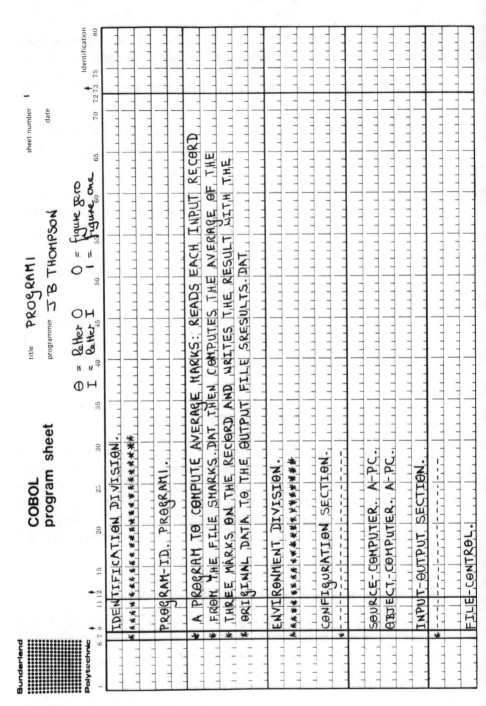

Figure 7.1 Completed COBOL coding sheet

130

number. This is a hangover from the days of punched cards when sequence numbers were needed in case the packs of cards on which the programs were held were misordered. In practice these days sequence numbers are left blank unless they are automatically provided by a system utility such as a text editor.

(ii) Column 7 (Indicator Area)

If this column is blank the compiler treats the remainder of the line as a normal source line. If the column contains an asterisk (*) the line is treated as a comment and is printed by the compiler but is otherwise ignored. Similarly a solidus (/) in the column causes the line to be treated as a comment but it also causes the compiler to advance the program listing to the start of a new page.

A hyphen (-) in the column indicates the continuation of source text from the previous line. This feature is normally used to continue a non-numeric literal from the previous line. The hyphen indicates that the first non-blank character in area B of the current line is the successor of the last non blank character on the preceeding normal COBOL line. If a non-numeric literal is to be continued, the first non-blank character on the continued line must be a quotation mark and all the spaces between the last non blank character and the start of column 73 on the preceding line are considered to be part of the literal. An example of such a continued non-numeric literal is given in the definition for the record TITLE-LINE shown in figure 10.2.

Column 7 can also contain a D signifying that the line of code is an optional debug line which can be used when the program is tested. This feature is part of the Debug module which has been designated as an obsolete element in the 1985 standard and hence will not be considered in this text.

(iii) Columns 8-11 (Area A)

This is used for starting division, section and paragraph headings and for certain entries regarding files and records, for example the FD entry and the level number 01.

(iv) Columns 12-72 (Area B)

All the divisional entries except those specified in (iii) are contained in area B. The programmer is free to choose his own format, however, it is normal practice to use the columns on the form to align like items, for example, commencing all 03 levels at column 12, commencing all 05 levels at column 14 and so on. Entries may be split over several lines so long as they remain in area B. Specific continuation lines are only needed in the case of split words or split non-numeric literals.

(v) Columns 73-80 (Identification)

These are intended to identify the source program and relate to punched card days. Normally these columns are left blank by the programmer.

Some compilers will accept a much more free format than that detailed above. For example some simply no longer use the sequence (columns 1-6) and identification (columns 73-80) areas. The code in these cases commences with the indicator column as the first entry and a much greater line length is often also allowed. Some text editors are, or can be, oriented towards standard COBOL format and these sometimes insert line numbers automatically in the sequence positions and provide tabbing to selected columns, for example, to the start of areas A and B.

7.3.2 Blank Lines

Blank lines may be included in the source text to improve the layout and readability of the code. They are simply printed out by the compiler but are otherwise ignored.

To indicate clearly on a coding sheet that a blank is to be included in the source code a convention such as a set of inverted or upright triangular characters in the first few columns are sometimes used.

7.3.3 Coding Standards

In many intallations there will be standards regarding the completion of COBOL coding sheets. This is particularly true in installations where the programs are to be keyed in by data preparation staff. Such standards normally include conventions regarding the writing of characters which could easily be confused, for example the letter O and the digit 0, the letter I and the digit 1. A typical convention would be to ensure that all letters that could lead to confusion are crossed (i.e. have horizontal bars clearly written or bars are added), for example, we could write the letters O and I as:

θ and I

7.4 Notation Used to Express the COBOL Language

To describe the permitted syntax and semantics of a language we use a higher level language referred to as a Meta-language, i.e. a language to describe a language. The meta-language for COBOL is referred to as the COBOL Notation.

The COBOL Notation consists of a format specification plus a set of rules for each COBOL element. The rules detail and clarify the format specification and describe any restrictions that apply. The form of the notation used in this text is based on that which the UK National Computing Centre have used in their COBOL reference summaries for the 1974 and 1985 standards [29 and 21]. Those given in the COBOL Reference Manuals for different compilers may differ very slightly in form but will be following the same general approach.

An example of the format, which specifies a form of the ADD statement, is shown in figure 7.2. The conventions used within the notation are as follows:

(i) Underlined, upper case words, such as ADD, are used to indicate mandatory reserved words. They must be written in the position shown in the format.

(ii) Non-underlined, upper case words, such as ON, are used to indicate optional reserved words. Such words may be included, in the positions shown in the format, to improve the readability of the code but their omission would not affect the execution of the element being described.

(iii) Lower case words represent a word or an entry which must be specified by the programmer. The lower case word indicates the type of word or entry which the programmer has to supply. For example, in the format for the ADD statement reference is made to three different identifiers and two literals. The suffix (-1, -2, etc) is used to assist in the referencing of the item in any rules which follow the format specification.

$$\underline{\textbf{ADD}} \begin{Bmatrix} \text{identifier--1} \\ \text{literal--1} \end{Bmatrix} \begin{Bmatrix} \text{identifier--2} \\ \text{literal--2} \end{Bmatrix} \cdots$$

$$\underline{\textbf{GIVING}} \begin{Bmatrix} \text{identifier--3} \ \underline{\textbf{[ROUNDED]}} \end{Bmatrix} \cdots$$

[ON SIZE ERROR imperative statement]

Figure 7.2 A format specification for the ADD statement.

(iv) Brackets, [and], indicate an optional feature which can be omitted, for example [ROUNDED].

(v) Braces, { }, show that a choice has to be made. Where alternatives are given within the braces one of these must be selected, for example, the programmer must either specify an identifier or a literal as the first operand in the ADD statement. If there is only one entry within the braces, it will be found that the braces are followed by ellipsis indicating repetition (see below), in this case the programmer must choose how many times the entry is used, but the entry must be written at least once. For example, in the ADD statement at least one identifier must be specified to receive the result of the addition. However, more resultants can be named if required. Also note, as shown in the example, brackets and braces can be nested.

(vi) Ellipsis, ... , indicates that the item immediately preceeding the ellipsis may be repeated as many times as required. If the ellipsis follow a closing bracket or brace the whole entry in the brackets or braces is repeated. Otherwise the word immediately preceeding the ellipsis is repeated. For example our specification for the ADD statement details that the programmer must decide if more than two operands are to be added and how many resultants are to be produced.

(vii) Full Stop, . , shows where a full stop is required. This is the only explicit punctuation shown in the formats detailed in this text and its importance has already been explained in section 7.2.3. However in some COBOL Reference Manuals the positions where optional punctuation, using commas or semicolons, can be used are also specified.

Now that we have a means of specifying the syntax and semantics of the language we can proceed to look at the elements within each division.

7.5 IDENTIFICATION DIVISION

The Identification Division provides a name for the source program. It will be printed on compiler listings and may also be used as the name of the object file generated by the compiler.

Format

```
IDENTIFICATION DIVISION.

PROGRAM-ID.  program-name.
```

The program-name must follow the rules for a user-defined name. It may also have to conform to rules specific to the COBOL implementation if it is to use outside the program by the computer's operating system; such an instance is illustrated by the VME example given in section 1.5.4.

Additional paragraphs in the Identification Division may be used by the programmer to detail Author, Installation, Date-Written, Date-Compiled and Security. However, all these paragraphs have been designated as obsolete elements in the 1985 Standard and hence will not be detailed in this text.

Examples of Identification Division code and that for the Environment and Data Divisions are given in sections 3.5 and 7.8.

7.6 ENVIRONMENT DIVISION

7.6.1 Structure

The Environment Division describes the compile time and run time environments for the program

Format

```
ENVIRONMENT DIVISION.

CONFIGURATION SECTION.

SOURCE-COMPUTER.      computer-name-1.

OBJECT-COMPUTER.      computer-name-2.

[SPECIAL-NAMES.  special-names entry]

[INPUT-OUTPUT SECTION.

FILE-CONTROL.

        [select entry] ... ]
```

The CONFIGURATION SECTION must be present. It documents the name of the computer system or systems to be used to compile and run the program. Some compilers will expect the computer-names to be in a prescribed form (the details will be given in the COBOL Reference Manual for the compiler). However, the majority of compilers treat the names as documentary and any COBOL name will be acceptable. A special-names paragraph may also be included in the CONFIGURA-TION SECTION. This provides a means of defining implementation-dependent features. Some examples of these are given in the following section.

The INPUT-OUTPUT SECTION must be included if the program handles any files. Then, as described in section 7.6.3, select entries in the FILE-CONTROL will be used to provide a link between internal and external file names and specify how each file is organised and accessed.

136

7.6.2   SPECIAL-NAMES Paragraph

The special-names entry within the SPECIAL-NAMES paragraph is used to relate user-defined names to features of the implementor's operating environment, and to redefine the representation of the currency sign and decimal point. Except in a few clearly defined circumstances it is rarely used.

Format

    SPECIAL-NAMES. [implementor-name IS mnemonic-name] ...

        [CURRENCY SIGN IS literal]

        [DECIMAL-POINT IS COMMA] .

The implementor-name clause allows a relationship to be defined between a mnemonic-name, which can be referenced in an ACCEPT, DISPLAY or WRITE statement, and an implementor-name associated with a hardware device or system file.

Examples

(i)   LINE-PRINTER IS LP1

Allows DISPLAYs referencing the mnemonic LP1 to be directed to a device known to the run time system by the logical name LINE-PRINTER.

(ii)   C01 IS START-OF-PAGE

This VAX COBOL example shows the association of the system code C01, which refers to the first line of a logical printed page, with the mnemonic START-OF-PAGE. This can then be used with a WRITE statement when required to move to the start of a new page viz:

    WRITE REPORT-RECORD AFTER START-OF-PAGE.

(iii)   CONSOLE IS CRT

This example relates to programs implemented using Micro Focus's CIS Cobol or LEVEL II COBOL. It changes the compiler default on ACCEPTs and DISPLAYS from CONSOLE, when the verbs would handle data on a line by line basis, to CRT. In this mode full screen addressing facilities are provided which is an extension to the 1974 and 1985 standards.

The CURRENCY clause allows specification of a local currency sign. The default value is normally a $ so in the UK you may need to specify:

```
CURRENCY SIGN IS "£"
```

The DECIMAL-POINT clause specifies that numeric data is to be handled in the format often encountered in continental Europe. There the comma is used as a decimal point and the decimal point is used as a comma, viz:

```
Britain     1,005.05
European    1.005,05
```

to achieve the latter format you specify:

```
DECIMAL-POINT IS COMMA
```

7.6.3 Select Entry for Sequential Files

A select entry must be included in the File-Control paragraph for each file that the program handles. The entry associates the internal name used to reference the file within the program with an external name by which the file is known outside the program. The entry also specifies how the file is organised and how it is to be accessed.

Format (Sequential Files)

```
SELECT file-name ASSIGN TO implementor-name

[ORGANIZATION IS SEQUENTIAL]

[ACCESS MODE IS SEQUENTIAL] .
```

The name used for file-name must be the internal name of the file whose format is specified in a corresponding File Description (FD) entry in the File Section of the Data Division. The form of implementor-name (the external name) is dependent upon the COBOL implementation. It may be a literal giving the actual name of the file (i.e. the name used by the computer's operating system), or it may be a logical name which is then associated with the actual name via an operating system command. The exact format for implementor-name will be specified in the COBOL Reference Manual or the COBOL User Guide for the system you are using.

The ORGANIZATION (note the spelling) and ACCESS clauses are optional and are usually omitted for sequential files as sequential is the default for both organisation and access mode. Thus the select entry for the input file for PROGRAM1 was simply:

```
SELECT IN-FILE ASSIGN TO "SMARKS.DAT".
```

here IN-FILE is the internal file-name and the literal's value SMARKS.DAT is the actual name of the external file. An alternative to this could be to reference a data-item which holds the name of the file or we may have

```
SELECT IN-FILE ASSIGN TO DATAFILE.
```

where DATAFILE is a logical name which will be used in an operating system command to link with the actual external file name.

In some COBOL implementations the select entry simply links the file name with a logical device name, for example DISK, and additional information is provided in the FD entry to identify the file. This option is detailed in section 7.7.2.

7.7   DATA DIVISION

7.7.1 Structure

The Data Division provides data descriptions for the records on each file that is to be handled by the program and for each internal data item that is required. The compiler then uses these descriptions to allocate the areas of program store needed to hold the data. The records read from or written to files are described in the File Section and the data items which exist only within the program are described in the Working-Storage Section.

Format (basic entries)

```
DATA DIVISION.

  FILE SECTION.

  [file description entry
    [record description entry] ... ] ...

  WORKING-STORAGE SECTION.

    [record description entry] ...
```

The FILE SECTION is required if any files have been defined in the File-Control paragraph in the Environment Division. Each file description is followed by record descriptions for each type of record that can occur on the file. Although many different types of record may reside on a file, the various record descriptions for them will only generate one storage area whose size is equal to that of the largest record which has been defined for the file. All the record descriptions for the file are simply different ways of picturing this storage area.

The WORKING-STORAGE SECTION is required to define any internal data items which the program uses, such as counters, end of file indicators and preset headings for reports.

7.7.2 Basic File Description Entry

The File Description entry provides a means of describing the particular physical characteristics of a file.

Format (Basic)

```
FD  file-name

    LABEL  { RECORD  IS  } { STANDARD }
           { RECORDS ARE }  { OMITTED  }
```

140

```
[ VALUE OF   {implementor-name IS {literal    }} ... ] .
                                  {data-name }
```

The letters FD must appear in area A, the remainder of the entry is written in area B. The file-name is the internal name for the file as was specified in the corresponding select entry.

The LABEL clause is used to indicate whether or not standard labels are used within the file. This clause has been designated as an obsolete element in the 1985 standard and is actually treated as optional in most implementations based on the 1974 standard. It will therefore be omitted from the examples given in this text.

The VALUE OF clause is used by some COBOL implementors as an extension of the select entry. This has been designated as an obsolete element in the 1985 standard and hence its use should be avoided if possible. However, with some compilers currently available the select clause simply assigns the internal name of the file to a general device name such as DISK. The VALUE OF clause must then be used to provide a link with the external file. For example, it may be necessary to write

```
        SELECT IN-FILE ASSIGN TO DISK.
            :
            :
            :
            :
    FD   IN-FILE.
         VALUE OF FILE-ID IS "SMARKS.DAT".
```

to associate the internal name IN-FILE with the actual external file name SMARKS.DAT.

7.7.3   Basic Record Descriptions

The file description for each file is followed by record descriptions for each type of record on the file. Each of these record descriptions consists of a set of one or more data description entries. Each data description entry consists of a level number followed by a data-name, followed by a series of independent clauses which specify the item's attributes. As described in chapter 3 the level numbers are used to specify the hierarchy of groups and fields within the record. Analogous record descriptions to these are used in the Working Storage Section to define internal data items. The following sections provide the basic formal specifications for records and some coded examples are given in section 7.9.

(a) Record Description Entry

Records are described by a series of data description entries. Single data items in the Working-Storage Section, such as counters, which are not part of a record are described by a single level data description entry.

Format

```
data-description-entry-1
[data-description-entry-2] ...
```

The level number within a record for data-description-entry-1 must be 01 and each subsequent data-description-entry must have a level number in the range 02-49. Level numbers 01-09 may be written 1-9. Single data items in Working-Storage can be allocated the level number 01 or the special level number 77. However, the use of this latter level is no longer recommended within most installations as the 01 level is equivalent and there has been clear indications that the 77 level will becme an obsolete element in the future.

(b) Data Description Entry (Basic)

Each data description consists of a level number, a data-name and a number of optional clauses which provide further information on the item.

Format (Basic)

```
level-number ┌ data-name ┐   [PICTURE clause]
             │           │
             └ FILLER    ┘   [USAGE clause]

                             [SIGN clause].
```

Level-number 01 should appear in area A, all other level-numbers may appear in area A or area B. The data-name, FILLER and any descriptive clauses must appear in area B. However, it should be noted that many compilers do relax the rule regarding the placement of the 01 level.

The name FILLER may be given to all those data items which do not require unique identification, for example, space filled fields between data fields on input and output records. The PICTURE, USAGE and SIGN clauses define the format of elementary items and how their values are represented within the computer.

7.8 PICTURE, USAGE and SIGN Clauses

7.8.1 PICTURE Clause (Basic)

As outlined in chapter 3 the Picture clause defines the format of elementary items.

Format

$$\left\{ \begin{array}{l} \underline{\texttt{PICTURE}} \\ \underline{\texttt{PIC}} \end{array} \right\} \texttt{IS picture-string}$$

The characters that make up picture-string primarily specify the data items category and its size. The three simplest categories of data item are alphabetic, alphanumeric and numeric. Alphabetic data items are composed of characters from the character set: A through to Z plus space. Alphanumeric data items are composed of any characters from the computer's character set. Numeric data items are composed of the digits 0 through to 9 and may have an operational sign and assumed decimal point position associated with them. The category of an item is specified by the categorisation characters that appear in the picture-string and the size of the data item is given by the number of times these characters are repeated. A categorisation character can be repeated either explicitly or a single occurrence of it can be followed by the number of repeats in brackets, for example:

        PIC AAAAAAAA   and   PIC A(8)

are equivalent.

The picture-string specification itself must not exceed 30 characters, the maximum size for a COBOL word. However, this constraint is not usually a problem when using the second approach to define the item's size. For although PIC A(80) defines an item 80 characters in size the picture-string itself is only 5 characters long. COBOL does not place a limit on the size of individual alphabetic and alphanumeric data items, though there may be system limits on total record size, but it does limit numeric data items to 18 digits.

Although individual data items can be categorised as alphabetic, alphanumeric or numeric, all group items are categorised as alphanumeric regardless of the categories of the data items within the group. For example, suppose we had part of a record which represented three numbers:

```
03   S-COUNTERS-1.
    05   S-COUNT-1      PIC 9(3).
    05   S-COUNT-2      PIC 9(3).
    05   S-COUNT-3      PIC 9(3).
```

here although the elementary data items are all numeric the group item S-COUNTERS would be treated by COBOL as alphanumeric.

The formation rules for picture-strings which specify alphabetic, alphanumeric and numeric data items are as follows:

(a) Alphabetic Data Items

These are specified by picture-strings which are primarily composed of the character A. Each occurrence of A in the picture-string represents an occurrence in the data item of a character from the set A through to Z plus space.

The character B may also appear in the picture-string. It causes a space to appear at the indicated position in the data item whenever a value is moved to the data item.

Examples

```
PIC AA
PIC A(10)
PIC A(5)BA(8)
```

these specify items whose lengths are 2, 10 and 14 characters respectively. Note that moving the character string "COBOLLANGUAGE" to an item described by the last picture would cause a space to appear between the two Ls.

(b) Alphanumeric Data Items

These are specified by picture-strings which are composed of the characters X, A or 9 but not all As or all 9s. Each occurrence of X in the picture-string represents an occurrence in the data item of any character from the computer's character set. An occurrence of A in the picture-string represents an occurrence in the data item of a character from the set A through to Z plus space and an occurrence of 9 represents an occurrence of a digit in the data item.

Examples

```
PIC X(10)
PIC 99X(5)AA
```

Note that the latter picture would be compatible with the character string "12*****AB".

(c) Numeric Data Items

The characters 9, V, S and P may appear in the picture-strings for numeric data items. Each occurrence of 9 in the picture-string represents an occurrence of a digit in the data item and an S at the start of the picture-string shows that the data item can be signed.

The position of a V in the picture-string represents the position of an assumed decimal point within the data-item. If no V is present in the picture-string the decimal point is assumed to be at the right of the data item i.e. the data item is an integer.

Occurrences of P at the left or right of the picture-string represent scaling factors. There may be a total of between 1 and 18 occurrences of 9 and P in a picture string.

Examples

(i)	`PIC 99`	specifies a two digit integer.
(ii)	`PIC S99`	specifies a signed two digit integer which can take negative as well as positive values.
(iii)	`PIC S99V99`	specifies a signed four digit number whose decimal point is assumed to be between the second and third digit. An actual decimal point must not appear in the number.
(iv)	`PIC V99`	specifies a fractional decimal number with two digits following the assumed decimal point.
(v)	`PIC VPP99`	specifies a fractional decimal number which is treated as if the two digits are preceeded by .00.
(vi)	`PIC 99PP`	specifies an integer which is to be treated as if the two digits had two zeroes following them.

The scaling factor P is used to specify the location of an assumed decimal point at some position to the left or the right of the item. Each P on the left of the picture-string specifies that the assumed decimal point is moved one place to the right. The difference between the two forms is that moving the number 56 to an item specified by picture (v) would result in a value for the item of .0056 while moving 56 to an item specified by picture (vi) would result in a value for the item of 5600.

7.8.2   USAGE Clause

This clause specifies the way in which the data values are held within the computer. The main options are character format or a format suitable for efficient arithmetic computations.

146

Format

$$
[\text{USAGE IS}] \quad \left\{ \begin{array}{l} \underline{\text{COMPUTATIONAL}} \\ \underline{\text{COMP}} \\ \underline{\text{DISPLAY}} \end{array} \right\}
$$

Specifying DISPLAY means the data is held in character format. COMPUTATIONAL and COMP are synonymous and they may only be applied to numeric items. They specify that the data is held in a form suitable for computation rather than in character format. The choice of format is left to the implementor but binary format is usual. The default usage is DISPLAY i.e. if no usage is explicitly specified then the data item is held in character format. Note also that the word USAGE is optional and is usually omitted.

Examples

(i)   PIC X(3)   specifies a three character alpha-
                         numeric item

(ii)   PIC 9(3)   specifies a 3 digit numeric item
                         held in character format

(iii)   PIC 9(3) COMP   specifies a 3 digit numeric item
                         held in computational format

The usage may be specified at group level. This is equivalent to specifying that usage for all the elementary items in the group. In these circumstances none of the subordinate elementary items may have a conflicting usage specified for them. However, it should be noted that specifying USAGE IS COMP at group level does not permit the group name to be treated as a numeric item, since COBOL still regards it as a alphanumeric item.

7.8.3   SIGN Clause

The sign clause is only used with numeric items which contain an S in the picture string and whose usage is display. It specifies how the sign is held.

147

Format

[SIGN IS] { LEADING
            TRAILING } [SEPARATE CHARACTER]

If SEPARATE is specified, then the sign will be represented by a + or - character. If LEADING is specified the relevant character will precede the digits of the item, if TRAILING is specified it follows the digits. The sign character adds one digit to the length of the data item in both cases.

If SEPARATE is not specified the sign is combined with the first (LEADING) or last (TRAILING) digit in the item and hence does not add to the length of the data item. The method of combination is left to the implementor of the compiler but is normally achieved by setting or unsetting a high order bit in the binary patterns that represent the digits in the computers character set. For example, in a computer which uses the EBCDIC character set, where 8 bits represent each character, the digit 1 is represented by the hexadecimal value F1. To represent +1 and -1 explicitly the hexadecimal values C1 and D1, which represent the characters A and J could be used instead.

The following examples show how the value -1221 would be held in data item specified as PIC S9(4) for different sign clause specifications assuming that the convention detailed above is used for combining characters:

(i)   LEADING SEPARATE   -1221

(ii)   TRAILING SEPARATE   1221-

(iii)   LEADING   J221

(iv)   TRAILING   122J

The default specification varies from compiler to compiler but is typically TRAILING. In programs where portability is of importance the SEPARATE option should be specified. However, in most programs the sign clause is not specified and the default specification applies.

It should be remembered that the sign clause is not used with computational signed numeric items. This is because the sign is taken care of

148

within the computational form used to represent the numeric value, for example by using 2s complement to represent binary numbers.

7.9 Further Examples

Figure 7.3 shows the first three divisions of a program which has been created to illustrate different file and record descriptions. The definitions for two files, whose internal names are FILE-1 and FILE-2, are given along with the Working-Storage descriptions of two single data items and an internally processed record. FILE-1 consists of three different types of record and hence its FD entry contains three different record descriptions each commencing with a 01 level. FILE-2 consists of only one type of record.

```
IDENTIFICATION DIVISION.

PROGRAM-ID. PROGRAM2.
* SOME EXAMPLE DATA DESCRIPTIONS

ENVIRONMENT DIVISION.

CONFIGURATION SECTION.
SOURCE-COMPUTER. A-PC.
OBJECT-COMPUTER. A-PC.

INPUT-OUTPUT SECTION.
FILE-CONTROL.
     SELECT FILE-1 ASSIGN TO "DATFILE1.DAT".
     SELECT FILE-2 ASSIGN TO "DATFILE2.DAT".

DATA DIVISION.

FILE SECTION.
FD   FILE-1.
     01  F1-RECORD-TYPE1.
         03   F1-RT1-INDICATOR        PIC X.
         03   F1-RT1-VALUE1           PIC 9(4).
     01  F1-RECORD-TYPE2.
         03   F1-RT2-INDICATOR        PIC X.
         03   F1-RT2-DATA1            PIC X(4).
         03   F1-RT2-DATA2            PIC X(7).
     01  F1-RECORD-TYPE3.
         03   F1-RT3-INDICATOR        PIC X.
         03   F1-RT3-DATA             PIC X(5).
```

149

```
FD  FILE-2.
    01 F2-RECORD.
        03  F2-FIELD1          PIC A(3).
        03  FILLER             PIC X.
        03  F2-FIELD2          PIC X(30).
        03  FILLER             PIC X.
        03  F2-FIELD3          PIC S9(3) SIGN IS LEADING
                                         SEPARATE CHARACTER.

        03  FILLER             PIC X.
        03  F2-FIELD4          PIC S9(3)V99.

WORKING-STORAGE SECTION.
    01  EOF-FILE1              PIC 9.
    01  EOF-FILE2              PIC 9.


    01  WS-RECORD1.
        03  WS-R1-COUNTERS  USAGE IS COMPUTATIONAL.
            05  WS-R1-COUNT1      PIC 9(3).
            05  WS-R1-COUNT2      PIC 9(3).
            05  WS-R1-COUNT3      PIC 9(3).
        03  WS-R1-DATA.
            05  WS-R1-FIELD1      PIC AA9(4)A.
            05  WS-R1-FIELD2      PIC X(100).
```

Figure 7.3 Example file and data descriptions

The compiler uses each data description to allocate the areas of program store needed for each type of record and single item. For example, twelve characters of program store will be reserved for records from FILE-1 i.e. space that is large enough to hold the longest type of record (F1-RECORD-TYPE2). The first five characters of this storage will also be used to hold the records described by F1-RECORD-TYPE1 and the first six characters will be used to hold the records described by F1-RECORD-TYPE3 viz

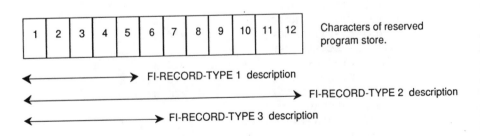

If a different character (e.g. 1, 2 or 3) is held in the first character position of each of the three types of record the programmer can check this position once a record has been accessed to determine what type of record has been retrieved from the file.

The data descriptions for FILE2 illustrate some different forms of the display picture clause and show the use of the reserved word FILLER to name fields which do not need to be uniquely identified.

Within the Working-Storage Section two individual numeric items EOF-FILE1 and EOF-FILE2 are defined as well as the internal record WS-RECORD1. You should remember that all group items are categorised as alphanumeric including WS-R1-COUNTERS. The usage clause given with this relates to the elementary numeric items within it and not to the group level. Also note that WS-R1-FIELD1 is classed as an alphanumeric item as the definition contains a mixture of As and 9s. The category of data items becomes very important when transfers are made between them as we will see when we consider the MOVE statement in detail.

TASKS - CHAPTER 7

1. As has been pointed out not all COBOL compilers agree exactly with the 1974 or 1985 Standard. They often allow more flexibility and include suppliers' "enhancements". Check each of the definitions and rules given in this chapter with those detailed in the COBOL Reference Manual for your compiler. Don't worry if you don't understand all the technical details following each entry - this will get easier with time and experience. However, it is important that you get used to referring to the manual and you understand the COBOL notation used in it.

2. Look at some example programs written for the COBOL compiler you are going to use. Are there any implemention differences between those and the programs illustrated in Figure 3.1 and 7.3? Does your compiler require the LABEL clause and/or the VALUE OF clauses in an FD (see section 7.7.2)? Check with your COBOL Reference Manual if you are not sure.

3. Obtain some COBOL coding forms.

4. If you intend to use data preparation facilities to create your programs check what coding standards (see section 7.3.3) they expect you to adhere to.

5. If you are going to enter your own programs via a terminal it will save time and reduce errors if you set up a 'skeleton' program containing all the Division and Section headings - i.e. those that are underlined in Figure 3.1. A copy of the skeleton can then be used each time you need to create a new program. Include the commented underlines shown in Figure 3.1, if you wish because these will help easy identification of the Divisions and Sections in your final programs.

6. Check your COBOL Reference Manual for the following:

(a) The maximum length of a non-numeric literal.

(b) How the data item F2-FIELD3 of FILE-2 shown in Figure 7.3 would be represented (see also section 7.8.3).

(c) How computational data items are represented in the implementation of COBOL you are using.

CHAPTER 8
The Procedure Division and Basic COBOL Verbs

8.1 Procedure Division

8.1.1 Description

The Procedure Division is used to specify the operations which the computer has to carry out. It is comprised of paragraphs each of which has its own paragraph-name. The paragraphs can be grouped together into sections, if required, with each section having its own section-name. Paragraph-names and section-names provide the destinations and delimiters for procedural control statements (i.e. GO TO and PER-FORM) and can also be used to provide meaningful headings for groups of operations. For example, in a program which implements a JSP design the paragraph and section names should relate to components within the program structure.

A paragraph may simply consist of the paragraph-name, but normally it will also contain one or more sentences each terminated by a full stop. COBOL sentences are comprised of one or more statements each of which defines an operation which the computer has to carry out. Each statement consists of a COBOL verb followed by an appropriate number of operands, for example:

```
ADD 1 TO M-COUNT
```

Here the operands are a literal value 1 and a data-name M-COUNT.

153

8.1.2 Statements

There can be three types of statements within the Procedure Division: imperative, conditional or compiler directing.

(a) Imperative Statements

These specify unconditional operations which the computer has to carry out, for example

```
(i)       MOVE INPUT-RECORD TO OR-ORIGINAL-DATA
(ii)      GO TO PROCESS-FILE-ITER
```

(b) Conditional Statements

These specify that the subsequent operation of the program depends on the evaluation of a condition, for example:

```
(i)         IF EOF-INPUT-FILE = 0 NEXT SENTENCE
                ELSE GO TO PROCESS-FILE-ITER-END.


(ii)        READ INPUT-FILE
                AT END MOVE 1 TO EOF-INPUT-FILE.
```

It should be noted that many COBOL statements such as the READ have an imperative basic form and an extended conditional form which includes an exception conditional such as AT END.

In the COBOL Notation the formats for conditional statements often include the term "imperative statement". Where this occurs it is understood to represent a sequence of one or more individual imperative statements. The sequence must be terminated by a full stop or a phrase (such as ELSE) which is associated with the conditional statement (for example IF) that contains the term "imperative-statement".

(c) Compiler Directing Statements

These are statements which specify actions which are to be carried out at compilation time, for example to copy into the source program some text from another file.

8.1.3 Structure of an Un-sectionalised Procedure Division

Format

```
PROCEDURE DIVISION.

{paragraph-name.

    [sentence] ... } ...
```

Paragraph-names must be unique within an un-sectionalised Procedure Division. They commence in area A and must be terminated by a full stop. Sentences are written in area B and they may comprise one or more statements, but the last statement in the sentence must be followed by a full stop. An example of a program implemented without sections is PROGRAM1 whose code was given in figure 3.1.

8.1.4 Structure of a Sectionalised Procedure Division

Format

```
PROCEDURE DIVISION.

{section-name SECTION.

{paragraph-name.

    [sentence] ... } ... } ...
```

Section-names must be unique within the Procedure Division. They begin in area A and are followed by the word SECTION which is terminated by a full stop. Paragraph-names must be unique within a section. If they are not unique within the program they must be qualified by the section name when they are referenced i.e. paragraph-name OF/IN section-name. The remaining rules are the same as for an unsectionalised Procedure Division.

A JSP diagram outlining the logical composition of a sectionalised

155

Procedure Division is given in figure 8.1. The logical structure for an unsectionalised Procedure Division would simply omit components B, C, D, E and F.

Sectionalisation is often used in the implementation of large programs where each section is concerned with a particular logical aspect of the processing. For example, we could have:

```
PROCEDURE DIVISION.
AN-INITIALISATION SECTION.
   :
   :        paragraphs that specify initialisation operations
   :
   :
MAIN-PROCESSING SECTION.
   :
   :        paragraphs that specify processing operations
   :
   :
THE-TERMINATION SECTION.
   :
   :        paragraphs that specify terminal operations
   :
   :
```

Since most of the programs that we will be considering in this text are relatively small it will generally be unnecessary to consider sectionalising them.

8.1.5 Punctuation

In the Procedure Division a full stop must terminate all occurrences of the word SECTION, all paragraph names and all sentences. Statements within a sentence may be separated by one or more occurrences of a space, a comma followed by a space or a semicolon followed by a space. The final statement in a sentence is obviously terminated by a full stop.

The coding standard adopted in this text is to keep things as simple as can be and wherever possible commence each statement on a separate line and terminate it with a full stop, i.e. make each statement into a sentence. The main exception to this will be in the coding of statements associated with conditionals where, as is explained in the relevant

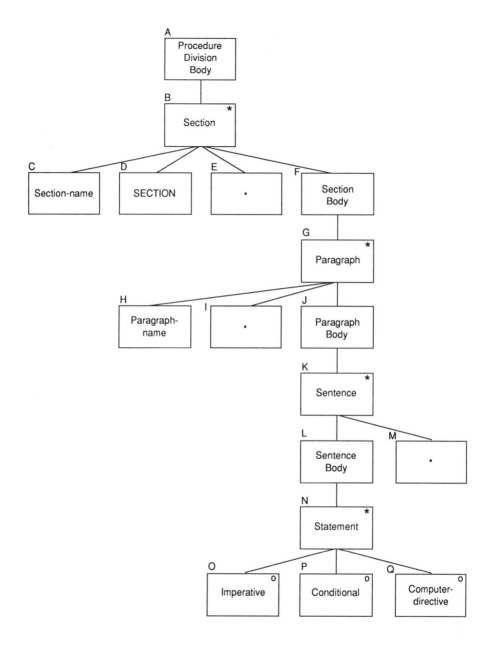

Figure 8.1 Logical Composition of a Sectionalised Procedure Division (omitting all separators except full stops)

sections, the full stop is a delimiter for the operations which depend on the evaluation of the condition.

The reason for making each statement a sentence is that it makes the code more robust to change. Amendments which involve the insertion of conditional statements into code made up of sequences of individual statements are more liable to lead to logical errors than amendments which are made to code where each sentence contains only one statement.

8.2 Basic COBOL Verbs

To implement the types of program we have considerd up to now we need to be able to carry out the following classes of operation:

(i)   Simple file handling.

(ii)   Input and Output to a terminal.

(iii) Simple data manipulation which involves the transfer of data from a sending data item to a receiving one.

(iv)   Incrementing counters.

(v)   Straightforward procedural control.

(vi)   Evaluation of simple conditions.

The following sections are concerned with the COBOL verbs relevant to the implementation of operations (i) to (v) viz.

(i)   OPEN, CLOSE, READ, WRITE

(ii)   ACCEPT, DISPLAY

(iii) MOVE

(iv)   ADD

(v)   GO TO, STOP RUN

Simple control structures supported by IF and IF...ELSE statements are considered in the next chapter along with details of the conventions relating to in-line COBOL coding of JSP designs.

8.3 SEQUENTIAL File Operations

The sequential input-output verbs support the transfer of records between a COBOL program and external files. In the Environment Division an internal name must have been associated with each external file via a select entry and program store must have been allocated for the file's records by a corresponding file description entry in the Data Division.

8.3.1 OPEN Statement

Before any records can be read from a file or written to a file the file must be opened. The availability of the file is then checked and it is made ready for the first record to be transferred. The file is then said to be in open mode.

Format

```
OPEN    ┌ INPUT  file-name ... ┐  ...
        └ OUTPUT file-name ... ┘
```

OPEN INPUT positions the file at the first record currently existing in the file and permits the use of the READ statement. If there are no records on the file the end of file condition will be detected when the first READ statement is executed. OPEN OUTPUT positions the file at its beginning and permits use of the WRITE statement. As many files as are desired can be opened in a single OPEN INPUT or OPEN OUTPUT statement, no matter what their organisation or access mode. Also a file may be opened several times within a program, so long as it has been closed before the second and any subsequent OPEN.

Examples

```
(i)         OPEN INPUT STUDENT-FILE, MARKS-FILE.
(ii)        OPEN OUTPUT RESULTS-FILE.
```

these may be combined into one OPEN statement viz.

```
OPEN INPUT STUDENT-FILE, MARKS-FILE,
     OUTPUT RESULTS-FILE.
```

Note that in these examples the optional separator comma has been used to improve legibility.

8.3.2 CLOSE Statement

When the processing of a file is finished it must be closed before the program ends.

Format

```
CLOSE file-name ...
```

The files named in the CLOSE statement must be in open mode when the statement is executed. A single close statement may be used for all the files that are open regardless of their organisation and access mode.

Examples

```
(i)     CLOSE INPUT-FILE.
(ii)    CLOSE STUDENT-FILE, MARKS-FILE,
              RESULTS-FILE.
```

8.3.3 READ Statement for SEQUENTIAL Files

The READ statement for sequential files is used to obtain the next logical from an input file which is in open mode.

Format

```
READ file-name RECORD   [ INTO identifier]
         AT END imperative-statement
```

The READ causes the next logical record on the file, if there is one, to be transferred to the record area which has been defined by the file-name's FD in the Data Division. The INTO phrase, if present, causes a copy of the record to be transferred to the named identifier. The phrase thus provides a convenient means of transferring the input record to a working storage record area. However, it must not be used when the input file contains records of varying sizes.

If, on execution of a READ statement, the end of file is encountered, the imperative statement(s) in the AT END exception phrase will be actioned. The last of these statements will normally be terminated by a full stop which delimits the exception processing to be carried out. Often on encountering the end of file it will be sufficient to simply set an end-of-file indicator, that is associated with the file, which can then be tested at the beginning of the relevant 'process record' iteration.

Examples

```
(i)       READ INPUT-FILE AT END MOVE 1 TO EOF-INPUT-FILE.
(ii)      READ PRODUCT-FILE INTO WS-PRODUCT-DETAILS
                    AT END MOVE "E100" TO ERROR-CODE
                    GO TO ERROR-ROUTINE.
```

8.3.4 WRITE Statement for SEQUENTIAL Non-Print Files

This section describes the form of the WRITE statement for simple sequential files i.e. those whose records do not require special formatting for printing. The statement releases a record to an output file which is in open mode.

Format

```
WRITE record-name [ FROM identifier]
```

The WRITE causes the record which has been created in the area record-name to be released to the relevant file. Record-name must be the name of a record within the FD of a file which has been opened for output. The FROM phrase allows a record to be built up in a different area, for example in Working-Storage, and then transferred to the output record area associated with the file just before output.

Examples

```
(i)       WRITE OUTPUT-RECORD.
(ii)      WRITE MARKS-RECORD FROM WS-MARKS-AREA.
```

161

The second example is equivalent to

```
MOVE WS-MARKS-AREA TO MARKS-RECORD
WRITE MARKS-RECORD.
```

8.3.5 Read and Write Transfers

When your program executes a read or a write statement it does not communicate directly with the device but instead communicates with routines provided by the implementor of your compiler. These routines in turn communicate with the computer's operating system and this actually transfers data to or from the device. Sequential and serial transfers to devices usually take place at device block level where a block is the device's logical unit of storage. In the case of storage devices which use magnetic disk or tape, a block is typically several thousand characters long and hence will normally hold many individual records.

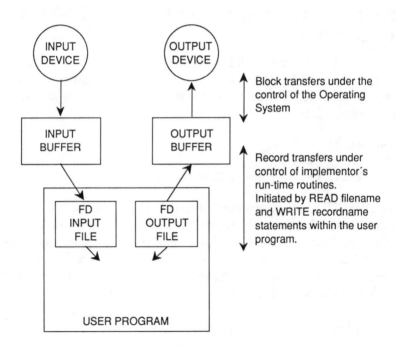

Figure 8.2 Data transfers in a COBOL run-time system.

Figure 8.2 depicts the operations that typically take place in transferring data between a COBOL program and a device. The implementor's routines will include appropriate I/O buffers for each file which the COBOL program uses. These buffers are filled/emptied by the operating system as required. The implementor's routines in turn control the transfer of individual records between the relevant FD record areas in the COBOL program and the I/O buffers. To understand the sequence of operations we will consider the production of the results file by PROGRAM1 which was detailed in section 3.5.1. The relevant extracts of code are reproduced in figure 8.3. Though not all systems will operate exactly as detailed below they will follow the same general principles.

```
ENVIRONMENT DIVISION.
       :
       :
INPUT-OUTPUT SECTION.
FILE-CONTROL.

    SELECT OUTPUT-FILE ASSIGN TO "SRESULTS.DAT".

DATA DIVISION.
FILE SECTION.

FD  OUTPUT-FILE.
    01  OUTPUT-RECORD.
      03  OR-ORIGINAL-DATA.
        05  OR-NAME            PIC X(20).
        05  OR-MARK-1          PIC 99.
        05  OR-MARK-2          PIC 99.
        05  OR-MARK-3          PIC 99.
      03  OR-AVE-MARK          PIC 99.

PROCEDURE DIVISION.
       :
       :
    OPEN OUTPUT OUTPUT-FILE.
       :
       :
    WRITE OUTPUT-RECORD.
       :
       :
    CLOSE OUTPUT-FILE.
       :
       :
```

Figure 8.3 COBOL code to produce an output file.

In PROGRAM1 when OUTPUT-FILE is opened the implementor's routines will set up the output buffer. The operating system will be called to check the availability of the device and if it is available an entry for the file SRESULTS.DAT will be set up in the file directory for the device. Also one or more header blocks may be created at the start of the physical file. Each WRITE OUTPUT-RECORD signals to the implementor routines that a record held in the record area OUTPUT-RECORD is ready to be released to file SRESULTS.DAT. The implementor routines will then attempt to place a copy of the record in the next available space in the output buffer. If there is no room for the current record, the operating system will be called to transfer the records from the full buffer to the file. Once this has been accomplished the record can be placed in the now empty buffer. This process will be repeated for each WRITE until the statement CLOSE OUTPUT-FILE is executed. When this happens the implementor routines will check the state of the buffer and if any records remain in it the operating system will be called to transfer them to the device. Finally the operating system will be instructed to close the file. This will probably involve writing some end of file blocks and updating the file directory for the device.

8.3.6   READ file-name WRITE record-name

Students new to COBOL sometimes encounter problems with the READ and WRITE statements. The reason why the formats are: READ filename, WRITE record-name may be understood by reference to the following extracts of Data Division code which define an input and an output file both of which contain three different types of record each supposedly of a different size.

```
FD   IN-FILE
  01   IN-REC-TYPE1.
          :
          :
  01   IN-REC-TYPE2.
          :
          :
  01   IN-REC-TYPE3.
          :
          :
```

```
FD   OUT-FILE.
  01   OUT-REC-TYPE1.
          :
          :
  01   OUT-REC-TYPE2.
          :
          :
  01   OUT-REC-TYPE3.
          :
          :
```

When a record is transferred from the file to the record-area for IN-FILE the programmer does not know in advance which particular type of record will be transferred so the instruction must be -

```
READ IN-FILE.
```

However, when a record has to be transferred to the output file the programmer must explicitly specify which record description applies and the instruction must therefore be either -

```
        WRITE OUT-REC-TYPE1.
or
        WRITE OUT-REC-TYPE2.
or
        WRITE OUT-REC-TYPE3.
```

8.4 Low Volume Input and Output

The ACCEPT and DISPLAY statements allow input and output of small amounts of data without having to define files or records.   They are primarily used for handling data to/from a user's terminal but can be used for data transfers between a program and a slow hardware device, such as a card reader or printer, or a system file which represents a hardware device.   In these latter cases the ACCEPT or DISPLAY will reference a mnemonic name which, as has been described in section 7.6.2, will have been associated with the relevant hardware device or system file via a Special-Names entry in the Environment Division. However, it is more normal for bulk transfers from card readers and to printers to be carried out via spooler files.   These files can then be handled more efficiently by COBOL programs using normal read and write statements.

When the phrase specifying the mnemonic name is omitted a standard device specified by the implementor is assumed. This is normally the user's terminal if the program is being run interactively and either the operator's console or a system file if the program is being run in batch mode. In the following descriptions it is assumed that the user's terminal is the default device.

8.4.1 ACCEPT Statement

The statement causes low volume data to be placed in a named identifier.

Format

```
ACCEPT  identifier [ FROM mnemonic-name]
```

On execution of the ACCEPT the program waits for data to be typed in at the terminal. Once the data has been typed and the "enter" or "return" key has been pressed the data will be transferred to the identifier. It will be left-aligned and will be truncated if the identifier is not large enough to hold it. Any implementation limits on the maximum size of item that can be accepted will be defined in your COBOL Reference Manual as will any rules relating to the situation when the data transferred does not fill the identifier. In the remainder of this text it will be assumed that the maximum size is 80 characters and that any unfilled character positions in the identifier will be set to spaces.

Examples

Using the following data descriptions

```
01   YOUR-NAME          PIC X(30).
01   PARAMETER-CARD     PIC X(80).
```

then

```
(i)        ACCEPT YOUR-NAME.
```

166

would cause characters typed at the terminal to be transferred to the left-most character positions of the data item YOUR-NAME.

(ii)   `ACCEPT PARAMETER-CARD FROM CR1.`

If we suppose that the mnemonic name CR1 has been associated with a card reader known to the system as CARD-READER via a Special-Names entry viz.

```
SPECIAL-NAMES.
    CARD-READER IS CR1.
```

Then a card will be read at the device and an 80 character card image will be transferred to the identifier

```
PARAMETER-CARD.
```

8.4.2 DISPLAY Statement

The statement causes specified data values to be transferred to the user's terminal or an appropriate hardware device.

Format

$$\underline{\text{DISPLAY}} \left\{ \begin{array}{l} \texttt{identifier} \\ \texttt{literal} \end{array} \right\} \quad \dots \quad [\ \underline{\text{UPON}}\ \texttt{mnemonic-name}]$$

A 'display line' is created by concatenating the values of the specified items. Spaces are not inserted between items, and figurative constants, ZEROES etc, will only produce a single occurrence of that character. If the 'display line' exceeds the line size of the output device the excess characters may be output on the next line or they may be ignored depending upon the implementation (check your COBOL Reference Manual). Note also that if the literal is a numeric it must be an unsigned integer, and that the figurative constant ALL is not allowed.

Examples (using the data descriptions defined for the ACCEPT)

(i)   `DISPLAY "PLEASE TYPE YOUR NAME".`
               `ACCEPT  YOUR-NAME.`
               `DISPLAY "HELLO ", YOUR-NAME.`

This sequence would output the request, accept the user's name and display a welcoming message, for example

```
PLEASE TYPE YOUR NAME
RICHARD
HELLO RICHARD
```

Note that any spaces needed in the output must be allowed for in the literal.

(ii)   `DISPLAY PARAMETER-CARD ON LP1.`

If, as above the mnemonic name LP1 has been associated via Special-Names with a particular hardware device, then the 80 character value of PARAMETER-CARD will be transferred to that device.

8.4.3 Message Pairs and Handling Numeric Data

Example (i) in the previous section illustrates the use of message pairs - a request from the program prompts the user to supply the correct information. It is obviously bad practice to produce programs for interactive environments which contain ACCEPTs without preceeding explanatory DISPLAYs. You cannot expect the users of your program to remember exactly what information they have to type and in what format it is required.

Helpful user prompts specifying the required formats for input are of particular importance when we wish to ACCEPT numeric data into our programs. This is because, unlike other languages such as BASIC, the ANS standards for COBOL do not specify any implementator rules for checking the input for non numeric characters nor for the alignment of ACCEPTed numeric strings by any embedded decimal point. Although some implementors have enhanced their COBOL to provide such facilities, many have not and it is left to the programmer in these cases, to ensure that such data is handled correctly.

Let us assume that the compiler we are using adheres to an ANS standard and that we wish to input a four-digit decimal value that represents a percentage interest rate, for example, 10.25. The input consists of two digits before the decimal point, the decimal point itself and two digits after it. The data item which is to receive this could be defined as:

```
01  PERCENT-RATE.
    03  FIRST-PART    PIC X(2).
    03  FILLER        PIC X.
    03  LAST-PART     PIC X(2).
```

To access this value from the user we could then code our routine as follows:

```
DISPLAY "PLEASE SUPPLY PERCENTAGE RATE FORMAT IS".
DISPLAY "99.99 INCLUDE LEADING AND TRAILING ZEROS".
ACCEPT PERCENT-RATE.
```

The second message should be designed so that when it is output the figures 99.99 are aligned directly above the position where the user response will be entered. The value typed in, which hopefully is in the correct format, will be accepted into the three alphanumeric fields FIRST-PART, FILLER (for the decimal point) and LAST-PART. The first and last field can be validated for numeric values (this is described in section 14.1.1) and then transferred to parts of a numeric item which includes the positioning of an assumed decimal point.

8.5 MOVE Statement

The MOVE statement is one of the most powerful in the COBOL language as it not only causes a copy of a sending item to be transferred to one or more receiving items, but it will also cause the received copy to be formatted according to the receiving identifier's description.

Format

$$\underline{\text{MOVE}} \left\{ \begin{array}{c} \text{identifer-1} \\ \text{literal} \end{array} \right\} \quad \underline{\text{TO}} \quad \text{identifier-2} \ \ldots$$

The result of each MOVE depends on the data descriptions for the sending and receiving data items. Some combinations of sending and receiving data types are not allowed, for example, a MOVE from a numeric integer data item to an alphabetic data item is not permitted. After the execution of a legal MOVE the sending item will still retain its original value but the original values of the receiving items will have been replaced by the transferred data.

For the moment we will consider only the simplest types of MOVEs i.e. those involving only elementary alphanumeric andelementary numeric items and those which involve group items. To illustrate these operations we will make use of the data descriptions given in figure 8.4 which relate to an enhanced version of our student marks program (PROGRAM1) which was first described in section 3.5.1.

```
DATA DIVISION.

FILE SECTION.

FD   STUDENT-MARK-FILE.
   01   STUDENT-RECORD.
      03   SR-NUMBER              PIC 9(7).
      03   SR-NAME.
         05   SR-FORENAME         PIC X(10).
         05   SR-SURNAME          PIC X(20).
      03   SR-RESULTS.
         05   SR-SUBJECT1.
            07   SR-SUBJECT1-NAME  PIC X(15).
            07   SR-SUBJECT1-MARK  PIC 99.
         05   SR-SUBJECT2.
            07   SR-SUBJECT2-NAME  PIC X(15).
            07   SR-SUBJECT2-MARK  PIC 99.
         05   SR-SUBJECT3.
            07   SR-SUBJECT3-NAME  PIC X(15).
            07   SR-SUBJECT3-MARK  PIC 99.

FD   RESULT-FILE.
   01   RESULT-RECORD.
      03   RR-STUDENT-DETAILS.
         05   RR-NUMBER           PIC 9(7).
         05   RR-NAME             PIC X(30).
         05   RR-RESULTS          PIC X(51).
      03   RR-AVERAGE             PIC 99V99.

WORKING-STORAGE SECTION.

   01   DISPLAY-AREA.
      03   DA-PART1               PIC X(50) JUSTIFIED RIGHT.
      03   DA-PART2               PIC X(20).
```

Figure 8.4 Data descriptions for illustrative MOVE statements.

8.5.1 MOVEs between elementary alphanumeric items

Unless the receiving item is explicitly defined as JUSTIFIED RIGHT the transferred data is left justified in the receiving item. If the receiving item is larger than the sending item it is right-filled with spaces. If it is smaller the excess characters are not transferred.

Examples

```
(i)        MOVE SR-NAME TO DA-PART2.
           PIC X(20)   PIC X(20)
```

After execution the contents of the two data items will be identical.

```
(ii)       MOVE SR-SUBJECT1-NAME TO DA-PART2.
           PIC X(15)             PIC X(20)
```

The contents of SR-SUBJECT1-NAME are copied to the first 15 character positions in DA-PART2 and the remainder is space filled.

```
(iii)      MOVE RR-NAME TO DA-PART2.
           PIC X(30)   PIC X(20)
```

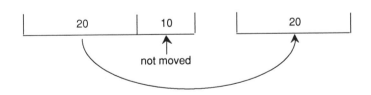

Only the first 20 characters of RR-NAME are copied to DA-PART2.

If the receiving item is explicitly defined as JUSTIFIED RIGHT the transferred data will be right justified in the receiving item with space filling to the left if necessary.

Example

```
MOVE RR-NAME TO DA-PART1.
     PIC X(30)  PIC X(50) JUSTIFIED RIGHT
```

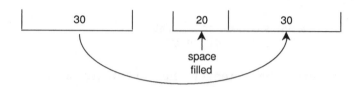

Note also that non-numeric literals are treated as elementary alphanumeric sending items.

Example

```
MOVE "JOHN" TO SR-FORNAME.
                PIC X(10)
```

This would result in the characters JOHN being copied to the first 4 character positions of SR-FORNAME and the last 6 character positions would be spaced filled.

8.5.2 MOVEs between elementary numeric items

Alignment of the transferred data is by decimal point position which is assumed to be at the right of any integer item. Unused digit positions are zero filled and excess digits are truncated.

Examples

(i)   Suppose the value held in SR-NUMBER is 1234567 then

```
MOVE SR-NUMBER TO RR-NUMBER
     PIC 9(7)     PIC 9(7)
```

would result in the value of RR-NUMBER becoming 1234567.

(ii) If, however, the picture for RR-NUMBER was PIC 9(8) its value after the MOVE would be 01234567. Alignment has taken place by the assumed decimal point to the right of the item and the unused leading digit position has been zero filled.

(iii) alternatively if the picture for RR-NUMBER was PIC 9(6) its value after the MOVE would be 234567 i.e. the excess digit after alignment has been truncated.

Numeric literals are treated as elementary numeric sending items. Any decimal point contained within them is treated as an assumed decimal point position and is used for alignment of the value in the receiving item.

Example

Suppose we have the definition

```
01  NUMERIC-VALUES.
    03  ITEM-A    PIC 9(3).
    03  ITEM-B    PIC 9(3) COMP.
    03  ITEM-C    PIC 9(3)V99.
    03  ITEM-D    PIC 9(3)V99 COMP.
```

and we then MOVE the value 12.34 to each of the elementary items viz.

```
MOVE 12.34 TO ITEM-A, ITEM-B,
              ITEM-C, ITEM-D.
```

the values that would result are -

ITEM-A would contain the characters 012,
ITEM-B would contain the value 12 in computational format,
ITEM-C would contain the characters 01234,
ITEM-D would contain the value 12.34 in computational format.

Note that not only is the value of the item transferred but if necessary it is also converted into the format (character or computational) speci-fied by the receiving item's data description.

For example if we had

```
MOVE ITEM-D TO ITEM-C.
```

a copy of the value of ITEM-D would be converted from computational format to character format and stored in ITEM-C aligned on the assumed decimal point position.

8.5.3 MOVEs between elementary alphanumeric and elementary numeric items

(a) Sending item alphanumeric, receiving item numeric

The sending alphanumeric item is assumed to contain an unsigned integer and the rules for an elementary numeric to elementary numeric MOVE are followed. If the sending item does not contain an unsigned integer an unexpected result is likely.

Examples

```
(i)        MOVE "12" TO RR-AVERAGE.
                         PIC 99v99
```

after the transfer RR-AVERAGE would contain the characters 1200 representing a value 12.00.

```
(ii)       MOVE "+12.57" TO RR-AVERAGE.
                         PIC 99v99
```

after the transfer RR-AVERAGE would contain the   characters 5700 which is unlikely to be what the programmer intended! The alphanumeric character string has been treated as a 6 digit number with an assumed decimal point to the right of it. This has been transferred to RR-AVERAGE and aligned on the assumed decimal point position between the second and third characters. Hence the first four characters (i. e. +12.) are truncated and we are left with the string 5700.

(b) Sending item numeric, receiving item alphanumeric

The MOVE is only legal if the numeric item is defined as an integer. The sending integer is regarded as an unsigned string of digit characters i.e. any operational sign is ignored and a computational item is converted to character format. The character string is then transferred to the receiving item as detailed in section 8.5.1 for MOVEs between elementary alphanumeric items.

Examples

```
(i)        MOVE SR-NUMBER TO DA-PART2.
                PIC 9(7)    PIC X(20)
```

This is legal and would result in the number being transferred to the seven left most character positions of DA-PART2. The remainder would be space filled.

```
(ii)       MOVE RR-AVERAGE TO DA-PART2.
                PIC 99v99    PIC X(20)
```

This is illegal as RR-AVERAGE is not an integer.

8.5.4 Group MOVEs

If either the sending or receiving item is a group item the transfer is treated as if both items were elementary alphanumeric items. Any named group level item is treated as an alphanumeric item equal in size to the total area defined by the data descriptions of the group's subordinate elementary items. Even if all the subordinate items are defined as computational numeric the MOVE will be as detailed for alphanumeric items.

Examples

```
(i)        MOVE SR-NAME TO RR-NAME.
(ii)       MOVE SR-RESULTS TO RR-RESULTS.
(iii)      MOVE SR-RESULTS TO DISPLAY-AREA.
(iv)       MOVE "******" TO NUMERIC-VALUES.
```

The first two examples represent straightforward copying of data values. In the third example the data will be left justified in the receiving field despite the JUSTIFIED RIGHT clause on the first subordinate field. Also it should be noted that the final example represents a perfectly legal COBOL MOVE. However, any intepretation of the receiving area according to its subordinate item's pictures is

175

likely to produce some very strange numeric values as they will be inter-
pretations of binary patterns representing asterisks or spaces!

8.6   Incrementing Counters

In many programs we will be concerned with the handling of counters,
control totals and the like. The data items that are used should always
be explicitly initialised at the appropriate time, for example, start of
program, start of group processing, start of sub-group processing etc. by

```
MOVE initial-value TO identifier
```

for example

```
MOVE ZERO TO M-COUNT.
```

Counters can then be incremented using the basic form of the ADD
statement.

Format

$$\underline{ADD} \left\{ \begin{array}{l} \text{identifier-1} \\ \text{numeric-literal} \end{array} \right\} \underline{TO} \text{ identifier-2}$$

The value of identifier-1 or the value of the numeric-literal is added to
the existing value of identifier-2.

Examples

```
ADD 1 TO M-COUNT.
ADD SUB-TOTAL TO GRAND-TOTAL.
```

8.7   Procedural Control Statements

8.7.1   GO TO Statement

The GO TO allows control to be transferred from one part of the
Procedure Division to another.

Format

```
GO TO procedure-name
```

Control is passed to the first statement in the named paragraph or section. The GO TO must be used with care as indiscriminate use of it can obviously lead to very tangled program logic. It should only be used in a controlled manner to implement standard control structures or provide direct transfers to exception or error handling routines.

Examples

```
(i)        GO TO PROCESS-FILE-ITER-END.
(ii)       GO TO ERROR-ROUTINE.
```

8.7.2 STOP RUN Statement

This causes the program to terminate execution and control is then normally passed back to the computer's operating system.

Format

```
STOP RUN
```

The statement may be written anywhere in the Procedure Division though it is logically the last statement in the program. It is permissible to have more than one STOP RUN statement in a program but good programming practice should lead to only one clearly defined terminal routine which includes the STOP RUN statement.

Example

```
PROGRAM-TERMINATION.
    CLOSE INPUT-FILE , OUTPUT-FILE.
    STOP RUN.
```

TASKS - CHAPTER 8

1. Once again try and become acquainted with the COBOL Reference Manual for your compiler. Look up each of the statements given in this chapter. Many, you will find, have more complex formats than are given here. For the moment ignore those additions. Simply ensure you understand the basic forms. Discuss any problems you encounter with an experienced programmer.

2. Look at the Procedure Division of some example programs written for the COBOL compiler you are going to use. Try and understand their logic - could this be improved by better layout?

3. The format for the READ statement is

    ```
    READ filename RECORD [ INTO identifier]
         AT END imperative-statement
    ```

    (i) Why must the statement reference a file-name and not a record-name (see section 8.3.6)?

    (ii) Can the INTO phase always be used (see section 8.3.3)?

    (iii) What constitutes and what normally terminates "imperative-statement" (see section 8.1.2)?

    (iv) What chain of events do you think will occur when the first READ in a program is executed (see section 8.3.5)?

4. Implement and run a simple COBOL program which will ask the user his name and then print out a welcoming message. The basic Procedure Division statements are given in section 8.4.3. You will need to add a paragraph heading, a STOP RUN statement and define a suitable item in Working-Storage to hold the name.

5. Assume we have the following definitions

    ```
    01  ALPHANUMERIC-ITEMS.
        03  ALPHANUM-1          PIC X(6).
        03  ALPHANUM-2          PIC X(5).
        03  ALPHANUM-3          PIC X(4).
    ```

```
01  NUMERIC-ITEMS.
    03  NUMBER-1              PIC 999V99.
    03  NUMBER-2              PIC 999.
    03  NUMBER-3              PIC 9V99 COMP.
```

Detail the contents of the receiving items after the following MOVES:

(i)   MOVE "ABCDE" TO ALPHANUM-1, ALPHANUM-2, ALPHANUM-3.

(ii) MOVE 15.06 TO NUMBER-1, NUMBER-2, NUMBER-3.

(iii) MOVE "ABC" TO NUMBER-2.

(iv) MOVE "12" TO NUMBER-2.

(v)   MOVE 15.06 TO ALPHANUM-1.

(vi) MOVE 15 TO ALPHANUM-3.

(vii) MOVE "ABCD" TO ALPHANUMERIC-ITEMS, NUMERIC-ITEMS.

To check your answers you could implement a simple test program which incorporates the above code and which DISPLAYS the results of the MOVEs.

6. How does the compiler recognise the end of your program? How does the run-time system (the execution system) know when it has reached the end of your program?

7. Check your COBOL Reference Manual to see how the COBOL you are using ACCEPTs numeric values. Does it follow the 1974 and 1985 standards as detailed in section 8.4.3 or does it provide enhanced features?

CHAPTER 9

Control Structures and Implementation of JSP Designs

9.1 Conditional Expressions

As was explained in Chapter 1 structured programs are composed of three basic logical structures - sequence, selection and iteration. The control flow through the latter two structures are dependent upon the evaluation of conditionals i.e. the execution path taken depends on whether a conditional expression is true or false.

9.1.1 Relation Conditions

The commonest conditional expressions in COBOL are simple relation conditions which involve comparisons of two operands.

Format

$$\text{operand-1 IS [}\underline{\text{NOT}}\text{]} \left\{ \begin{array}{l} \underline{\text{GREATER}}\text{ THAN} \\ \underline{\text{LESS}}\text{ THAN} \\ \underline{\text{EQUAL}}\text{ TO} \\ > \\ < \\ = \end{array} \right\} \text{operand-2}$$

Operand-1 and operand-2 may be identifiers, literals or arithmetic expressions. If both operands are numeric, the comparison is by their algebraic values, for example, 56, 56.0 and 056 are all equal and -56 is less than 56.

If both operands are non-numeric they are compared character by character according to the computer's collating sequence, for example, SMITH is less than SMYTH as I precedes Y in the collating sequence. If one operand is shorter than the other it is extended to the same length with spaces. For example, if a PIC X(4) field was being compared with a PIC X(5) field the value of the PIC X(4) field would have a space character added to the right of it.

Note that in the above format the relational operators >, < and = are not underlined although they are mandatory reserved words. This is so there can be no confusion with the symbols that represent operators such as greater than or equal to.

Examples

Assume the following data items and values:

item	picture	value
EOF-INPUT-FILE	PIC 9	1
VALUE-2	PIC 9	2
VALUE-3	PIC 9	3
VALUE-6	PIC 9V99	6.00
ITEM-1	PIC X(5)	BARRY
ITEM-2	PIC X(6)	BARRIE

The evaluations of the following conditional expressions are:

conditional expression	evaluation
EOF-INPUT-FILE IS EQUAL TO 0	FALSE
(VALUE-2 + VALUE-3) < VALUE-6	TRUE
ITEM-1 IS LESS THAN ITEM-2	FALSE
ITEM-1 = "BARRY "	TRUE

9.1.2 Compound Conditions

Simple conditions such as relation conditions may be combined using the logical operators AND or OR into a compound condition.

Format

```
simple-condition-1 { ⎧ AND ⎫ simple-condition-2} ...
                     ⎩ OR  ⎭
```

An ANDed compound condition is true if all the constituent simple conditions are true, or else it is false. An ORed compound condition is true if any constituent condition is true. It is only false if all the constituent simple conditions are false.

Parenthesis may be used to clarify a compound condition and any conditions may be negated by

        NOT   condition

Examples (using the data items and values from 9.1.1)

```
conditional expression                       evaluation

VALUE-2 = 2  AND  VALUE-3 = 3                 TRUE
VALUE-2 = 2  AND  VALUE-3 = 1                 FALSE
VALUE-2 = 2  OR   VALUE-3 = 1                 TRUE
VALUE-2 = 1  OR   VALUE-3 = 1                 FALSE
NOT (VALUE-2 = 1  OR  VALUE-3 = 1)            TRUE
```

When simple relational conditions which all refer to the same subject and which involve no parenthesis are combined it is only necessary to specify the subject once. For example, we can write the expression

        VALUE-3 IS > VALUE-2 AND < VALUE-6

which is true.

9.2 IF Statement

The IF statement causes a conditional expression to be evaluated. The subsequent operation of the program depends on whether the resultant value of the conditional expression is true or false.

9.2.1 Basic IF

Format

```
IF  condition imperative-statement
```

If the value of the condition is true the imperative statement(s) which follow the condition, and are terminated by a full stop, are executed.

Examples

```
(i)        IF EOF-INPUT-FILE = 1
                    GO TO PROCESS-FILE-ITER-END.
(ii)       IF LINE-COUNT = 60
                    ADD 1 TO PAGE-COUNT
                    WRITE OUTPUT-RECORD FROM HEADING-LINE1
                    WRITE OUTPUT-RECORD FROM WS-DATA-RECORD
                    MOVE 2 TO LINE-COUNT.
```

If the value of the condition is false the imperative statements associated with the condition are skipped over. Execution then continues at the first statement following the full stop which terminated the imperative statements, i.e. at the first statement in the next sentence.

Example

```
           IF EOF-INPUT-FILE = 1
                    GO TO PROCESS-FILE-ITER-END.
           ADD 1 TO RECORD-COUNT.
```

If the value of EOF-INPUT-FILE is not equal to 1 control will pass to the ADD statement.

9.2.2 IF ... ELSE

With a basic IF we are able to specify that particular actions are to be taken when a condition is true. With the IF ... ELSE we are able to specify particular actions for the situation when the condition is true and for the situation when the condition is false.

Format

```
IF   condition    {  {statement-1} ...  }
                  {  NEXT SENTENCE      }

            ELSE  {  {statement-2} ...  }
                  {  NEXT SENTENCE      }
```

In the format statement-1 and statement-2 represent either one or more imperative statements or a conditional statement. If any of the conditional statements is an IF statement we have a more complex structure known as a nested IF which is explained in the next section.

The "ELSE" terminates the action to be taken if the condition is true. Hence, there must be no full stop between the IF and the ELSE. The "ELSE" and the statement's terminating full stop delimit the action to be taken if the condition is false. NEXT SENTENCE causes control to be transferred to the first statement following the terminating full stop.

The operation may therefore be depicted as

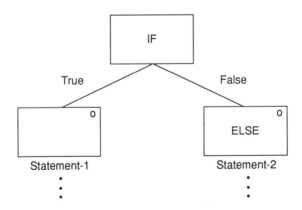

185

Examples

```
(i)         IF RECORD-TYPE = "A"
                        ADD 1 TO A-COUNT
                        MOVE IN-DATA TO OUT-DATA
                    ELSE ADD 1 TO OTHERS-COUNT.
(ii)        IF EOF-INPUT-FILE = 0 NEXT SENTENCE
                    ELSE GO TO PROCESSS-FILE-ITER-END.
```

9.2.3 Nested IFs

Either leg of an IF ... ELSE may contain further IF statements which themselves may contain further IFs and so on. Such a structure is said to be nested.

Example

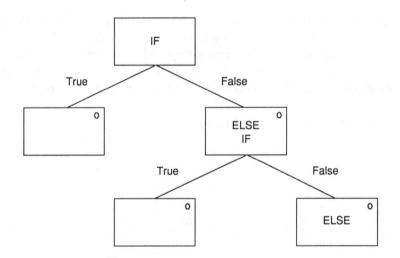

```
IF RECORD-TYPE = "A"
       ADD 1 TO A-COUNT
       MOVE IN-DATA TO OUT-DATA
   ELSE
       IF RECORD-TYPE = "B"
           ADD 1 TO B-COUNT
       ELSE
           ADD 1 TO OTHERS-COUNT.
```

Nested IFs should always be used with care. The programmer must ensure that IF and ELSEs are correctly matched and the intended logic is clear. Indentation of the code as above will often help.

However, deeply nested IFs probably cause more problems at maintenance time than any other statement - the logic is often far from clear and the matching of which ELSE belongs to which IF becomes extremely difficult. They are therefore best avoided and in this text we will be implementing our multiway selected structures via a series of separate IF ... ELSE statements.

9.3 Implementation of JSP Designs in In-line Code

Sections 6.3 and 6.4 described the production of schematic logic from a final JSP program structure and outlined how the design could be implemented in COBOL using either hierarchic or in-line code. As was explained in section 6.4 in-line coding is compatible with both the basic and more advanced techniques used within the JSP method and hence is the preferred technique for implementation. It mirrors the schematic logic in layout and uses straightforward IF statements and controlled GO TOs to implement the JSP structures that involve conditionals. The following sub-sections describe how each type of schematic logic block can be converted into in-line Procedure Division code.

The paragraph naming convention used in the majority of COBOL examples given in this text is to generate each paragraph name from a program identifying code, program structure page number and component label. For example, we will have paragraph names of the form

187

"AOP1E-SEQ." i.e. names analogous to those given to schematic logic blocks shown in figure 6.5 for the Analysis of Orders Program. If you prefer to use names generated from the text within the boxes on the program structure, for example, names of the form "P-ORDER-SEQ.", this is perfectly permissable. All you need to do is to simply replace the identifiers used in the examples (e.g. AOP1E) with the corresponding textual description for the component.

The examples given in the following subsections all relate to the Analysis of Orders Program which we developed in chapters 5 and 6. For ease of reference the schematic logic for this program (figure 6.5) is reproduced as figure 9.1.

```
AOP1A-SEQ
   AOP1B
      Open monthly orders file
      Set count of cash orders (M-COUNT) = 0
      Set count of credit orders (C-COUNT) = 0
      Set value of EOF-ORDERS-FILE = 0
      Read record from monthly orders file at end set
                    the value of EOF-ORDERS-FILE = 1
   AOP1C-ITER while not end of monthly orders file
                    (while EOF-ORDERS-FILE = 0)
      AOP1E-SEQ
         AOP1F-SEL if cash order (OR-PAYMENT-TYPE = M)
            AOP1H
               Add 1 to count of cash orders (M-COUNT)
         AOP1F-OR1 if credit order (OR-PAYMENT-TYPE = C)
            AOP1I
               Add 1 to count of credit orders (C-COUNT)
         AOP1F-SEL-END
         AOP1G
            Read record from monthly orders file at end set
                       the value of EOF-ORDERS-FILE = 1
      AOP1E-SEQ-END
   AOP1C-ITER-END
   AOP1D
      Display counts of cash and credit orders with
                       explanatory text
      Close monthly orders file
      Stop program run
AOP1A-SEQ-END.
```

Figure 9.1 Schematic Logic for Analysis of Orders Program Version 2

9.3.1 Procedure Division Code for Sequences

Construct

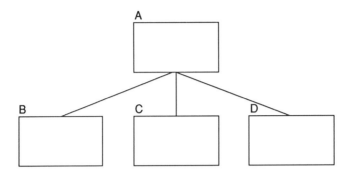

Schematic Logic

```
A-SEQ
    :
    :   schematic logic for lower level components
    :
A-SEQ-END
```

Code

```
A-SEQ.
    :
    :   paragraphs for lower level components
    :
A-SEQ-END.
```

Here the conversion into code simply involves writing the schematic logic block identifiers as paragraph names.

Example: Component A of figure 9.1

```
AOP1A-SEQ.
    :
    :
    :
AOP1A-SEQ-END.
```

9.3.2 Procedure Division Code for Selections

Construct

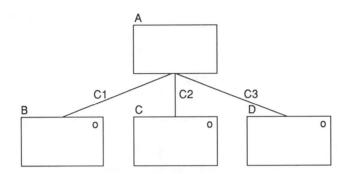

Schematic Logic

```
A-SEL if C1
   :
   : schematic logic for lower level components
   :
A-OR1 if C2
   :
   : schematic logic for lower level components
   :
A-OR2 if C3
   :
   : schematic logic for lower level components
   :
A-SEL-END
```

Code

```
A-SEL.
    IF condition-C1 NEXT SENTENCE
                    ELSE GO TO A-OR1.
  :
  :  paragraphs for lower level components
  :
    GO TO A-SEL-END.
```

```
A-OR1.
      IF condition-C2 NEXT SENTENCE
                      ELSE GO TO A-OR2.
   :
   :  paragraphs for lower level components
   :
         GO TO A-SEL-END.
A-OR2.
*     condition-C3
   :
   :  paragraphs for lower level components
   :
A-SEL-END.
```

The three schematic logic blocks: A-SEL to A-OR1, A-OR1 to A-OR2 and
A-OR2 to A-SEL-END have each been converted to a self contained block
of Procedure Division code. At the start of each block, except the last, an
IF ... ELSE statement is used to test the condition which is shown on the
schematic logic. If the condition is true execution continues (NEXT
SENTENCE) but if the condition is false control is passed to the start of
the next block (A-OR1, A-OR2). At the end of each of these blocks a
controlled GO TO statement (GO TO A-SEL-END) is coded to transfer
control to the end of the selection. If these GO TOs were not included
execution would incorrectly continue into the next leg of the selection.
Note that in the last part of the selection no condition is coded as all the
alternatives will already have been covered in the preceding blocks.
However, a comment can be included in the code giving the condition
that relates to this final leg of the selection. Also no GO TO is obviously
needed at the end of this final block.

In the above implementation the conditions are coded as given in the
schematic logic and use is made of the NEXT SENTENCE phrase of the
IF statement. An alternative approach is to use only basic IFs and
negate the conditions as shown below:

```
A-SEL.
      IF NOT condition-C1 GO TO A-OR1.
   :
   :  paragraphs for lower level components
   :
         GO TO A-SEL-END.
```

191

```
A-OR1.
    IF NOT condition-C2 GO TO A-OR2.
:
: paragraphs for lower level components
:
    GO TO A-SEL-END.
A-OR2.
*   condition-C3
:
: paragraphs for lower level components
:
A-SEL-END.
```

The main problem with the second approach is that the conditions no longer exactly mirror those in the schematic logic and this can produce problems at maintenance time. Also the negation of the conditions at coding time may not be easy if they are complex. Therefore, the first approach will be used in this text.

Example : Component F of figure 9.1

```
AOP1F-SEL.
    IF OR-PAYMENT-TYPE = "M" NEXT SENTENCE
                ELSE GO TO AOP1F-OR1.
:
:
:
    GO TO AOP1F-SEL-END.
AOP1F-OR1.
*   CREDIT ORDER  OR-PAYMENT-TYPE = "C"
:
:
:
AOP1F-SEL-END.
```

9.3.3 Procedure Division Code for Iterations

Construct

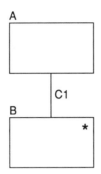

Schematic Logic

```
A-ITER while C1
    :
    :   schematic logic for lower level components
    :
A-ITER-END
```

Code

```
A-ITER.
      IF condition-C1 NEXT SENTENCE
                      ELSE GO TO A-ITER-END.
    :
    :  paragraphs for lower level components
    :
         GO TO A-ITER.
A-ITER-END.
```

The schematic logic block is implemented by following the A-ITER paragraph name by a test which will cause execution to continue while the condition is true. Once the condition is not true control is transferred to the end of iterative block i.e. the A-ITER-END paragraph name. The block of iterated code is terminated by a controlled GO TO statement (GO TO A-ITER) which transfers control back to the start of the iteration where the test will be re-evaluated.

As in the case of selections, iterations may alternatively be implemented by negating the iterative condition and using a simple IF i.e.

```
A-ITER.
    IF NOT condition-C1 GO TO A-ITER-END.
:
:  paragraphs for lower level components
:
    GO TO A-ITER.
A-ITER-END.
```

Athough this second approach also suffers from the disadvantages described in section 9.3.2, it can prove useful if the while condition is itself a negative condition or if the controlling condition has been expressed as an until condition. However, in most cases it is best to use the first approach.

Example : Component C of figure 9.1

```
AOP1C-ITER.
    IF EOF-ORDERS-FILE = 0 NEXT SENTENCE
                    ELSE GO TO AOP1C-ITER-END.
:
:  paragraphs for lower level components
:
    GO TO AOP1C-ITER.
AOP1C-ITER-END.
```

9.3.4   Procedure Division Code for Elementary Components

Construct

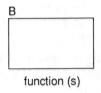

function (s)

Schematic Logic

```
B
    function(s) associated with component B
```

Code

```
B.
        COBOL statement(s)/sentence(s) implementing the
        function(s)
```

The component label becomes a paragraph name and then the function(s) associated with the component are converted in turn into COBOL statement(s)/sentence(s).

Example : Component H of figure 9.1

```
AOP1H.
    ADD 1 TO M-COUNT.
```

9.3.5 Controlled GO TOs

You should note that although GO TOs have been used in the implementation of selections and iterations their use is strictly controlled. They are simply being used to implement in-line control structures and have therefore only been used in the following circumstances:

(i)   To transfer control from the start of one leg of a selection to the following OR leg i.e. GO TO ... -ORn.

(ii) To transfer control from the end of one leg of the selection to the end of the selected component i.e. GO TO ... -SEL-END. This type of controlled GO TO must immediately precede each -ORn paragraph name.

(iii) To transfer control from the start of an iteration to the end i.e. GO TO ... -ITER-END.

(iv) To return control to the start of an iteration i.e. GO TO ... ITER. This type of controlled GO TO must immediately precede each -ITER-END paragraph name.

195

9.4 Implementation of Analysis of Orders Program

Now that we have covered the implementation of each of the schematic logic constructs we can produce the Procedure Division code for Analysis of Orders Program from the schematic logic given in figure 9.1. The completed code for the program is shown in figure 9.2 and some sample test data and the resultant output is given in figure 9.3. In the program (figure 9.2) the two counters have been given computational data descriptions as they are involved in arithmetic operations. Also space lines have been inserted into the procedure division code to help in delimiting the schematic logic blocks as COBOL paragraph names must all start in area A. Note that the functions to zeroise the counters and the EOF-ORDERS-FILE data item could have been combined into one COBOL statement viz.

```
MOVE ZERO TO M-COUNT, C-COUNT, EOF-ORDERS-FILE.
```

Also it should be noted that the selection AOP1F-SEL is a simple binary selection of two elementary components and it could have been implemented as

```
AOP1F-SEL.
    IF OR-PAYMENT-TYPE = "M" ADD 1 TO M-COUNT
            ELSE ADD 1 TO C-COUNT.
AOP1F-SEL-END.
```

However, if either component H or I in the original program later had to be further subdivided or if the selection itself was extended (for example to allow for another type of payment) this simplified form of coding would no longer be sufficient. Therefore it is always best to follow the general implementation rules given in section 9.3.

This completes the production of the Analysis of Orders Program. The approach that we have taken may appear to be excessively detailed for such a simple program. However, as you will see in the remaining chapters of this text the method of design and implementation adopted here can be just as effective and straightforward for programs of a much more complex nature.

```
IDENTIFICATION DIVISION.
PROGRAM-ID. AOP.
* A PROGRAM TO PROCESS MONTHLY ORDERS FILE PRODUCING COUNTS
* OF CASH AND CREDIT ORDERS

ENVIRONMENT DIVISION.

CONFIGURATION SECTION.
SOURCE-COMPUTER. A-PC.
OBJECT-COMPUTER. A-PC.

INPUT-OUTPUT SECTION.
FILE-CONTROL.
    SELECT ORDERS-FILE ASSIGN TO "ORDERS.DAT".

DATA DIVISION.

FILE SECTION.
FD  ORDERS-FILE.
    01  ORDER-RECORD.
        03  OR-AGENT-CODE.
            05  OR-AREA-CODE        PIC X(2).
            05  OR-AGENT-NUMBER     PIC 9(4).
        03  OR-CATALOGUE-REF        PIC X(6).
        03  OR-CATALOGUE-PRICE      PIC 9(3)V99.
        03  OR-NO-ORDERED           PIC 9(2).
        03  OR-PAYMENT-TYPE         PIC X.

WORKING-STORAGE SECTION.
    01  EOF-ORDERS-FILE     PIC 9.
    01  M-COUNT             PIC 9(3)   COMP.
    01  C-COUNT             PIC 9(3)   COMP.

PROCEDURE DIVISION.
AOP1A-SEQ.
AOP1B.
    OPEN INPUT ORDERS-FILE.
    MOVE ZERO TO M-COUNT.
    MOVE ZERO TO C-COUNT.
    MOVE ZERO TO EOF-ORDERS-FILE.
    READ ORDERS-FILE AT END MOVE 1 TO EOF-ORDERS-FILE.

AOP1C-ITER.
    IF EOF-ORDERS-FILE = 0 NEXT SENTENCE
                ELSE GO TO AOP1C-ITER-END.
AOP1E-SEQ.
```

197

```
AOP1F-SEL.
     IF OR-PAYMENT-TYPE = "M" NEXT SENTENCE
               ELSE GO TO AOP1F-OR1.
*    PROCESS CASH ORDER
AOP1H.
     ADD 1 TO M-COUNT.
     GO TO AOP1F-SEL-END.

AOP1F-OR1.
*    PROCESS CREDIT ORDER
AOP1I.
     ADD 1 TO C-COUNT.
AOP1F-SEL-END.

AOP1G.
     READ ORDERS-FILE AT END MOVE 1 TO EOF-ORDERS-FILE.
AOP1E-SEQ-END.
     GO TO AOP1C-ITER.
AOP1C-ITER-END.

AOP1D.
     DISPLAY "NUMBER OF CASH ORDERS ", M-COUNT,
             "   NUMBER OF CREDIT ORDERS ", C-COUNT.
     CLOSE ORDERS-FILE.
     STOP RUN.
AOP1A-SEQ-END.
```

Figure 9.2 Analysis of Orders Program

```
Input data

AA1234ZW49471499901C
AA1234TW19400125001C
AA1234TW26280099504C
AA1235YW74320099902M
AA1236WW09330129901M
AB0070WW65931199501M
AB0070ZX48630749901C
     :
     :
     :


Output results

NUMBER OF CASH ORDERS 157    NUMBER OF CREDIT ORDERS 226
```

Figure 9.3 Sample input and output for Analysis of Orders Program

TASKS - CHAPTER 9

1. The following terms were explained in section 9.1; look up each of them in your COBOL Reference Manual and ensure that you understand their meaning:

    conditional expressions
    complex conditions
    a relation condition

2. In an IF statement which COBOL character or word terminates the imperative statement(s) that will be executed if the condition is true?

3. For each of the following specify where control will be transferred to, after execution of the IF statement assuming the data definitions and values given in section 9.1.1.

(i)   IF EOF-INPUT-FILE = 0 NEXT SENTENCE
                ELSE GO TO A-ITER-END.

(ii)   IF ITEM-1 = "JOHN" GO TO PARAGRAPH-A.

(iii)   IF VALUE-1 + VALUE-2 = 6 GO TO PARAGRAPH-A
            ELSE
                IF VALUE-1 > VALUE-2 GO TO PARAGRAPH-B
                ELSE GO TO PARAGRAPH-C.

(iv)   IF VALUE-1 = 1 AND VALUE-2 = 3 GO TO PARAGRAPH-A.

(v)   IF VALUE-1 = 1 OR VALUE-2 = 3 GO TO PARAGRAPH-A.

(vi)   IF VALUE-6 IS NOT EQUAL TO 6.00 NEXT SENTENCE
                ELSE GO TO PARAGRAPH-B.

(vii)   IF VALUE-6 IS EQUAL TO 6 GO TO PARAGRAPH-D

(viii)   IF VALUE-1 IS EQUAL TO "1" GO TO PARAGRAPH-E.

Check with your COBOL Reference manual for the evaluation of (viii). Could a similar test have been made on VALUE-6?

If you are unsure of your answers set up simple test programs which will execute the relevant conditional statement and display a resultant message. Your programs must include the relevant data descriptions, to which the appropriate literal values can be moved, and the destination paragraphs. The latter need only consist of a paragraph-name and an appropriate display.

4. List the controlled GO TOs that would occur in a COBOL implementation of the schematic logic depicted in figure 2.3. check your answer with the list given in section 9.3.5.

5. Implement on your computer the code for the Analysis of Orders Program as detailed in figure 9.2. Generate some test data of your own and execute the program. See if you obtain the results you expected.

6. Implement your solution to the JOHN SMITH count problem (see task 1 in chapter 6). Get a friend to generate a test data file for the program. Does your program work with his/her test data?

CHAPTER 10

Report Production and Arithmetic Operations

10.1 Producing Reports

In commercial data processing departments a significant proportion of the work is concerned with the production of textual output and much of this is in the form of printed reports. To produce such reports usually involves processing one or more input files, carrying out analysis and straightforward computations on the accessed data and generating formatted output which can then be printed. A simple example of a formatted report is illustrated in figure 10.1. This report provides a hard copy print of each of the student records held on the output file produced by the student mark analysis program (PROGRAM1) which was described in section 3.5.

To be able to produce printed reports you need to be familiar with the way COBOL handles the files which are to be printed, how print lines can be defined and how to access run-time information such as the current date and time. Also you will probably need to be conversant with COBOL's arithmetic verbs and its facilities for reformatting data. Sections 2 to 6 of this chapter cover the technical details associated with each of these areas, section 7 details the COBOL program which generated the report shown in Figure 10.1 and the next chapter on Fusing Data Structures includes examples of both the design and implementation of various report programs.

NAME	MARK 1	MARK 2	MARK 3	AVERAGE
AHMAD J	60	50	55	55
BELL R	65	60	50	58
BLOOR C	65	70	50	62
BROWN A	50	45	45	47
CLARK I	45	65	65	58
:	:	:	:	:
:	:	:	:	:
:	:	:	:	:
THOMPSON J	60	50	50	53
WISEMAN J	70	60	60	63
WYVILL M	75	60	60	65

XXXXXXXXXXXXXXXXXXXXXXXXXXXXXXXXXXXXXXXXXXXXXXXXXXXXXXXXXXXXXXXXX

Figure 10.1 Printed report of student marks. Each detail line is double spaced and the report is terminated by a line of Xs.

10.2   Handling Printer Files

10.2.1 File-Control Entry

To produce printed output it would be feasible to simply assign the name of the output file given in the appropriate FD clause to the printer itself. Unfortunately this would mean that the execution of the program would be constrained by the speed and availability of this slow output device. It is therefore normal practice to write the output to a file on magnetic media which can later be directed to the printer. With most COBOL implementations the relevant select entry would simply take the same form as for other sequential files viz.

```
SELECT file-name ASSIGN TO implementor-name.
```

for example

```
SELECT PRINT-FILE ASSIGN TO "REPORT.DAT".
```

However, some non-standard versions of COBOL may require additional clauses which explicitly identify that the file is to contain printed output, for example the format may be:

```
SELECT file-name ASSIGN TO implementor-name
     USE FOR PRINTING.
```


10.2.2 Procedure Division Entries

Printer files are OPENed and CLOSEd in exactly the same way as any other output file. But since we normally need paged hard copy output to be formatted (headings must appear at the top of pages and blank lines are often required between print lines) COBOL provides an extended form of the WRITE statement specifically for printer files. In fact, it is the use of this form of the WRITE statement within standard COBOL which identifies that the file is intended for printing, as its use will cause special printer control characters to be included in the file.

Format for extended WRITE

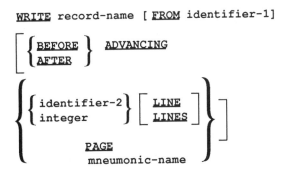

The additional part of the statement allows the programmer control over the format of the printed pages. The AFTER ADVANCING clause causes the paper to be moved prior to printing while the BEFORE ADVANCING clause causes the paper to be moved after the record is printed. The number of lines by which the paper is advanced is specified by the integer literal or the value of identifier-2 which must be an elementary integer data item. Neither of these may have a negative value, but a zero value is allowed which will cause no printer movement and hence allow overprinting. If PAGE is specified the paper is moved so that the print head is aligned with the top of the next page. Similarly page control which has been defined by the COBOL implementor can be achieved by specifying a mneumonic name which, as described in section 7.6.2, must have been defined in the Special-Names paragraph within the Configuration Section.

Examples

(i)   `WRITE PRINT-RECORD AFTER ADVANCING 3 LINES.`

This will cause the paper to be advanced by three lines and the record will be printed at that position, i.e. it will cause two blank lines to be generated.

(ii)   `WRITE PRINT-RECORD AFTER ADVANCING 0 LINES.`

This will cause the record to be printed at the position where the paper is currently positioned, overprinting any details that are already present.

(iii)   `WRITE PRINT-RECORD AFTER ADVANCING 1 LINE.`

This will cause the record to be printed on the next line and is equivalent in most COBOL implementations to simply specifying:

`WRITE PRINT-RECORD.`

(IV)   `WRITE PRINT-RECORD BEFORE ADVANCING 2 LINES.`

This will cause the record to be printed where the paper is currently positioned (overprinting any details that are already present) and then the paper will be advanced by two lines.

204

(v)   WRITE PRINT-RECORD AFTER ADVANCING PAGE.

This causes the record to be printed at the top of the next page.

(vi)   WRITE PRINT-RECORD BEFORE ADVANCING PAGE.

The record will be printed where the paper is currently positioned which will then be advanced so that the print head is aligned at the top of the next page.

10.3 Defining Data: The Value Clause

The value of data items, such as those which represent preset print lines, can be defined by adding a value clause to an item's data description.

Format

```
VALUE IS literal
```

The value of the literal must obviously confirm with the data item's picture for example:

```
01   A-HEADING        PIC X(25)
         VALUE "  PRINT OF MONTHLY ORDERS".
```

The VALUE clause may also be used to define the initial value of variables such as counters, for example:

```
01   NO-OF-ORDERS PIC 9(6) COMP VALUE 0.
```

However, many installations regard it as better practice to reserve the VALUE clause only for the definition of those items which have constant values. The initial values of variables being set by explicit Moves in the Procedure Division.

You should note that the VALUE clause may only be used to define the value of a data item within the Working-Storage Section. The clause is not allowed within record descriptions in the File Section as these are volatile areas whose values will change as each record is input or output, and thus attempting to allocate an initial value to a data item here is meaningless. This restriction on the use of the VALUE clause means that we must create in Working-Storage definitions for each print line that we wish to output. A single data record description will then be given in the output file's FD to which each print line will be moved before output. For example, in the program which processes the student results file generated by PROGRAM1 and produces the report shown in Figure 11.1 four different print lines need to be defined in the Working-Storage Section. These are detailed in the extract of code shown in Figure 11.2 which also includes the FD output record description which obviously must be big enough to hold the largest record which is to be written out.

```
FD   PRINT-FILE.
   01   PRINT-RECORD           PIC X(60).

WORKING-STORAGE SECTION.

   01   STUDENT-PRINT-RECORD.
      03   SPR-NAME               PIC X(20).
      03   FILLER                 PIC X(4)       VALUE SPACES.
      03   SPR-MARK-1             PIC 99.
      03   FILLER                 PIC X(8)       VALUE SPACES.
      03   SPR-MARK-2             PIC 99.
      03   FILLER                 PIC X(8)       VALUE SPACES.
      03   SPR-MARK-3             PIC 99.
      03   FILLER                 PIC X(8)       VALUE SPACES.
      03   SPR-AVE-MARK           PIC 99.
      03   FILLER                 PIC X(4)       VALUE SPACES.

   01   PAGE-HEADING-LINE.
      03   FILLER                 PIC X(36)
                  VALUE "   STUDENT RESULTS              DATE   ".
      03   PHL-DAY                PIC 99.
      03   FILLER                 PIC X          VALUE "/".
      03   PHL-MONTH              PIC 99.
      03   FILLER                 PIC X          VALUE "/".
      03   PHL-YEAR               PIC 99.
      03   FILLER                 PIC X(12)
                  VALUE "     PAGE   ".
      03   PHL-PAGE-NO            PIC Z9.
      03   FILLER                 PIC XX         VALUE SPACES.

   01   TITLE-LINE.
      03   FILLER                 PIC X(60)
                  VALUE "NAME                     MARK 1     MARK 2     MA
 -                "RK 3   AVERAGE ".

   01   END-LINE                  PIC X(60)      VALUE ALL "X".
```

Figure 10.2 Data definitions needed for the production of the report shown in figure 10.1.

206

The relevant WRITEs in the Procedure Division would then be:

(i)   `WRITE PRINT-RECORD FROM PAGE-HEADING-LINE`
                               `AFTER ADVANCING PAGE.`

(ii)   `WRITE PRINT-RECORD FROM TITLE-LINE`
                               `AFTER ADVANCING 3 LINES.`

(iii)   `WRITE PRINT-RECORD FROM STUDENT-PRINT-RECORD`
                               `AFTER ADVANCING 2 LINES.`

(iv)   `WRITE PRINT-RECORD FROM END-LINE`
                               `AFTER ADVANCING 1 LINE.`

These will respectively cause:

(i) Printing at the top of the page.

(ii) Printing after two blank lines.

(iii) Printing which is double spaced.

(iv) Printing on the next line.

10.4 Accessing Run-Time Information

Printed reports such as that depicted in Figure 10.1 often require run-time information such as the current date, day or time. COBOL programs can access this information from the computer's operating system via a second form of the accept statement.

Format

$$\underline{\text{ACCEPT}} \text{ identifier } \underline{\text{FROM}} \left\{ \begin{array}{l} \underline{\text{DATE}} \\ \underline{\text{DAY}} \\ \underline{\text{TIME}} \end{array} \right\}$$

Examples

Assuming the following data definitions:

```
01   CURRENT-DATE      PIC 9(6).
01   CURRENT-DAY       PIC 9(5).
01   CURRENT-TIME      PIC 9(8).
```

we would access the relevant run-time information by:

(i)   ACCEPT CURRENT-DATE FROM DATE.

This causes a 6 digit number to be placed in CURRENT-DATE which represents the date in terms of year number, month number and day number within month. The format is YYMMDD.

(ii)   ACCEPT CURRENT-DAY FROM DAY.

This causes a 5 digit number to be placed in CURRENT-DAY which represents the current day in terms of year number and day number within year. The format is YYDDD.

(iii)   ACCEPT CURRENT-TIME FROM TIME.

This causes an 8 digit number to be placed in CURRENT-TIME which gives the time elapsed since the most recent midnight in terms of hours, minutes, seconds and hundredths of a second. The format is HHMMSScc where cc represents the hundredths of a second.

Unfortunately the format in which COBOL supplies the date is different to that which we normally use viz DDMMYY. Thus to set up the date in the title line specified in figure 11.2 it would be necessary to define an accepting identifier such as

```
01   CURRENT-DATE
     03   CD-YEAR      PIC 99.
     03   CD-MONTH     PIC 99.
     03   CD-DAY       PIC 99.
```

and then move the individual elementary items to the relevant fields in the title line, for example:

```
MOVE CD-YEAR TO PHL-YEAR.
etc.
```

10.5 Arithmetic Operations

COBOL provides various arithmetic operations which perform addition, subtraction, multiplication, division and compound calculations with each of the basic operations existing in more than one form.

10.5.1 ADD Statement

The ADD statement causes two or more numeric operands to be added and the result to be stored.

Format 1

$$\underline{ADD} \left\{ \begin{array}{l} \text{identifier-1} \\ \text{numeric-literal-1} \end{array} \right\} \ldots \underline{TO} \text{ identifier-2} \ldots$$

The basic form of the format 1 ADD statement was considered in section 8.6. In its full form the values of all the operands between the ADD and the TO are added together. The resulting value is then added in turn to each identifier-2 which follows the TO.

Examples

```
ADD 1 TO A-COUNT.
ADD SUB-TOTAL-1, SUB-TOTAL-2 TO TOTAL-1, TOTAL-2.
```

In the first example the value of A-COUNT will be incremented by 1. In the second example both the value of TOTAL-1 and TOTAL-2 will be incremented by the sum of SUB-TOTAL-1 and SUB-TOTAL-2.

Format 2

$$\underline{ADD} \left\{ \begin{array}{l} \text{identifier-1} \\ \text{numeric-literal-1} \end{array} \right\} \left\{ \begin{array}{l} \text{identifier-2} \\ \text{numeric-literal-2} \end{array} \right\} \ldots$$

$$\underline{GIVING} \text{ identifier-3} \ldots$$

With format 2 ADD statements the values of all the operands between the ADD and the GIVING are added together. The resulting value is then transferred to each identifier-3 which follows the GIVING.

Example

```
ADD SUB-TOTAL-1, SUB-TOTAL-2 GIVING GRAND-TOTAL.
```

The two sub-totals are added together and the result is transferred to GRAND-TOTAL replacing any previous value. But note that SUB-TOTAL-1 and SUB-TOTAL-2 both retain their original values.

10.5.2 SUBTRACT Statement

The SUBTRACT statement is used to subtract one, or the sum of two or more, numeric data items from one or more items, and to set the value of one or more items equal to the results.

Format 1

$$\underline{\text{SUBTRACT}} \left\{ \begin{array}{l} \text{identifier-1} \\ \text{numeric-literal-1} \end{array} \right\} \ldots \underline{\text{FROM}} \quad \text{identifier-2} \ldots$$

In format 1 SUBTRACT statements the values of all the operands between the SUBTRACT and the FROM are added together. The resulting value is then subtracted in turn from each identifier-2 which follows the FROM.

Examples

```
SUBTRACT 1 FROM TOTAL-1, TOTAL-2.
SUBTRACT ISSUE-A, ISSUE-B FROM TOTAL STOCK.
```

In the first example both TOTAL-1 and TOTAL-2 are decremented by 1. In the second the value of TOTAL-STOCK is reduced by the sum of ISSUE-A and ISSUE-B. Both these latter items retain their original values.

Format 2

$$\underline{\text{SUBTRACT}} \left\{ \begin{array}{l} \text{identifier-1} \\ \text{numeric-literal-1} \end{array} \right\} \ldots \underline{\text{FROM}} \left\{ \begin{array}{l} \text{identifier-2} \\ \text{numeric-literal-2} \end{array} \right\}$$

$$\underline{\text{GIVING}} \text{ identifier-3} \ldots$$

With format 2 SUBTRACT statements the value of all the operands

210

between the SUBTRACT and the FROM are added together. The resulting value is subtracted from the value of the operand following the FROM, and this final value is transferred to each identifier-3 which follows the GIVING. The original values of each identifier-3 are replaced but all the others retain their original contents.

Example

```
SUBTRACT INCOME-TAX, SUPERANNUATION, NI-CONTRIBUTION
FROM GROSS-PAY GIVING NET-PAY.
```

The values of INCOME-TAX, SUPERANNUATION and NI-CONTRI-BUTION are added together. This value is then subtracted from the value of GROSS-PAY and the result is moved to NET-PAY. Only the value of the item NET-PAY is changed while all the others retain their original values.

10.5.3 MULTIPLY Statement

The MULTIPLY statement causes two numeric data items to be multiplied together, and sets the value of one or more items equal to the result.

Format 1

```
MULTIPLY { identifier-1       } BY  identifier-2 ...
         { numeric-literal-1  }
```

In format 1 MULTIPLY statements each identifier-2 following the BY has its value multiplied by the value of the operand following the MULTIPLY. The result replaces the original value of the relevant identifier-2.

Example

Assuming the following data items and values

```
01    ITEM-A    PIC 9(3)    VALUE 10.
01    ITEM-B    PIC 9(3)    VALUE 6.
01    ITEM-C    PIC 9(3)    VALUE 3.
```

then

```
MULTIPLY ITEM-A BY ITEM-B, ITEM-C.
```

will result in the following values

```
ITEM-A = 10
ITEM-B = 60
ITEM-C = 30
```

You must remember that with this form of MULTIPLY, as is normal in COBOL, the result(s) are placed in the rightmost operand(s).

Format 2

$$\underline{MULTIPLY} \left\{ \begin{array}{l} \texttt{identifier-1} \\ \texttt{numeric-literal-1} \end{array} \right\} \underline{BY} \left\{ \begin{array}{l} \texttt{identifier-2} \\ \texttt{numeric-literal-1} \end{array} \right\}$$

$$\underline{GIVING} \texttt{ identifier-3 } \ldots$$

In format 2 MULTIPLY statements the value of the two operands separated by the BY are multiplied together and the result is moved to identifier-3.

Example

Using the data items defined above with their original values the statement:

```
MULTIPLY ITEM-A BY ITEM-B GIVING ITEM-C
```

will result in the following values

```
ITEM-A = 10
ITEM-B =  6
ITEM-C = 60
```

10.5.4 DIVIDE Statement

The DIVIDE statement is used to divide one numeric data item into one or more other numeric data items, and then set the values of one or more items equal to the result.

Format 1

$$\text{DIVIDE} \left\{ \begin{array}{l} \text{identifier-1} \\ \text{numeric-literal-1} \end{array} \right\} \text{INTO} \quad \text{identifier-2} \ \dots$$

In format 1 statements each identifier-2 following the INTO has its value divided by the value of the operand following the DIVIDE. The resulting quotient replaces the original value of the relevant identifier-2.

Examples

```
DIVIDE 3 INTO ITEM-A, ITEM-B.
DIVIDE ITEM-C INTO ITEM-D
```

If the initial values of ITEM-A to ITEM-D are 9, 18, 5 and 10 respectively their values after execution of the above statements will be:

```
ITEM-A = 3
ITEM-B = 6
ITEM-C = 5    (unchanged)
ITEM-D = 2
```

Format 2

$$\text{DIVIDE} \left\{ \begin{array}{l} \text{identifier-1} \\ \text{numeric-literal-1} \end{array} \right\} \left\{ \begin{array}{l} \text{INTO} \\ \text{BY} \end{array} \right\} \left\{ \begin{array}{l} \text{identifier-2} \\ \text{numeric-literal-2} \end{array} \right\}$$

$$\text{GIVING} \quad \text{identifier-3} \ \dots$$

In format 2 statements if INTO is specified the result is obtained by dividing the operand which precedes the INTO (the divisor) into the operand (the divident) which follows it. If BY is specified the operand which follows the BY (the divisor) is divided into the operand which precedes the BY (the divident). The resultant quotient is moved to each identifier-3. The divisor and divident both retain their original values.

Examples

```
DIVIDE TIME-ELAPSED INTO DISTANCE-TRAVELLED
        GIVING AVERAGE-SPEED.

DIVIDE DISTANCE-TRAVELLED BY TIME-ELAPSED
        GIVING AVERAGE-SPEED.
```

As can be seen these two statements are equivalent.

Format 3

$$\underline{\text{DIVIDE}} \left\{ \begin{array}{l} \text{identifier-1} \\ \text{numeric-literal-1} \end{array} \right\} \left\{ \begin{array}{l} \underline{\text{INTO}} \\ \underline{\text{BY}} \end{array} \right\} \left\{ \begin{array}{l} \text{identifier-2} \\ \text{numeric-literal-2} \end{array} \right\}$$

```
GIVING identifier-3 ...

REMAINDER identifier-4
```

Format 3 DIVIDE statements operate in the same way as format 2 with the addition that the remainder calculated according to:

remainder = divident - (truncated quotient x divisor)

is moved to identifier-4. The truncated quotient is the value of the quotient according to identifier-3's picture clause.

Example

Assuming the following data items and values

```
01  A-QUOTIENT    PIC 99.
01  A-REMAINDER   PIC 99.
```

then

```
DIVIDE 100 BY 15 GIVING A-QUOTIENT
        REMAINDER A-REMAINDER
```

would result in

```
A-QUOTIENT  =  6
A-REMAINDER = 10
```

Divide by Zero

With all forms of the divide statement care must be taken to ensure that the divisor does not have zero value as this will result in a run-time error which will cause the program to fail. Thus it should be normal practice to check the value of a divisor before the divide statement is executed.

10.5.5 COMPUTE Statement

The COMPUTE Statement is used to assign the value of an arithmetic expression to one or more data items. It thus provides a more convenient way of handling complex arithmetic operations than having to code them as a series of individual ADD, SUBTRACT, MULTIPLY or DIVIDE statements.

Format

```
COMPUTE identifier-1 ... = arithmetic expression.
```

The arithmetic expression is evaluated and the result is transferred to each identifier-1. An arithmetic expression may simply be an identifier or a numeric literal. However, it is normally a combination of identifiers, numeric literals, arithmetic operators and where necessary parenthesis.

The arithmetic operators are

+   for addition
-   for subtraction
*   for multiplication
/   for division
** for exponentiation (raising to a power)

Each arithmetic operator must always be preceded and followed by a space. The COBOL order of precedence in evaluating arithmetic expressions is as in normal mathematics viz exponentiation then multiplication and division and finally addition and subtraction. Though again, as normal, this order can be over-ruled by the use of parenthesis, as expressions in parenthesis will always be evaluated first.

Examples

```
COMPUTE AVERAGE-MARK = (MARK-1 + MARK-2 + MARK-3) / 3.

COMPUTE NET-PAY = HOURS-WORKED * HOURLY-RATE
                + MISC-ALLOWANCES
                - (INCOME-TAX + PENSION-CONTRIBUTIONS).
```

As with the Divide statement care must be taken to ensure that during the evaluation of any arithmetic expression division by zero does not occur.

10.5.6 Identifiers Used in Arithmetic Statements

The identifiers which are referenced in any arithmetic statement must obviously be defined as numerics. The basic rule is that each identifier must relate to a normal numeric data item as defined in section 7.8.1(c) i.e. the picture string that describes it is comprised of characters from the set 9, V, S and P. The only exceptions to this rule are that where the GIVING form of a statement is used or where the COMPUTE is used the item(s) where the result is placed can be defined either as numeric data items or as numeric-edited data items. This later type of numeric is intended for textual output and its composition is covered in section 10.6.1.

Care must be taken to ensure that the items which receive the results of arithmetic operations are of suitable size. Transfers to receiving fields are governed by decimal point alignment, as with the Move statement, and where the defined length is insufficient truncation will occur. It may be acceptable to have the fractional part of a number truncated but truncation of the integer part is obviously unacceptable. Also for efficient processing you should ensure that any data item that is involved in a significant number of arithmetic operations is defined as Computational. Such items can later be moved to an appropriate PIC 9 display field when they need to be output in textual form.

10.5.7 Accuracy of Results - ROUNDED Option

As described in the previous section if the receiving field of an arithmetic operation is not large enough truncation will take place. For example execution of the statement:

```
            DIVIDE TIME-ELAPSED INTO DISTANCE-TRAVELLED
            GIVING AVERAGE-SPEED.
```

with
```
       TIME-ELAPSED = 10, DISTANCE-TRAVELLED = 58
```
and
```
       01  AVERAGE-SPEED      PIC 99.
```

would generate a result of 5.8 but when this is stored in AVERAGE-SPEED the fractional part would be lost and AVERAGE-SPEED would have a value of 5!

To overcome this problem any receiving item in an arithmetic statement can have the ROUNDED option specified so that rounding takes place instead of truncation. This option is reflected in the full format specifications given in appendix C for the arithmetic statements. When the ROUNDED option is specified the result is that if the most significant digit being truncated is equal to or greater than 5 then the least significant digit of the stored result is increased by 1.

For example using the data values given above execution of:
```
            DIVIDE TIME-ELAPSED INTO DISTANCE-TRAVELLED
            GIVING AVERAGE-SPEED ROUNDED.
```

would result in a value of 6 being stored in AVERAGE-SPEED. A much more accurate value than previously.

10.5.8 Intercepting Errors: ON SIZE ERROR Phrase

A size error occurs in an arithmetic statement when the integer part of the result is too large to be stored in the appropriate data item without truncation taking place. A size error will also occur with a Multiply or Divide statement if an intermediate result is too large or if divide by zero is attempted.

Specifying the ON SIZE ERROR phase makes the arithmetic statement a conditional statement and allows interception of errors. If a size error occurs and the ON SIZE ERROR phase is specified the resultant item is unchanged and the imperative statement(s) associated with the ON

SIZE ERROR phase are executed. If the phase is not specified and a size error occurs the values in the relevant data items will be unpredictable or there may be run-time error which will cause the program to fail.

Example

```
MULTIPLY HOURS-WORKED BY HOURLY-RATE
    GIVING BASIC-PAY
    ON SIZE ERROR GO TO ERROR-ROUTINE.
```

If the result of the multiplication produces a size error control would be transferred to ERROR-ROUTINE.

The full definitions for the arithmetic statements including the ON SIZE ERROR phrase are given in Appendix C. Note that when both ROUNDED and ON SIZE ERROR are specified in a statement rounding is done first.

10.6 Reformatting Data: Edited Moves

In section 7.8.1 we considered the basic types of item that could be defined by the Picture clause viz:

> alphabetic
> alphanumeric
> numeric

and in section 8.5 descriptions of the operation of COBOL Moves between these different data types were given. COBOL also supports two additional data types:

> numeric edited
> alphanumeric edited

which support formatted textual output of the type that business often requires. To achieve this formatting special editing characters are used in the picture strings which define the items. Data when moved to these 'edited' items will then be modified according to the specified picture.

10.6.1 Numeric Editing

Numeric editing takes place whenever a numeric data value is transferred to a field which has a numeric edited picture. The transfer may result from an explicit Move statement between elementary numeric items, or from an implicit Move caused by the Giving option of an arithmetic statement, or by the final assignment in a Compute statement of a value to the identifier(s) which appear to the left of the equals sign. The numeric editing options which are available are as follows:

(a) Decimal point insertion and alignment

The position where an actual decimal point is to be inserted is specified by a full stop in the appropriate position in the item's Picture. For example

    PIC 9(6).99

The position of the full stop also specifies the position of decimal point alignment. Where alignment is required, at a position other than the rightmost, but no decimal point is to be printed a V may be used instead of the full stop to specify an assumed decimal point position.

(b) Insertion of Zeros and Commas

Zeros and commas may both be edited into data items by including '0' and ',' in the appropriate places. For example

    PIC 9(4)00

would scale a value up by a factor of a hundred and

    PIC 99,999,999.99

will show the division of a value into millions and thousands.

(c) Insertion of Spaces or Solidi

Spaces and/or Solidi may be edited into a field - for example to act as separators between the day, month and year in a number which represents a date - by including 'B' or '/' in the appropriate places. For example

    PIC 99B99B99
    PIC 99/99/99

(d) Zero Suppression

It is not normally required for leading zeros to be printed. For example a four digit field which holds the value 56 should normally be printed as:

```
56
```

and not as:

```
0056
```

To replace such non significant zeros by spaces Zs are substituted for the relevant 9s in the Picture. For example:

```
PIC Z(3)9
```

will produce the output specified above.

Also the insertion characters: '0'; ','; 'B' and '/' when used within zero suppression strings will each be replaced by a space when non significant. For example movement of the value 56 to a field described as:

```
PIC ZZ,ZZZ,ZZ9.99
```

would produce the character string

```
56.00
```

where all the character positions to the left of the 5 have been space filled.

(e) BLANK WHEN ZERO Clause

A complete elementary item can be specified to be space filled, irrespective of its Picture clause, when a zero value is moved to it by adding the clause

```
BLANK WHEN ZERO
```

to its description. For example

```
03   TOTAL-CHARGE PIC Z(4)9.99   BLANK WHEN ZERO.
```

(f) Editing in Signs + and -

The plus and minus signs may be edited into either the leftmost or rightmost position of a character string. The options are

(i) If the sign is always to be printed write a '+' in the picture string.

(ii) If the sign is to be printed only when the number is negative write a '-' in the picture string.

Examples:

```
PIC +9(5)
PIC ZZ9-
```

Moving the value 56 to these fields would result in +00056 and 56 respectively.

(g) Editing Cash Fields

In business applications the handling of cash fields is of particular importance. COBOL provides the following facilities:

(i) Insertion of a Currency Sign ($ or £)

The currency sign appearing as the leftmost character in a picture string will cause it to be edited into the data item at that position. For example

```
PIC £99.99
```

You should note that with many COBOL implementations the currency sign £ will have to be defined in a CURRENCY clause within SPECIAL-NAMES.

(ii) Floating Currency Signs

Suppose the value 56 is moved to a field with a picture £ ZZ,ZZ9.99 the result would be:

```
£    56.00
```

This is not aesthetically pleasing and more importantly it could be fraudulently altered. To overcome this problem currency symbols are written instead of the Zs in the picture string. The effect is to suppress leading currency symbols in a similar way as leading zeros are suppressed except that a leading currency sign is always printed. For example if our picture was £ £ £, £ £ 9.99 the result would be:

```
£56.00
```

which is much safer.

This principle of a floating character may also be applied to '+' and '-' signs appearing at the left-hand end of a picture string.

(iii) Cheque Protection

In a similar manner to zero suppression, non significant zeros may be replaced by asterisks to prevent output being fraudulently altered. For example moving 56 to an item specified as:

```
PIC £****9.99
```

would result in

```
£***56.00
```

(iv) Credits and Debits: CR and DB

As for plus and minus signs, specification of credit and debits is achieved by adding the characters "CR" and "DB" to the right hand side of the picture string. However, they are only edited in if the data is negative.

Examples

```
PIC ££,££9.99CR
PIC 99.99DB
```

Moving -56 to each of these items would result in the values £ 56.00CR and 56.00DB respectively.

(h) General Points Regarding Sizing

It should be remembered that:

(i) a maximum of 30 symbols is allowed in any picture string,

(ii) editing characters define actual character positions in the data item they are specifying.

For example the picture string £*(6)9.99 consists of 9 symbols and defines an item which is 11 characters long.

10.6.2 Alphanumeric Editing

Limited editing facilities also exist for alphanumeric data. Zeros, spaces and solidi can be edited into alphanumeric items in the same way as for numeric edited items by specification of the characters '0', 'B' and '/'. For an item to be classed as alphanumeric edited it must be pictured using characters from the set 'A', 'X', '9', '0', 'B' and '/' and the picture must contain at least one 'X' or 'A' and at least one '0', 'B' or '/'.

10.6.3 Group Move Limitations

It should be remembered that with the MOVE statement, as described in section 8.5.4, if either the sending or receiving item is a group item the MOVE is treated as pure alphanumeric. Thus if a group item is the sending field in a MOVE, which uses an edited receiving field, the data transfer will also be treated as a pure alphanumeric MOVE and no editing will take place.

10.7 A Report Program

The complete code for the program which processes the student results file, generated by PROGRAM1, and which produces the report illustrated in figure 10.1 is given in figure 10.3. The corresponding basic program structure is shown in figure 10.4. Each result record is read in turn, reformatted and written to the output file. At the start of each page, the page heading and title lines are written out and finally once all the results records have been processed a line of Xs is written. The program has been designed so that a maximum of 20 result records will be reported on each page.

```
IDENTIFICATION DIVISION.

PROGRAM-ID. PRINTSR.
* A PROGRAM TO PROVIDE A PRINTOUT OF STUDENT RESULTS: RECORDS
* ARE READ FROM THE FILE SRESULTS.DAT, REFORMATTED AND THEN
* WRITTEN ALONG WITH APPROPRIATE PAGE HEADINGS TO THE PRINT FILE
* SPRINT.DAT. THE PRINT FILE IS TERMINATED WITH A LINE OF Xs.

ENVIRONMENT DIVISION.

CONFIGURATION SECTION.
SOURCE-COMPUTER. A-PC.
OBJECT-COMPUTER. A-PC.

INPUT-OUTPUT SECTION.
FILE-CONTROL.
     SELECT RESULTS-FILE ASSIGN TO "SRESULTS.DAT".
     SELECT PRINT-FILE ASSIGN TO "SPRINT.DAT".

DATA DIVISION.

FILE SECTION.
FD   RESULTS-FILE.
     01   RESULTS-RECORD.
          03   RR-NAME          PIC X(20).
          03   RR-MARK-1        PIC 99.
          03   RR-MARK-2        PIC 99.
          03   RR-MARK-3        PIC 99.
          03   RR-AVE-MARK      PIC 99.

FD   PRINT-FILE.
     01   PRINT-RECORD          PIC X(60).

WORKING-STORAGE SECTION.
     01   EOF-RESULTS-FILE         PIC 9.
     01   PF-OUTPUT-COUNT          PIC 99   COMP.
     01   PF-PAGE-COUNT            PIC 99   COMP.

     01   CURRENT-DATE.
          03   CD-YEAR             PIC 99.
          03   CD-MONTH            PIC 99.
          03   CD-DAY              PIC 99.
```

224

```
01  STUDENT-PRINT-RECORD.
    03  SPR-NAME              PIC X(20).
    03  FILLER               PIC X(4)       VALUE SPACES.
    03  SPR-MARK-1           PIC 99.
    03  FILLER               PIC X(8)       VALUE SPACES.
    03  SPR-MARK-2           PIC 99.
    03  FILLER               PIC X(8)       VALUE SPACES.
    03  SPR-MARK-3           PIC 99.
    03  FILLER               PIC X(8)       VALUE SPACES.
    03  SPR-AVE-MARK         PIC 99.
    03  FILLER               PIC X(4)       VALUE SPACES.


01  PAGE-HEADING-LINE.
    03  FILLER               PIC X(36)
            VALUE "  STUDENT RESULTS              DATE  ".
    03  PHL-DAY              PIC 99.
    03  FILLER               PIC X          VALUE "/".
    03  PHL-MONTH            PIC 99.
    03  FILLER               PIC X          VALUE "/".
    03  PHL-YEAR             PIC 99.
    03  FILLER               PIC X(12)
            VALUE "      PAGE  ".
    03  PHL-PAGE-NO          PIC Z9.
    03  FILLER               PIC XX         VALUE SPACES.

01  TITLE-LINE.
    03  FILLER               PIC X(60)
            VALUE "NAME                    MARK 1    MARK 2    MA
-           "RK 3   AVERAGE ".

01  END-LINE                 PIC X(60)      VALUE  ALL "X".

PROCEDURE DIVISION.

PSR1A-SEQ.
PSR1B.
*    INITIALISATION OPERATIONS
     MOVE 0 TO EOF-RESULTS-FILE, PF-PAGE-COUNT.
     OPEN INPUT RESULTS-FILE.
     OPEN OUTPUT PRINT-FILE.
     ACCEPT CURRENT-DATE FROM DATE.
     MOVE CD-YEAR TO PHL-YEAR.
     MOVE CD-MONTH TO PHL-MONTH.
     MOVE CD-DAY TO PHL-DAY.
     READ RESULTS-FILE AT END MOVE 1 TO EOF-RESULTS-FILE.
```

```
 PSR1C-ITER.
     IF EOF-RESULTS-FILE = 0 NEXT SENTENCE
                               ELSE GO TO PSR1C-ITER-END.
 PSR1E-SEQ.
*    PROCESS PAGE
 PSR1F.
*    OUTPUT PAGE HEADINGS
     ADD 1 TO PF-PAGE-COUNT.
     MOVE PF-PAGE-COUNT TO PHL-PAGE-NO.
     WRITE PRINT-RECORD FROM PAGE-HEADING-LINE
                     AFTER ADVANCING PAGE.
     WRITE PRINT-RECORD FROM TITLE-LINE
                     AFTER ADVANCING 3 LINES.
     MOVE 0 TO PF-OUTPUT-COUNT.
 PSR1G-ITER.
     IF EOF-RESULTS-FILE = 0 AND PF-OUTPUT-COUNT < 20
             NEXT SENTENCE ELSE GO TO PSR1G-ITER-END.
 PSR1H.
*    PROCESS STUDENT RECORD
     MOVE RR-NAME TO SPR-NAME.
     MOVE RR-MARK-1 TO SPR-MARK-1.
     MOVE RR-MARK-2 TO SPR-MARK-2.
     MOVE RR-MARK-3 TO SPR-MARK-3.
     MOVE RR-AVE-MARK TO SPR-AVE-MARK.
     WRITE PRINT-RECORD FROM STUDENT-PRINT-RECORD
                     AFTER ADVANCING 2 LINES.
     ADD 1 TO PF-OUTPUT-COUNT.
     READ RESULTS-FILE AT END MOVE 1 TO EOF-RESULTS-FILE.
     GO TO PSR1G-ITER.
 PSR1G-ITER-END.
 PSR1E-SEQ-END.
     GO TO PSR1C-ITER.
 PSR1C-ITER-END.
 PSR1D.
*    TERMINAL ACTION
     WRITE PRINT-RECORD FROM END-LINE
                     AFTER ADVANCING 1 LINE.
     CLOSE RESULTS-FILE, PRINT-FILE.
     STOP-RUN.
 PSR1A-SEQ-END.
```

Figure 10.3   Code for program PRINTSR

In the program the variables EOF-RESULTS-FILE and PF-OUTPUT-COUNT are used to control the iterations. The former represents the state of the input file and the latter is used to count the number of sets

226

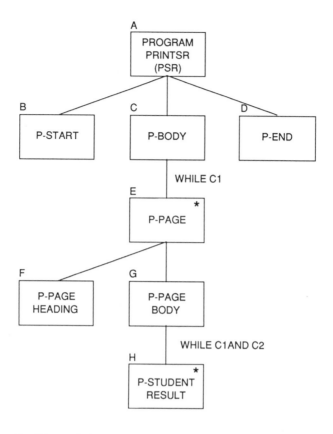

Conditions: C1 There is a student record still to process
            C2 There is room on the current page to output
               another set of student results

Figure 10.4 Basic program structure for PRINTSR.

of student results printed on each page. At the upper iterative level
(PSR1C-ITER) the condition is "while there is a student record still to
process" i.e. we have not yet reached the end of the results file hence
EOF-RESULTS-FILE will have a value of zero. At the lower iterative
level (PSR1G-ITER) we have a compound condition "while there is a
student record still to process AND there is room on the current page to
output another set of student results". The second part of the condition
is satisfied so long as PF-OUTPUT-COUNT is less than 20. This
variable is set to zero at the start of each new page (at component

PSR1F) and is incremented after each set of student results is output. Note it is necessary to repeat the higher level iterative condition at component PSR1G-ITER. This is because when the end of the input file is detected by the read at component PSR1H the program must first exit the lower level iteration (PSR1G-ITER) and then the upper level iteration (PSR1C-ITER). Thus we must check EOF-RESULTS-FILE at both levels.

In this chapter the design of program PRINTSR has been presented as a fait accompli. In the next chapter the design of such report programs will be considered in detail.

TASKS - CHAPTER 10

1. Look up in your COBOL Reference Manual each of the statements described in this chapter and ensure that you can answer the following questions.

(i) What is the form of the select entry for printer files on your system?

(ii) Are any special operating system commands needed when dealing with printer files? (You may need to consult the operating system manual for your system or the user manual for the COBOL run-time system to determine this).

(iii) Is WRITE record-name for a print file equivalent to:

WRITE record-name AFTER ADVANCING 1 LINE.

in the version of COBOL you are using?

(iv) With which data descriptions is a VALUE clause not allowed? Why?

(v) What do the ROUNDED option and ON SIZE ERROR phrases accomplish? If both occur in a COBOL statement which is carried out first?

2. Identify the COBOL Write statements that are needed to produce the printout detailed below. Assume that an output record PRINT-REC is to be used for the transfer and each line has been set up in Working-Storage.

(i) LINE-H is to be printed at the top of the next page.

(ii) Ten copies of LINE-D are to be printed with two blank lines before each.

(iii) LINE-A is to be printed on the next line and it is then to be overprinted by LINE-B.

(iv) LINE-C is to be printed after two or more blank lines and finally the printer is to be positioned at the top of the next page.

3. Implement a simple program which will access the current date and time and display the information with appropriate headings. Use the value clause to define appropriate display items in Working-Storage.

4. A set of data items have the following values:

```
01   ITEM-A          PIC S9(2)   COMP   VALUE 10.
01   ITEM-B          PIC S9(2)   COMP   VALUE  8.
01   ITEM-C          PIC S9(2)   COMP   VALUE 12.
01   ITEM-D          PIC S9(3)   COMP   VALUE  5.
```

(i) State what their values would be after execution of the following paragraph of code

```
A-CALCULATION.
    ADD ITEM-A TO ITEM-B.
    SUBTRACT 6 FROM ITEM-B, ITEM-A.
    MULTIPLY ITEM-B BY ITEM-A GIVING ITEM-D.
    DIVIDE ITEM-C INTO ITEM-D.
```

(ii) Rewrite the calculation of ITEM-D using a compute statement.

(iii) Implement a test program to see if your answers are correct.

(iv) Amend your code so that it will minimise any loss of accuracy due to the truncation of fractional values.

(v) Explain how you would trap "divide by zero errors".

5. Design and implement a program that will read integer numbers from a file, display each one and state whether they are odd or even.

6. State what the contents of ITEM-B would be after execution of

   `MOVE ITEM-A TO ITEM-B.`

   given the following pictures for ITEM-A and ITEM-B and initial values for ITEM-A.

ITEM A		ITEM B
PICTURE	VALUE	PICTURE
9(5)V99	12345.6	99,999.99
9(6)	010484	99/99/99
9(5)V99	12.3	ZZ,ZZ9.99
S9(5)V99	12.3	£Z,ZZ9.99+
S9(5)V99	12.3	££,££9.99−
S9(5)V99	−12.3	£****9.9DB
X(4)	ABCD	/X(2)BX(2)/

   Again check your answers via simple test routines.

7. Implement the report program detailed in section 10.7 and test it on output generated by your PROGRAM1 (see task 3 Chapter 3). Amend the program so that the result records are single spaced with a maximum of 30 on each page.

PART 4

THE DESIGN AND IMPLE-MENTATION OF TYPICAL DATA PROCESSING PROGRAMS

The following three chapters are concerned with the design and implementation of the types of programs frequently encountered in commercial data pocessing - report programs, analysis programs and programs which involve the matching of sequentially organised files. Chapter 11 covers the fusing of data structures and the development of straightforward report and analysis type programs. Chapter 12 develops further the concept of fusing and covers the design of programs which handle sequentially organised files. Finally chapter 13 is devoted to describing the design and implementation of programs which update sequentially organised master files.

Programs Which Handle More Than One File – the fusing of data structures

11.1 Introduction

Stage 2 of the JSP Method (Creating a Basic Program Structure) involves fusing the individual logical data structures on which the program is based into a composite fused data structure. As was outlined in section 5.4.1 this involves identifying correspondences between components within each data structure. Those components which correspond are then merged together to become fused components in the composite fused data structure. Those components within each data structure which do not correspond with any components in the other data structures are incorporated into the fused data structure as individual components which relate only to their own originating data structure.

The processes involved in producing a fused data structure are best understood by means of illustrative examples. Therefore to become acquainted with the basic techniques we shall consider a second version of the Analysis of Orders Program, first specified in section 5.1, which requires that, instead of simply counting the credit and cash orders and then displaying the results at the end of the program run, the following printed report is to be produced:

The report is to provide a copy of the agent orders that are held on the Monthly Orders File. Each order is to be printed on a new line with a space between each data field and there are to be a maximum of 50 such detailed lines per page of the report. Each page is to commence with a heading giving the report title "Print of Monthly Orders", the date and the page number. The heading is to be followed by a blank line. The final page is to contain only the page heading and details of the counts of cash and credit orders.

Part of two sample pages of the report to be produced by this Print of Monthly Orders Program is shown in figure 11.1 and the logical data structures for the Monthly Orders File and the Report File are shown in figure 11.2.

```
PRINT OF MONTHLY ORDERS        DATE   21/10/88        PAGE    1

AA1234 ZW4947 14999 01 C
AA1234 TW1940 01250 01 C
AA1234 TW2628 00995 04 C
AA1235 YW7432 00999 02 M
AA1236 WW0933 01299 01 M
AB0070 WW6593 11995 01 M
   :      :      :     : :
   :      :      :     : :
   :      :      :     : :




PRINT OF MONTHLY ORDERS        DATE   21/10/88        PAGE    9

NUMBER OF CASH ORDERS 157    NUMBER OF CREDIT ORDERS 226
```

Figure 11.1 Sample pages of the report to be produced by the Print of Monthly Orders Program

11.2 Correspondence

Two components are said to correspond when for every occurrence of one there is a corresponding occurrence of the other, i.e. there is a one to one correspondence between the individual occurrences of the components. The rules associated with correspondences and the production of a fused data structure, and hence a basic program structure, are:

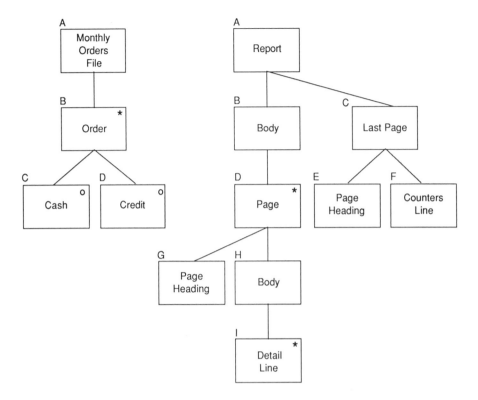

Figure 11.2 Logical Data Structures for Print of Monthly Orders Program.

(i) Corresponding components in the logical data structures are combined into one component in the fused data/basic program structure.

(ii) Every component of each data structure must correspond with a component in the fused data/basic program structure.

(iii) The structure produced by fusing the data structures must itself be logically sound i.e. it must represent the correct processing of each of its constituent data structures.

11.2.1 Identifying Correspondences between Data Structures

There is correspondence between components from different logical data structures if they -

(i)   occur the same number of times,
(ii) occur in the same order,
(iii) are processed together.

Correspondences are identified by working logically through the structures. Each component is considered in turn and checked to see whether it satisfies the above criteria with regard to a component in another structure. For example, between the logical data structures shown in figure 11.2 there is correspondence at File/Report level and also at Order/Detail Line Level. From a Monthly Orders File a Report File is produced and thus component A of the Monthly Orders File corresponds to component A of the Report. Also for every Order on the Monthly Orders File a Detail Line is produced on the Report. These obviously occur in the same order and are processed together - the first Order will produce the first Detail Line and so on. Thus there is correspondence between component B of the Monthly Orders File and component I of the Report.

11.2.2 Documenting Correspondences

In small programs, such as the Print of Monthly Orders where the data structures can be drawn on a single page, correspondences can be shown directly on the diagram by means of double headed arrows as in figure 11.3. However, it is more likely that each data structure will be drawn on a separate page in which case correspondences must be documented using a correspondence table as shown in figure 11.4. Here the identifiers of those components which correspond are listed side by side and where there is no correspondence a dash is inserted.

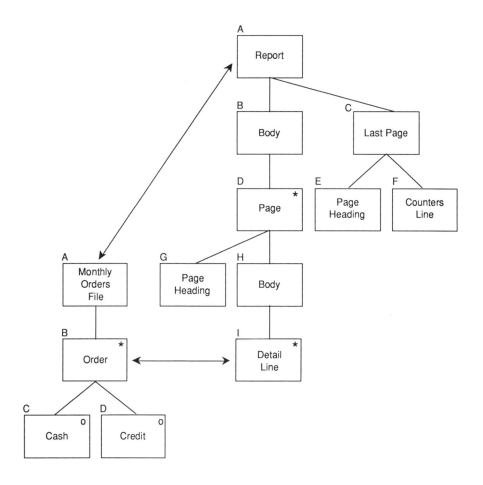

Figure 11.3 Correspondences between Data Structures for the Print of Monthly Orders Program.

11.3 Fusing the Logical Data Structures

Having identified those components which correspond, the logical data structures can be fused together. The links between corresponding components, which will fuse together to form single components in the composite data structure, provide guides for the merging together of the

Monthly Orders File	Report
A	A
–	B
–	C
–	D
–	E
–	F
–	G
–	H
B	I
C	–
D	–

Figur 11.4 Correspondence Table for the Print of Monthly Orders Program.

data structures and the placement of non-corresponding data structure components in the fused data structure. For example, in figure 11.3 components A and B of the Monthly Orders File correspond respectively with components A and I of the Report. Thus components B to H of the Report must be merged between these pairs of corresponding components and components C and D of the Monthly Orders File must follow the fused Order/Detail Line component. The resultant fused data structure and developed basic program structure are shown in figures 11.5 and 11.6.

In figure 11.6 extra components have been added to allow for initial program housekeeping (component B) and for processing the current record and accessing the next (components K and L).

11.4 Checking the Fused Structure

11.4.1 Consistency Checks

As stated in section 11.2, every component of each logical data structure must correspond with a component in the fused data structure and the fused data structure itself must be logically sound. The first requirement means that within the fused data structure we should be able to

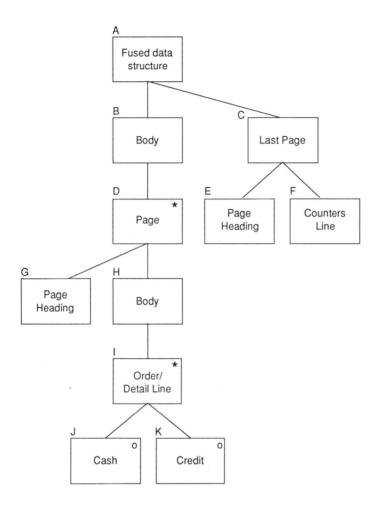

Figure 11.5 Fused Data Structure for the Print of Monthly Orders Program.

239

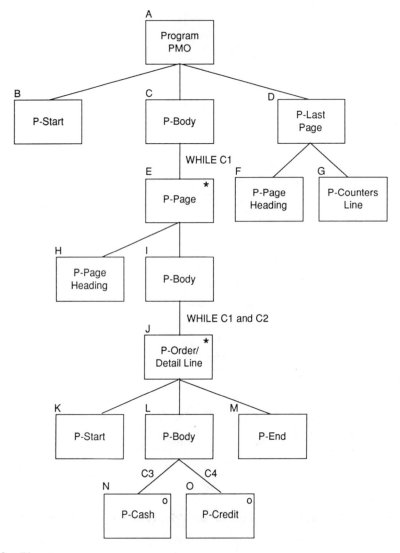

Conditions

C1 not end of Monthly Orders File – record(s) still to process (EOF-ORDERS-FILE = O)

C2 detail line count within page is less than 50 (DL-COUNT < 50)

C3 cash order (OR-PAYMENT-TYPE = M)

C4 credit order (OR-PAYMENT-TYPE = C)

Figure 11.6 Basic Program Structure for the Print of Monthly Orders Program.

240

identify a set of components which fully represent each of the constituent data structures. The correspondences between the individual data structures and the fused data structure can most easily be checked by adding an additional column to the correspondence table. This column is used to record the components of the fused data structure and each entry within it is aligned with those of the constituent data structure(s) to which the entry corresponds. Figure 11.7 illustrates such a correspondence table for the Print of Monthly Orders Program.

Monthly Orders File	Report	Fused Data Structure
A	A	A
–	B	B
–	C	C
–	D	D
–	E	E
–	F	F
–	G	G
–	H	H
B	I	I
C	–	J
D	–	K

Figure 11.7 Full correspondence table for the Print of Monthly Orders Program.

As can be seen from this correspondence table the components of the Monthly Orders File correspond with components A, I, J and K of the fused data structure and the components of the Report correspond with components A to I of the fused data structure. In the correspondence table each entry for a component from the fused data structure must be shown to correspond with at least one component from the constituent data structures. If a basic program structure is produced without first deriving the fused data structure the correspondence checks can be performed between the data structures and the basic program structure. However, in such cases it must be remembered that basic program structures do include additional components, such as components B, K, L and M of figure 11.6, which will not relate to any constituent data structure.

241

Ensuring that the fused structure is itself logically sound is best achieved by "reading" the structure in the order it will be executed. Carrying out this process by oneself or better still explaining the structure to another person will usually expose any logical inconsistencies, for example, showing a detail line before the relevant page heading. Such checks can alternatively be carried out on the the basic program structure.

11.4.2 Problems

Sometimes the above checks will reveal errors in the fused data structure and in some cases you will encounter difficulties in the actual production of the fused data structure itself. These problems are usually due to one of the following:

(i)   Errors in one or more of the logical data structures - you will find that producing correct logical data structures and their successful fusing is often an iterative process that may require several revisions before completion.

(ii) Errors in the fusing process - these are normally caused by incorrectly identifying correspondences, omitting correspondences, or incorrectly merging together the data structures. Most of these problems are overcome by carefully checking the work that has been carried out and usually they diminish as you gain experience with the method.

(iii) Logical structures which simply do not fuse together despite the fact that careful checking has indicated that their structures are logically correct. This problem occurs when the structures themselves are incompatible and is referred to as a structure clash. It is normally resolved by a JSP technique called Program Inversion which is fully described in Chapter 18 (within Volume 2).

11.5   Completion of Print of Monthly Orders Program

11.5.1 Schematic Logic and Coding

Following the production of the basic program structure as shown in figure 11.6 the functions for the program are identified by reference to the original specification. Once these have been allocated to the program structure the schematic logic can be drawn up and the program coded. The schematic for the program is given in figure 11.8 and the code is given in figure 11.9.

```
PMO1A-SEQ
   PMO1B
      Open monthly orders file
      Open report file
      Set count of cash orders (M-COUNT) = 0
      Set count of credit orders (C-COUNT) = 0
      Set value of EOF-ORDERS-FILE = 0
      Set report page count (R-PAGE-COUNT) = 0
      Access current date and set up in heading line
      Read record from monthly orders file at end set the
                        value of EOF-ORDERS-FILE = 1
   PMO1C-ITER while not end of monthly orders file
                        (EOF-ORDERS-FILE = 0)
      PMO1E-SEQ
         PMO1H
            Add 1 to report page count (R-PAGE-COUNT) and set
                  up in heading line
            Write heading line to report file followed by a
                  blank line
            Set detail line count within page (DL-COUNT) = 0
         PMO1I-ITER while not end of monthly orders file and
                        detail line count within page < 50
                     (EOF-ORDERS-FILE = 0 and DL-COUNT < 50)
            PMO1J-SEQ
               PMO1K
                  Set up detail line
               PMO1L-SEL if cash order (OR-PAYMENT-TYPE = M)
               PMO1N
                  Add 1 to count of cash orders (M-COUNT)
               PMO1L-OR1 if credit order (OR-PAYMENT-TYPE = C)
               PMO1O
                  Add 1 to count of credit orders (C-COUNT)
               PMO1L-SEL-END
               PMO1M
                  Write detail line to report file
                  Add 1 to detail line count within page
                                       (DL-COUNT)
                  Read record from monthly orders file at end
                        set the value of EOF-ORDERS-FILE = 1
            PMO1J-SEQ-END
         PMO1I-ITER-END
      PMO1E-SEQ-END
   PMO1C-ITER-END
```

```
PMO1D-SEQ
    PMO1F
        Add 1 to report page count (R-PAGE-COUNT) and set up
                in heading line
        Write heading line to report file followed by a blank
                line
    PMO1G
        Set up counters line
        Write counters line to report file
        Close monthly orders file
        Close report file
        Stop program run
PMO1D-SEQ-END
AOP1A-SEQ-END.
```

Figure 11.8 Schematic Logic for Print of Monthly Orders Program

```
IDENTIFICATION DIVISION.

PROGRAM-ID. PMO.
* A PROGRAM TO PROCESS MONTHLY ORDERS FILE PRODUCING A PRINT
* OF EACH ORDER AND COUNTS OF CASH AND CREDIT ORDERS

ENVIRONMENT DIVISION.

CONFIGURATION SECTION.
SOURCE-COMPUTER. A-PC.
OBJECT-COMPUTER. A-PC.

INPUT-OUTPUT SECTION.
FILE-CONTROL.
    SELECT ORDERS-FILE ASSIGN TO "ORDERS.DAT".
    SELECT REPORT-FILE ASSIGN TO "REPORT.DAT".

DATA DIVISION.

FILE SECTION.
FD   ORDERS-FILE.
    01   ORDER-RECORD.
        03   OR-AGENT-CODE.
            05   OR-AREA-CODE          PIC X(2).
            05   OR-AGENT-NUMBER       PIC 9(4).
        03   OR-CATALOGUE-REF          PIC X(6).
        03   OR-CATALOGUE-PRICE        PIC 9(3)V99.
        03   OR-NO-ORDERED             PIC 9(2).
        03   OR-PAYMENT-TYPE           PIC X.

FD   REPORT-FILE.
    01   REPORT-RECORD                 PIC X(60).

WORKING-STORAGE SECTION.

    01   EOF-ORDERS-FILE               PIC 9.
```

244

```
01  M-COUNT                      PIC 9(3)  COMP.
01  C-COUNT                      PIC 9(3)  COMP.
01  R-PAGE-COUNT                 PIC 99    COMP.
01  DL-COUNT                     PIC 99    COMP.


01  CURRENT-DATE.
    03  CD-YEAR                  PIC 99.
    03  CD-MONTH                 PIC 99.
    03  CD-DAY                   PIC 99.


01  DETAIL-LINE.
    03  OR-AGENT-CODE.
        05  OR-AREA-CODE         PIC X(2).
        05  OR-AGENT-NUMBER      PIC 9(4).
    03  FILLER                   PIC X         VALUE SPACES.
    03  OR-CATALOGUE-REF         PIC X(6).
    03  FILLER                   PIC X         VALUE SPACES.
    03  OR-CATALOGUE-PRICE       PIC 9(3)V99.
    03  FILLER                   PIC X         VALUE SPACES.
    03  OR-NO-ORDERED            PIC 9(2).
    03  FILLER                   PIC X         VALUE SPACES.
    03  OR-PAYMENT-TYPE          PIC X.


01  HEADING-LINE.
    03  FILLER                   PIC X(36)
            VALUE " PRINT OF MONTHLY ORDERS      DATE    ".
    03  CD-DAY                   PIC 99.
    03  FILLER                   PIC X             VALUE "/".
    03  CD-MONTH                 PIC 99.
    03  FILLER                   PIC X             VALUE "/".
    03  CD-YEAR                  PIC 99.
    03  FILLER                   PIC X(12)
            VALUE "      PAGE    ".
    03  HL-PAGE-NO               PIC Z9.
    03  FILLER                   PIC XX            VALUE SPACES.


01  COUNTERS-LINE.
    03  FILLER                   PIC X(23)
            VALUE " NUMBER OF CASH ORDERS ".
    03  CL-M-COUNT               PIC ZZ9.
    03  FILLER                   PIC X(27)
            VALUE "   NUMBER OF CREDIT ORDERS ".
    03  CL-C-COUNT               PIC ZZ9.

PROCEDURE DIVISION.

PMO1A-SEQ.
PMO1B.
*    INITIAL OPERATIONS
     OPEN INPUT ORDERS-FILE.
     OPEN OUTPUT REPORT-FILE.
     MOVE ZERO TO M-COUNT, C-COUNT, EOF-ORDERS-FILE,
                  R-PAGE-COUNT.
     ACCEPT CURRENT-DATE FROM DATE.
```

245

```
            MOVE CORRESPONDING CURRENT-DATE TO HEADING-LINE.
            READ ORDERS-FILE AT END MOVE 1 TO EOF-ORDERS-FILE.


        PMO1C-ITER.
            IF EOF-ORDERS-FILE = 0 NEXT SENTENCE
                       ELSE GO TO PMO1C-ITER-END.
        PMO1E-SEQ.
    *       PROCESS PAGE
        PMO1H.
    *       OUTPUT PAGE HEADINGS
            ADD 1 TO R-PAGE-COUNT.
            MOVE R-PAGE-COUNT TO HL-PAGE-NO.
            WRITE REPORT-RECORD FROM HEADING-LINE
                       AFTER ADVANCING PAGE.
            MOVE SPACES TO REPORT-RECORD.
            WRITE REPORT-RECORD AFTER ADVANCING 1 LINE.
            MOVE 0 TO DL-COUNT.


        PMO1I-ITER.
            IF EOF-ORDERS-FILE = 0 AND DL-COUNT < 50
                       NEXT SENTENCE ELSE GO TO PMO1I-ITER-END.
        PMO1J-SEQ.
    *       PROCESS ORDER RECORD
        PMO1K.
            MOVE CORRESPONDING ORDER-RECORD TO DETAIL-LINE.


        PMO1L-SEL.
            IF OR-PAYMENT-TYPE OF ORDER-RECORD = "M" NEXT SENTENCE
                       ELSE GO TO PMO1L-OR1.
    *       PROCESS CASH ORDER
        PMO1N.
            ADD 1 TO M-COUNT.
            GO TO PMO1L-SEL-END.
        PMO1L-OR1.
    *       PROCESS CREDIT ORDER
        PMO1O.
            ADD 1 TO C-COUNT.
        PMO1L-SEL-END.


        PMO1M.
            WRITE REPORT-RECORD FROM DETAIL-LINE
                       AFTER ADVANCING 1 LINE.
            ADD 1 TO DL-COUNT.
            READ ORDERS-FILE AT END MOVE 1 TO EOF-ORDERS-FILE.
        PMO1J-SEQ-END.
            GO TO PMO1I-ITER.
        PMO1I-ITER-END.


        PMO1E-SEQ-END.
            GO TO PMO1C-ITER.
        PMO1C-ITER-END.
```

```
      PMO1D-SEQ.
*         PROCESS FINAL PAGE AND TERMINATE PROGRAM
      PMO1F.
            ADD 1 TO R-PAGE-COUNT.
            MOVE R-PAGE-COUNT TO HL-PAGE-NO.
            WRITE REPORT-RECORD FROM HEADING-LINE
                              AFTER ADVANCING PAGE.
            MOVE SPACES TO REPORT-RECORD.
            WRITE REPORT-RECORD AFTER ADVANCING 1 LINE.
      PMO1G.
            MOVE M-COUNT TO CL-M-COUNT.
            MOVE C-COUNT TO CL-C-COUNT.
            WRITE REPORT-RECORD FROM COUNTERS-LINE
                              AFTER ADVANCING 1 LINE.
            CLOSE ORDERS-FILE, REPORT-FILE.
            STOP RUN.
      PMO1D-SEQ-END.
      PMO1A-SEQ-END.
```

Figure 11.9   Code for Print of Monthly Orders Program

To implement the solution two Working-Storage variables **R-PAGE-COUNT** and **DL-COUNT** have been defined to accumulate the count of output pages and the number of detail lines on each page respectively. **DL-COUNT** is set to zero at the start of each new page of printed orders and it is used to control the iteration (PMO1I-ITER) associated with the processing of orders.

11.5.2 MOVE CORRESPONDING

You should note that in the coding of the Print of Monthly Orders Program elementary data fields within ORDER-RECORD and DE-TAIL-LINE and also within CURRENT-DATE and HEADING-LINE have been given the same names. This is legal in COBOL as they can still be uniquely identified using qualification as explained in section 3.6.2. However, by using the same names we can simplify our coding of data transfers between these records by using the CORRESPONDING option with the relevant MOVE statements.

A MOVE CORRESPONDING statement between records or group items does not cause the referenced data items themselves to be moved but only those subordinate items which are not designated as FILLER and have the same data-names and the same qualification up to, but not including the referenced data items. Also at least one of the subordinate items must be elementary. For example:

247

will result in the same data transfers as those specified by the explicit MOVEs:

```
MOVE CD-YEAR OF CURRENT-DATE
              TO CD-YEAR OF HEADING-LINE.
MOVE CD-MONTH OF CURRENT-DATE
              TO CD-MONTH OF HEADING-LINE.
MOVE CD-DAY OF CURRENT-DATE
              TO CD-DAY OF HEADING-LINE.
```

Use of the CORRESPONDING option can save significant coding time in situations such as those illustrated in the Print of Monthly Orders Program where a number of data fields have to be moved, reformatted or reordered. The option is also available with the ADD and SUBTRACT statements.

11.6 Further Examples of Fusing

Fusing data structures becomes easier with experience. Hence the purpose of this section is to illustrate fusing for a number of commonly encountered data processing activities.

11.6.1 File Copy and Summary

Figures 11.10 a) to d) illustrate the data structures and correspondences for a program which produces a Value of Monthly Orders File which contains a copy of the records on the Monthly Orders File plus a summary record at the end which gives the total value of all the orders. Here the structure for the Monthly Orders File totally corresponds to components within the Value of Orders File. Thus we have a Fused Data Structure which is identical to the Value of Monthly Orders File itself.

11.6.2 Data Extraction

Figures 11.11a) - d) illustrate the data structures and correspondences for a program which produces an Extract File containing details of all orders with a value of £100 or more from the Value of Monthly Orders File detailed in section 11.6.1. The Extract File is terminated by a new total value record which gives the total value of orders copied to the file.

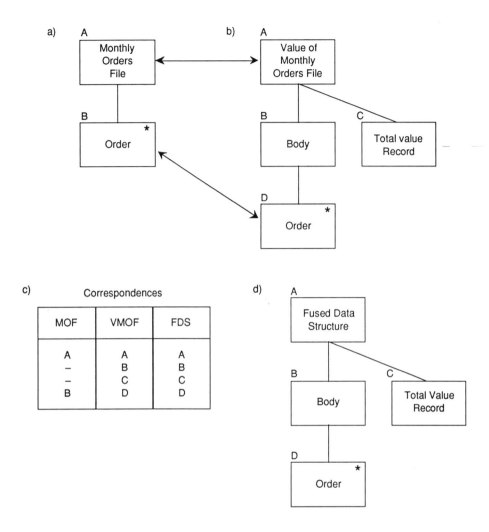

Figure 11.10 Data Structures and Correspondences for File Copy and Summary Program.

You should note that in this example component F of the Value of Monthly Orders structure corresponds with component D of the Extract structure despite the fact that one is a sequenced component and the other is an iterative component. This is quite a common occurrence because corresponding components do not need to be of the same type; they simply need to have a one to one corresponding relationship. Here the situation is that the selected component lies within an iteration and for every order record which has a value of £100 or more an extracted order is produced. Thus we have correspondence.

11.6.3   File Summary and Report

Figures 11.12 a) - d) illustrate the data structures and correspondences for a program which provides a summary report on the value of cash and credit orders recorded on the Monthly Orders File for each agent. The report has a single heading line, then a one line report for each agent and it is terminated by a summary line giving the total value of cash and credit orders. Note that here correspondence is between Agent on the Monthly Orders File and Detail Line on the Report File.

11.6.4   File Extract and Paged Report

Figures 11.13 a) to d) illustrate the data structures and correspondences for a program which extracts details of all the credit orders on Monthly Orders File and produces a Paged Report. Each page of the report commences with a heading which is then followed by details of twenty credit orders each forming one line of the report.

As before we have correspondence between a selected and iterated component. Also we have levels above each of these corresponding components which have to be meshed together to form the fused data structure. In cases such as these, when decisions have to be made concerning the form of the fused data structure, it is useful to consider how the parts of this composite structure will be processed.

To see how pages and orders interleave with each other note that the processing of the Monthly Orders File to produce the Paged Report will involve the processing of pages. The processing of each of these pages will involve processing orders and each order may either be a credit order, in which case it is ignored, or a cash order in which case its details are output on the report. Hence we have the fused data structure as shown.

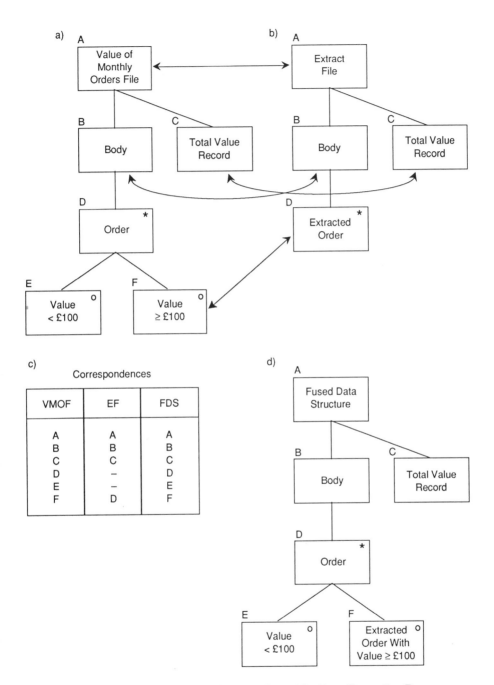

Figure 11.11 Data Structures and Correspondences for Data Extraction Program.

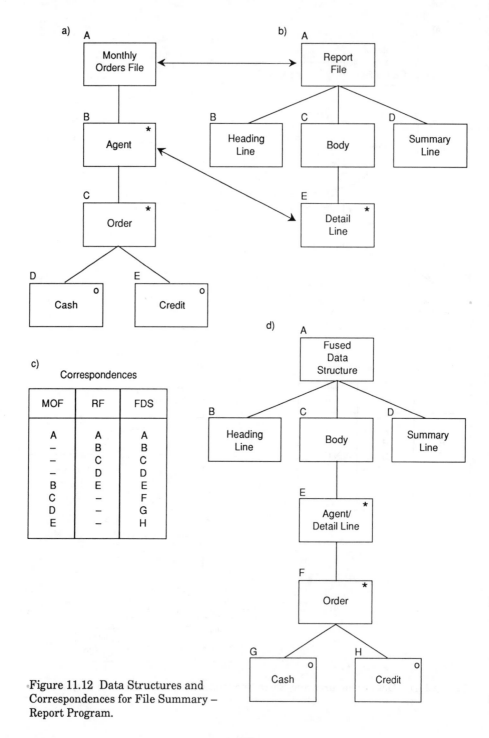

Figure 11.12 Data Structures and Correspondences for File Summary – Report Program.

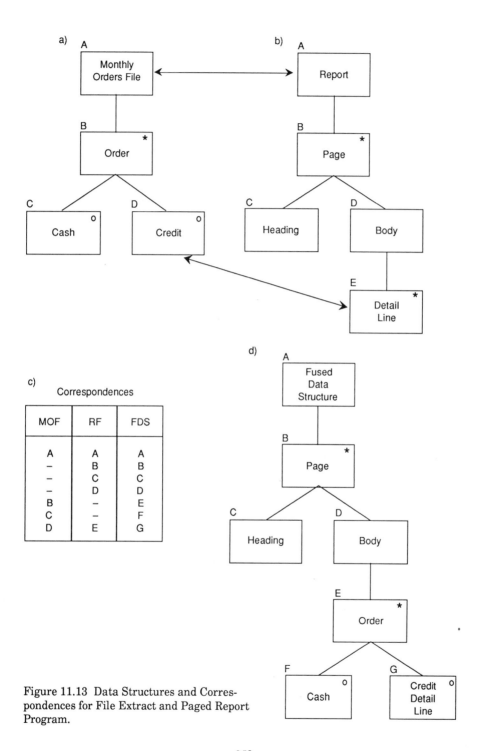

a)

A Monthly Orders File ⟷ b) A Report

B Order *

C Cash ○   D Credit ○

B Page *

C Heading   D Body

E Detail Line *

c)

Correspondences

MOF	RF	FDS
A	A	A
–	B	B
–	C	C
–	D	D
B	–	E
C	–	F
D	E	G

d)

A Fused Data Structure

B Page *

C Heading   D Body

E Order *

F Cash ○   G Credit Detail Line ○

Figure 11.13 Data Structures and Correspondences for File Extract and Paged Report Program.

253

You may also find it helpful at first, when fusing data structures, to add additional 'dummy' logical components to each data structure which reflect processing primarily based on the structure of the other file(s). Examples of such dummy components are shown in figures 11.14 a) and b) for the Monthly Orders File and the Report.

Component AA has been added to the structure for the Monthly Orders File and components EA and EB have been added to the structure for the Report. Component AA represents consideration of the Monthly Orders File as consisting of groups of orders where each group includes 20 credit orders plus an unspecified number of cash orders. This component obviously corresponds with component B, a page of the Report. Component EA and EB have been added to the Report to give correspondence with components C and D on the Monthly Orders File. EA represents the details of a cash order, which is not reported, and hence is absent from the Report. EB represents the details of a credit order, which is reported, and hence is present on the Report. The logical concept of items being present or absent from a file is difficult to grasp at first but once understood proves very useful when producing data structures.

11.6.5   File Breakdown (Double File Extraction)

Figures 11.15 a) to c) illustrate the data structures and correspondences for a program which processes the Monthly Orders File and produces two output files - one containing all the cash orders and one containing all the credit orders. In a simple instance such as this it is a relatively straightforward task to identify the correspondences between the three files at one time. In more complex situations, where there are more than two data structures to fuse, it is often easier to stage the process. First two data structures are fused to form a composite structure, then the third data structure is fused with this composite structure, and so on. Thus the final composite structure is built up by merging in one data structure at a time.

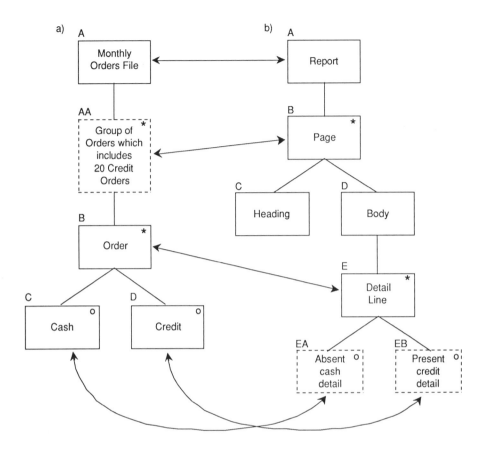

Figure 11.14 Use of Dummy Logical Components in showing Correspondences Between Two Files.

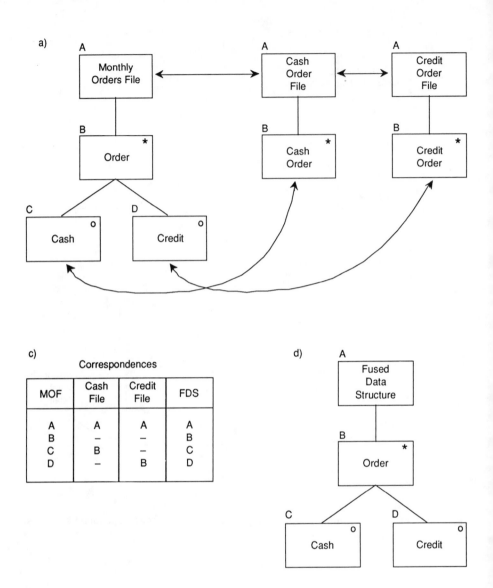

Figure 11.15 Data Structures and Correspondences For File Breakdown Program.

TASKS - CHAPTER 11

1. The following specification details two programs which process
    customer payment records:

    A transaction file contains customer payment records, where each
    record contains details of one customer payment and has the
    following format:

Item	Data
Sales area code	Three numeric digits in range 001-250
Customer number	Two numeric digits in range 01-30
Amount of payment	Six digits representing 9(4)V99

    There may be more than one payment per customer and more than
    one customer per sales area. The file is sorted in customer number
    within sales area code sequence.

    Program 1

    The transaction file is to be validated producing a file of valid
    payments and an error report. The error report is to be paged and
    is to consist of 2 line reports which detail each erroneous record. A
    blank line is to be left between each report and between the page
    heading (giving report title and date) and first report on the page.
    Validation is to be restricted to a single logical test which checks
    whether the data within a record is all numeric or not.

    Program 2

    The file of valid payments is to be analysed producing a summary
    report showing total payments for each customer, total payments
    for each sales area and a grand total for the whole file. The report
    is to be paged with each page commencing with a heading. The last
    page is to contain only the heading and the file grand total. The
    pages that form the body of the report are each to contain the
    summary for one sales area. This will consist of the customer totals
    and the area total for that sales area. It is to be assumed that, since
    there is a maximum of 30 customers per area, the summary for each
    area will fit on a single page.

Produce for each of the above programs:

(i) A system network diagram.

(ii) Logical data structure diagrams down to record level for each file.

(iii) A table showing any correspondences between the components of each logical data structure.

(iv) A fused data structure.

(v) An amended correspondence table which includes fused data structure entries.

2. Produce basic program structures showing conditions for each of the programs described in section 11.6

3. Referring only to section 11.1 draw up a function list for the Print of Monthly Orders Program. Allocate your functions to a copy of the basic program structure shown in figure 11.6 and then produce the schematic logic for your solution. Finally compare your schematic logic with that given in figure 11.8. Once you have corrected any errors in your solution implement it in COBOL, generate some test data and execute the program. Reference to a mail order catalogue or that for a catalogue shop will help you generate some realistic test data. While testing your program check each of the following for correctness:

(i) The format of the printed orders.

(ii) The page headings.

(iii) The number of items per page.

(iv) The details printed on the final page.

4. Look up the CORRESPONDING option for the MOVE, ADD and SUBTRACT statements in your COBOL Reference Manual and ensure that you understand how it operates in each case.

CHAPTER 12

Programs Which Match Sequentially Organised Files – the collation process

12.1 Sequential File Matching

A common type of task within D.P. departments is that which involves the matching together (collating) of two or more sequentially organised files according to key values which are held in the records. Typical of this type of task are the following:

(i) The comparison of files to determine information on matching and non-matching records.

(ii) The merging together of data from several input files into one output file.

(iii) The updating of a master file.

A standard approach to the production of programs which will support this type of task exists within JSP. The primary feature of this approach is the development of logical data structures which are centred around the key used for matching and which show all the match/non match combinations between the relevant input files. The next two sections cover in detail the development of file comparison type programs. In these particular attention is paid to the production of generalised logical data structures which can be used as a base in the design of any program which involves the matching of sequentially organised files. The remaining sections then show how such general structures can be used in the development of file merge and update programs. In this chapter we will mostly concentrate on the development of basic program structures. However, in chapter 13 complete design and implementation details for a major file update program will be given.

12.2 Comparison of Two Sequential Input Files

12.2.1 The JSP Approach

To understand the JSP approach to this type of problem we shall consider the following simple example:

Two sequentially ordered files reference F1 and F2 are to be matched according to the key values held in the records and the following counts are to be accumulated and displayed at the end of the program run:

(i) Count of matched records (MATCHED-COUNT).

(ii) Count of the number of records whose key value appears on file F1 only (F1-ONLY-COUNT).

(iii) Count of the number of records whose key value appears on file F2 only (F2-ONLY-COUNT).

The records on the two files have the following COBOL descriptions:

```
01  F1-RECORD.
    03  F1-KEY     PIC 9(3).
    03  F1-DATA    PIC X(40).

01  F2-RECORD.
    03  F2-KEY     PIC 9(3).
    03  F2-DATA    PIC X(40).
```

The key values held in F1-KEY and F2-KEY are unique within each file i.e. within each file there can only be a single instance of any particular key value. However, there need not be a record on the files for every possible key value. Both files are held in the same ascending sequence of key value.

The system network diagram for this problem is shown in figure 12.1 and initial data structures for each of the data streams are shown in figure 12.2. The data structures for the two files show each of them as a continuous iteration of ordered key values. In addition the structures show that each particular ordered key value may be present on the file or absent from the file at the time of the program run. The output structure (figure 12.2(c)) represents a simple single display line and for the present we will ignore it.

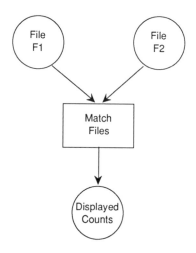

Figure 12.1 System Network Diagram for File Match Program.

Although the file structures shown in figure 12.2 illustrate the logical presence or absence of ordered key values they do not illustrate the main processing involved - the matching together of the two files according to these key values. This deficiency is corrected in the developed logical file structures illustrated in figures 12.3(a) and (b). If we consider first file F1, the data structure again shows that a particular ordered key value may be present or absent from the file. However, it also shows that a particular key value that is present on file F1 may also be present on file F2 (a match situation) or it may be absent from file F2 (a non-match

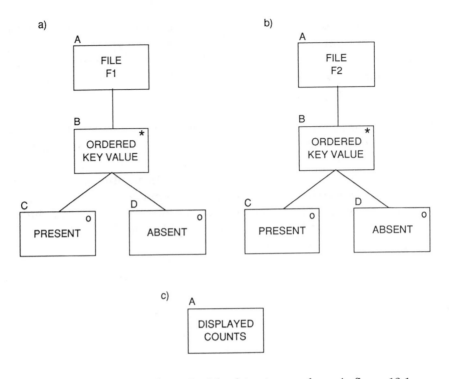

Figure 12.2 Data structures for each of the data streams shown in figure 12.1.

situation). Similarly a particular key value that is absent from file F1 may be present on file F2 (a non-match situation) or it may also be absent from file F2 (a situation which does not explicitly concern us in this problem). The structure for file F2 illustrates an analogous view of key values.

That these views are correct may be confirmed by checking that they do represent the following sample data:

Key Values on file F1	Key values on file F2
001	001
003	005
006	006
007	008

Remember in the logical data structures shown in figure 12.3 we are primarily viewing each file as an iteration of a continuum of key values

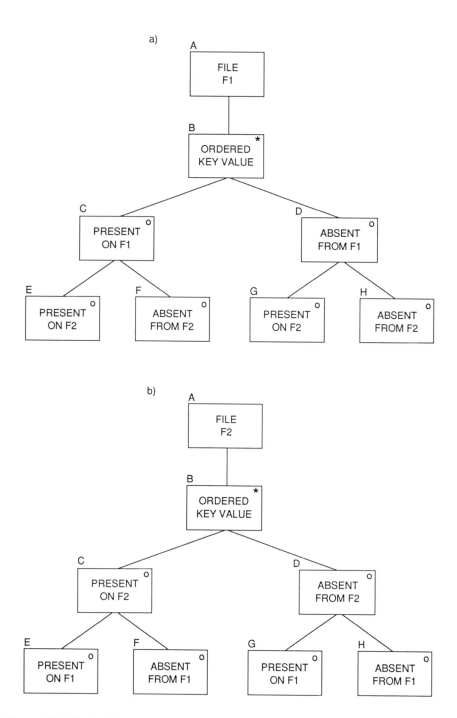

Figure 12.3 Logical data structures for files F1 and F2.

i.e. an iteration of all the possible values that can be on the file. We are not viewing each file as an iteration of the particular key values that lie just on it at run time. Hence we have the Present/Absent combinations that are shown.

To simplify matters we can redraw these logical structures combining the two selected levels into one as shown in figures 12.4(a) and (b). Correspondences between these structures and the displayed output can now be identified and a fused structure can be drawn up. The displayed counts line corresponds with the top most level of the two files viz. from one occurrence of file F1 and one occurrence of file F2 we generate one displayed counts line. The ordered key value components (B) correspond as their occurrences represent the complete range of ordered keys that can appear on either file i.e. a possible ordered key value that can occur on one file can also occur on the other. Once this is understood the correspondences for the lowest level components easily follow. All the correspondences between the logical data structures are detailed in figure 12.5 and the fused data structure is shown in figure 12.6. The correspondences between the fused data structure and the logical data structures are shown in the last column of figure 12.5.

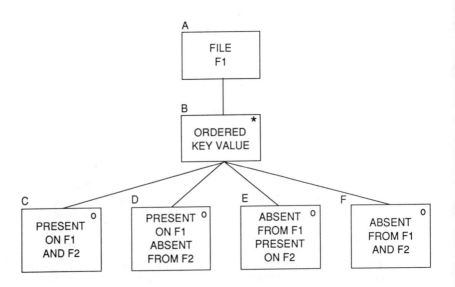

Figure 12.4a Redrawn logical data structures for files F1 and F2.

264

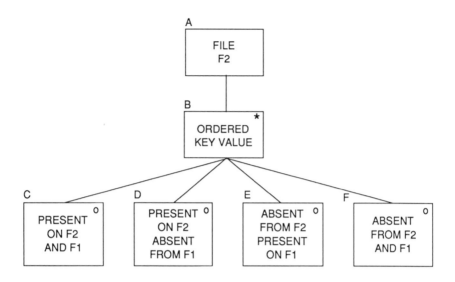

Figure 12.4b Redrawn logical data structures for files F1 and F2.

FILE F1	FILE F2	DISPLAYED COUNTS	FUSED DATA STRUCTURE
A	A	A	A
B	B	–	B
C	C	–	C
D	E	–	D
E	D	–	E
F	F	–	F

Figure 12.5 Correspondence table for the Match Files Program.

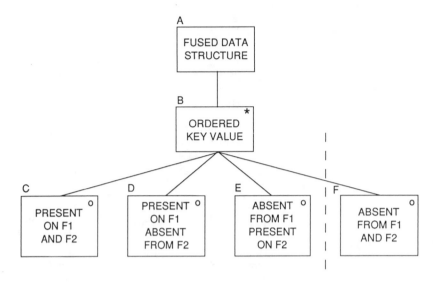

Figure 12.6 Fused data structure – component F can be neglected from futher considerations.

As was stated earlier in this problem we are not concerned with possible ordered key values which are absent from both files. Thus we can neglect the component in the fused data structure which represents this situation (component F of figure 12.6) from any further considerations.

12.2.2 Basic Program Structure and Controlling Conditions

A basic program structure for the File Match Program follows simply from the fused structure shown in figure 12.6. As described above, the component representing an ordered key value which is absent from both files (component F) can be neglected and all we need to add to the fused structure is a START/BODY/END sequence to allow for initial and terminal program actions. The result is shown in figure 12.7.

In programs such as this where two or more sequential files are to be matched together the conditions which control any iterations or selections generally need more care in their determination than those which apply to programs with only one input file. This is because in sequential

266

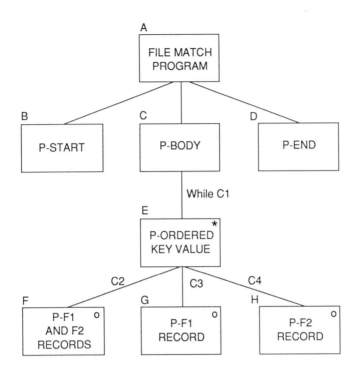

Figure 12.7 Basic program structure for File Match Program.
The conditions C1 – C4 are discussed in the text.

file match programs we are concerned both with the comparison of keys and the handling of end of file situations. For example, we would not want the File Match Program to enter its terminating actions until all the relevant key values and hence all the records on each input file have been processed. Also because one file may terminate before the other the conditions associated with the selection P-ORDERED KEY VALUE (component E) must also take account of possible end of file situations. In general terms the conditions identified in figure 12.7 may be expressed as:

C1: there are key values (i.e. records) still to process,
C2: there is a pair of matching records to process,
C3: there is a non matching record from file F1 to process,
C4: there is a non matching record from file F2 to process.

We will now consider three approaches that may be used to formalise the evaluation of these conditions.

(a) Use of boolean end of file indicators.

We define the following end of file indicators:

```
01  EOF-F1    PIC 9.
01  EOF-F2    PIC 9.
```

where a value of 1 represents end of file and a value of 0 represents not end of file. We also specify that these will be set 0 at the start of processing and that the relevant indicator will be set to 1 using the AT END exception phrase of the READ statement when appropriate. The conditions then become:

```
C1:   (EOF-F1 = 0  OR  EOF-F2 = 0)

C2:   (EOF-F1 = 0 AND EOF-F2 = 0 AND F1-KEY = F2-KEY)

C3:   (EOF-F1 = 0 AND EOF-F2 = 0 AND F1-KEY < F2-KEY)
           OR (EOF-F2 = 1 AND EOF-F1 = 0)
```

Here the second part of the condition caters for the situation where we have reached the end of file F2 but there are still records on file F1 to process.

```
C4:  (EOF-F1 = 0 AND EOF-F2 = 0 AND F2-KEY < F1-KEY)
          OR (EOF-F1 = 1 AND EOF-F2 = 0)
```

Here the second part of the condition caters for the situation where we have reached the end of file F1 but there are still records on file F2 to process.

It may first appear that these conditions are unnecessarily complicated and that the sub-conditions

```
EOF-F1 = 0

EOF-F2 = 0
```

could be omitted from within C2, C3 and C4. However, they do need to be included because once the end of file has been detected in a COBOL program the contents of the relevant record area are normally undefined. Hence any processing which relies only on values held in the key fields within the record areas may not execute correctly. For example if the following data is held on the files:

```
   Keys on file F1          Keys on file F2

          :                        :
          :                        :
         106                      106
         eof                      108
                                  109
                                  eof
```

We would process the two records with key 106 and would then attempt to access the next record from each file. This would result in

```
    EOF-F1 = 1          EOF-F2 = 0
    F1-KEY = undefined   F2-KEY = 108
```

condition C1 is satisfied and the iteration is continued. Condition C2 in its full form will be false as EOF-F1 = 1. If however, the end of file conditions were not included in C2 there is a chance that it may actually be satisfied as the value of F1-KEY is unpredictable.

An exact match being satisfied here is actually very unlikely but the chance of satisfying an inequality check such as

```
F1-KEY < F2-KEY
```

within C3 is much more likely if the value of F1-KEY is unpredictable. Hence all the end of file conditions should be included

(b) The use of special end records to identify the end processing.

The situation becomes much easier if each file is terminated with a special record which has the same predetermined highest value for its key. If the value of this special key is held in a Working-Storage data item MAX-KEY the conditions simplify to:

```
C1:   F1-KEY < MAX-KEY OR F2-KEY < MAX-KEY

C2:   F1-KEY = F2-KEY

C3:   F1-KEY < F2-KEY

C4:   F2-KEY < F1-KEY
```

Although this represents an easy programming solution and may be a feasible approach with files you create yourself, it is unlikely to occur in "real world" situations. The chance that system designers will have included such a high value key at the end of every file that is to be sequentially matched is to say the least highly improbable.

(c) Use of a programmer defined high value key.

A third approach is to use a high valued data item (higher valued than any that can occur on the files) and MOVE this to the relevant record key field once the end of file is detected. Suitable values for this item would be the literal value ALL "9" if the keys on the files are numeric and the literal value HIGH-VALUES if the keys on the file are alphanumeric. (HIGH-VALUES should not be used to represent numeric keys as its movement to a numeric field is usually prohibited). If the data item MAX-KEY represents the high valued item then this approach will give the same conditions as specified in section (b) above. Since this approach is relatively straightforward it will be the one used in the remainder of this chapter. Also it does maintain the concept that we are processing an iteration of key values. However, you should note that problems can arise with this approach, for example:

(i) the value chosen for the high value may actually occur on the file,

(ii) the file's input record area may be changed after the high value has been placed in the key field. This may happen if another read is issued for the file without resetting the high value or if the input record area is shared with another file,

(iii) the high value placed in the key field may be interpreted by the program logic as an actual key value that occurs on the file.

Thus care must be taken if errors are to be avoided.

12.2.3 Completing the Design

To complete the design we must draw up a function list (figure 12.8), allocate the functions to the program structure (figure 12.9a). The conditions are detailed in figure 12.9b. We can then produce schematic logic (figure 12.10). Note in the final program structure the allocation of the read functions. A record must be read from both files at the start of the program (component B) and there must be a read replace for each file after processing a successful match (component F). Single read replace functions are also needed for the relevant file after processing an unsuccessful match (components G and H). To check that the design is correct you should generate some test data and use it to "walk through" the schematic logic (see task 1 at the end of this chapter).

Function List

1. Open file F1.
2. Read record from file F1 at end move MAX-KEY to F1-KEY
3. Close file F1.
4. Open file F2.
5. Read record from file F2 at end move MAX-KEY to F2-KEY
6. Close file F2.
7. Zero counters (MATCH-COUNT, F1-ONLY-COUNT, F2-ONLY-COUNT)
8. Display counters (MATCHED-COUNT, F1-ONLY-COUNT,
                                        F2-ONLY-COUNT)
9. Add 1 to MATCHED-COUNT
10. Add 1 to F1-ONLY-COUNT
11. Add 1 to F2-ONLY-COUNT
12. Stop program run.

Figure 12.8   Function List for File Match Program

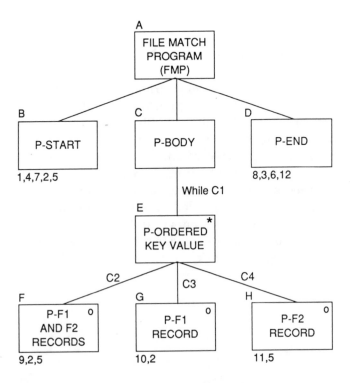

Figure 12.9a   Final program structure for File Match Program.

272

Condition List

C1. F1-KEY < MAX-KEY   or   F2-KEY < MAX-KEY
C2. F1-KEY = F2-KEY
C3. F1-KEY < F2-KEY
C4. F2-KEY < F1-KEY

MAX-KEY has the value 999.

Figure 12.9b Condition List for File Match Program

```
FMP1A-SEQ
   FMP1B
      Open file F1
      Open file F2
      Zero Counters (MATCHED-COUNT, F1-ONLY-COUNT, F2-ONLY-COUNT)
      Read record from file F1 at end move MAX-KEY to F1-KEY
      Read record from file F2 at end move MAX-KEY to F2-KEY
    FMP1C-ITER while F1-KEY < MAX-KEY or F2-KEY < MAX-KEY
      FMP1E-SEL if F1-KEY = F2-KEY
         FMP1F
            Add 1 to MATCHED-COUNT
            Read record from file F1 at end move MAX-KEY to F1-KEY
            Read record from file F2 at end move MAX-KEY to F2-KEY
      FMP1E-OR1 if F1-KEY < F2-KEY
         FMP1G
            Add 1 to F1-ONLY-COUNT
            Read record from file F1 at end move MAX-KEY to F1-KEY
      FMP1E-OR2 if F2-KEY < F1-KEY
         FMP1H
            Add 1 to F2-ONLY-COUNT
            Read record from file F2 at end move MAX-KEY to F2-KEY
      FMP1E-SEL-END
    FMP1C-ITER-END
    FMP1D
      Display counters
                    (MATCHED-COUNT, F1-ONLY-COUNT, F2-ONLY-COUNT)
      Close file F1
      Close file F2
      Stop program run
FMP1A-SEQ-END
```

Figure 12.10   Schematic Logic for File Match Program

12.3 Processing Multiple Input Files

12.3.1 Two Input Files

The basic logical view for a file which is to be sequentially matched with one other was given in figure 12.4. The view is that the file consists of an iteration of all the possible ordered key values that can occur and that each key value may be present on both files, only present on either one of the files or absent from both. These four alternatives for the selection are illustrated in the Venn diagram for the two files shown in figure 12.11.

In most cases the final leg of the selection (key value absent from both files) can be omitted as we are normally not concerned with processing total absences and thus the logical structure takes the form shown in figure 12.12. An exception to this would be the case where we do wish to process every possible key value and say whether it is present or absent from each file. Jackson's classic example: The Magic Mailing Company [30] typifies this type of problem. Here a report is required of record occurrences on both a numbered letters-sent-file and a cross referencing reply-received-file. For cases such as this the four way selection is used and the program structure takes the form shown in figure 12.13. Here it is necessary to introduce a controlling variable - the Key of Reference (KR) - which takes each value within the total range of possible key values. KR is set to the first possible key value at the start of the program (component B) and is set to the next possible value just before the end of each iteration (component G). As shown in figure 12.13 the values that KR takes controls the iteration and its comparison with the key values on the files (K1 and K2) controls the four way selection. To show how the files are accessed, the read operations' allocations are also included in figure 12.13. End of file situations are dealt with here by setting K1 and K2 as appropriate to a value greater than the highest possible value KR can take.

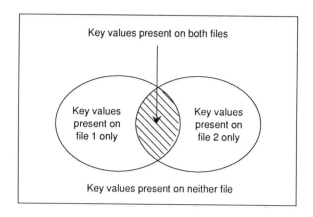

Figure 12.11 Venn diagram for the keys on two sequentially matched files. The outer rectangle represents the boundary of key values.

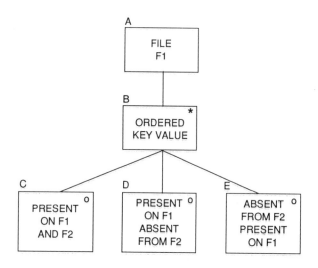

Figure 12.12 Logical data structure for file F1 which is to be sequentially matched with file F2 for the case where keys that appear on neither file do not have to be considered.

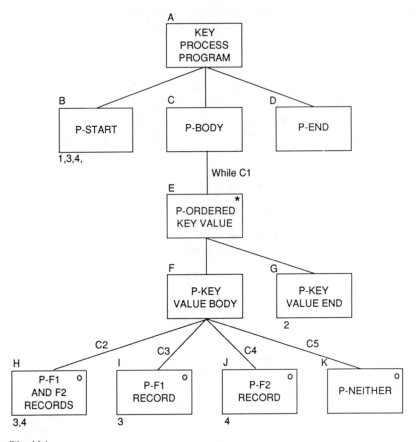

Condition List

Cl KR is within permissible range
C2 KR = K1 = K2
C3 KR = K1 and KR ≠ K2
C4 KR = K2 and KR ≠ K1
C5 KR ≠ K1 and KR ≠ K2

Function List (Key handling and record access only)

1 Set KR = first possible value
2 Set KR = next possible value
3 Read F1 record at end set K1 to a high value
4 Read F2 record at end set K2 to a high value

Figure 12.13 Program structure for a program which processes all possible key values on two files.

12.3.2 Three or More Input Files

As the number of files to be matched sequentially together increases, the structure diagrams naturally become more complex because the inter-relationships between each of the files have to be catered for. The Venn diagram illustrating these interrelationships for three input files is given in figure 12.14. Each additional file would add an additional selective level to the type of structures shown in figure 12.3 and on simplification would lead to a multiway selection with

$$2^n \text{ legs}$$

where n is the number of input files. For example there would be 8 possible combinations for 3 input files. Even allowing for the common case where we are not interested in totally absent keys the total number of selections would simply be reduced by 1. However, so long as care is taken, the same general approach that has been outlined in section 12.2 can be applied no matter how many input files are involved.

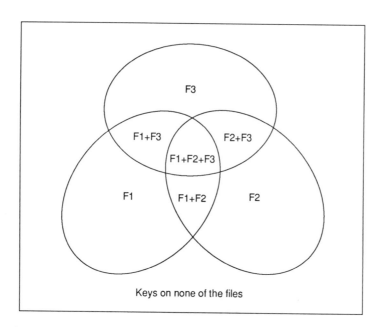

Figure 12.14 Venn diagram showing the interrelationships between key values on three sequentially matched files F1, F2 and F3. The outer rectangle represents the boundary of the key values.

12.4 Programs that Merge Sequentially Organised Data

In Section 4.5 we identified two types of merge processes. These were record merges where corresponding records from two or more files are combined into a single output record, and file merges where separate files of similar records are merged into one file but the records themselves are not combined together. In this section we will consider an example of each type of merge which is related to the case studies we have used so far.

12.4.1 Record Merge

This example is based on the student marks system which was first introduced in section 3.5. The specification is:

Two files SMARK1 and SMARK2 each contain the names of a class of students and their marks for three subjects. These names and the six marks are to be transferred to a single output file SMARK12. The relevant file details are:

(i) SMARK1 and SMARK2 are sequential files ordered alphabetically on student name. Their common record description is:

```
01   MARK-RECORD.
    03   STUDENT-NAME    PIC X(20).
    03   STUDENT-MARKS.
       05   MARK-1    PIC 99.
       05   MARK-2    PIC 99.
       05   MARK-3    PIC 99.
```

(ii) SMARK12 is a sequential file ordered alphabetically on student name. The record description for it is:

```
01   MARK12-RECORD.
    03   STUDENT-NAME    PIC X(20).
```

278

```
03   SMARK1-MARKS.
     05   MARK-1        PIC 99.
     05   MARK-2        PIC 99.
     05   MARK-3        PIC 99.
03   SMARK2-MARKS.
     05   MARK-1        PIC 99.
     05   MARK-2        PIC 99.
     05   MARK-3        PIC 99.
```

During the program run data is transferred to the output records from the corresponding fields in the relevant input records. If there is only a record for a student on one of the files the output is created from that single record and the output fields for which there is no data are set to zero.

In this problem we are concerned with matching records according to student name and thus our data structures must be centred around the processing of this entity. The logical data structures for the three files are shown in figure 12.15. These are based on the general structure shown in figure 12.12 because we are only interested in key values (student names) which actually appear on the input files. Normally it is sufficient to develop logical data structures down to record level but in this case I have taken them below this level to reflect the particular processing that will take place when a student record appears on only one of the input files. Note that in the structures for files SMARK1 and SMARK2, although the three combinations of present and absent key values are given in each structure, the components NAME and MARKS are only shown below 'present' components for the relevant file.

The correspondences between the three files are given in figure 12.16. These lead to a fused data structure which is identical to the data structure for file SMARK12. This can then be developed into the program structure shown in figure 12.17. This figure includes details of the controlling conditionals and the read/write functions. Here as detailed in section 12.2.2(c) the literal value HIGH-VALUES has been used to represent a maximum key value signifying the end of each file.

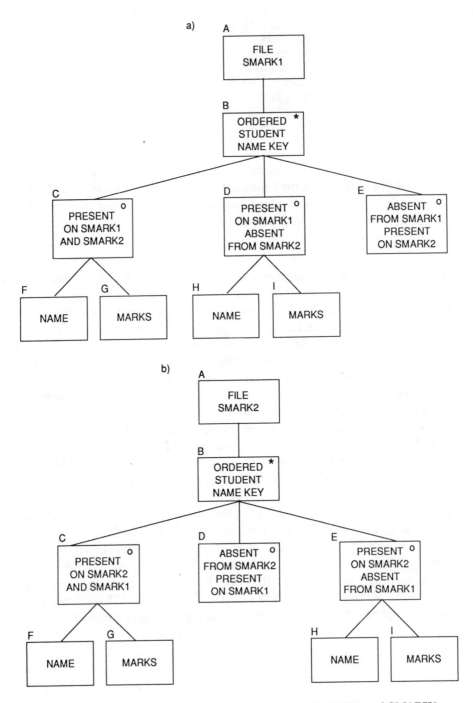

Figure 12.15a and b Logical data structures for files SMARK1 and SMARK2

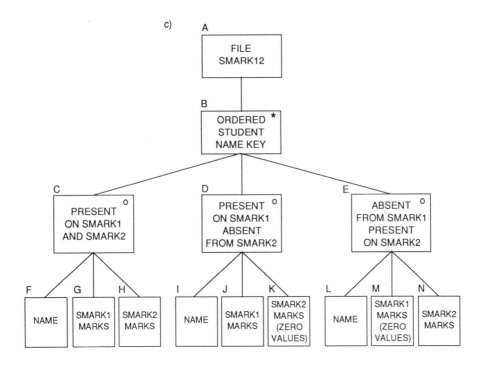

Figure 12.15c Logical data structures for file SMARK12

SMARK1	SMARK2	SMARK12
A	A	A
B	B	B
C	C	C
D	D	D
E	E	E
F	F	F
G	–	G
–	G	H
H	–	I
I	–	J
–	–	K
–	H	L
–	–	M
–	I	N

Figure 12.16 Correspondence table for Record Merge Program.

281

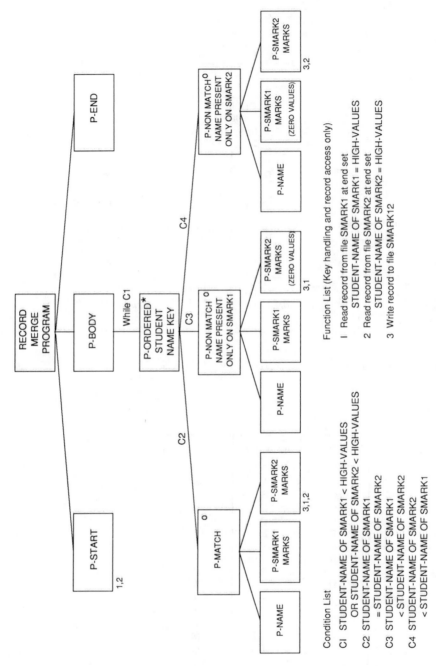

Condition List

C1 STUDENT-NAME OF SMARK1 < HIGH-VALUES
    OR STUDENT-NAME OF SMARK2 < HIGH-VALUES

C2 STUDENT-NAME OF SMARK1
    = STUDENT-NAME OF SMARK2

C3 STUDENT-NAME OF SMARK1
    < STUDENT-NAME OF SMARK2

C4 STUDENT-NAME OF SMARK2
    < STUDENT-NAME OF SMARK1

Function List (Key handling and record access only)

1   Read record from file SMARK1 at end set
    STUDENT-NAME OF SMARK1 = HIGH-VALUES

2   Read record from file SMARK2 at end set
    STUDENT-NAME OF SMARK2 = HIGH-VALUES

3   Write record to file SMARK12

Figure 12.17 Basic program structure and file operations for Record Merge Program.

282

12.4.2　File Merge

The example here is based on a part of the MOCO mail order operations introduced in Chapter 5. The specification is:

> Two Monthly Orders Files (OF1 and OF2) produced at the end of successive months are to be merged together into a single output file. This Merged File (MF) is to be in the same agent code sequence as the input files OF1 and OF2. In addition the orders for each agent are to be held so that where there are orders from an agent on both input files those for the first month (i.e. those on file OF1) precede those for the second month. The definitions for the records on each of the files are as specified in section 5.2 which detailed the Analysis of Orders Program.

In this program the records are matched according to agent code values and hence the files will be viewed as consisting of an iteration of ordered agent codes which may be present or absent on each of the files. We are not interested in codes which appear on neither of the input files so our logical data structures will again follow the form given in figure 12.12. The resultant logical data structures are shown in figure 12.18. Note that where an agent code can occur on a file an iteration of records is shown below the relevant 'present' leg of the selection because there can be many orders from an agent.

To be exact the text in the selected component boxes C, D and E in figure 12.18 in addition to referencing files OF1 and OF2 should also reference file MF. For example, a more descriptive text for component E would be "Present on OF1 and OF2 and MF". However, space limitations usually mean that only the input files are explicitly named as it is these that drive the processing. Having completed the data structures a table of correspondences can be compiled (figure 12.19), a fused data structure can be drawn (again this will be identical to the output data structure) and a basic program structure can then be produced (figure 12.20).

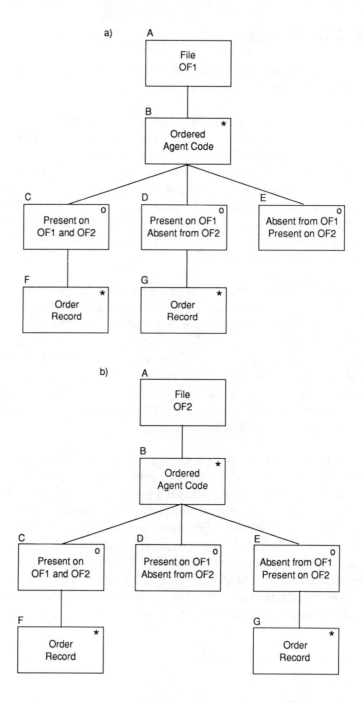

Figure 12.18a and b   Logical data structures for the files OF1 and OF2

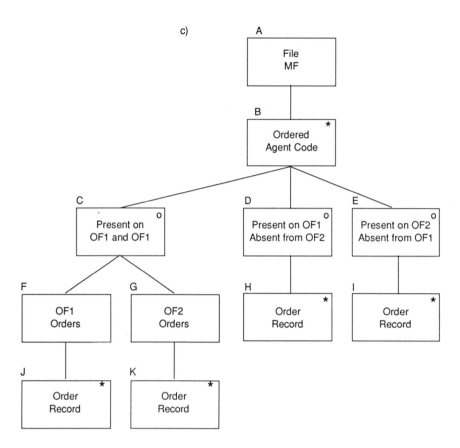

Figure 12.18c Logical data structures for the file MF

OF1	OF2	MF
A	A	A
B	B	B
C	C	C
D	D	D
E	E	E
–	–	F
–	–	G
G	–	H
–	G	I
F	–	J
–	F	K

Figure 12.19 Correspondence table for File Merge Program

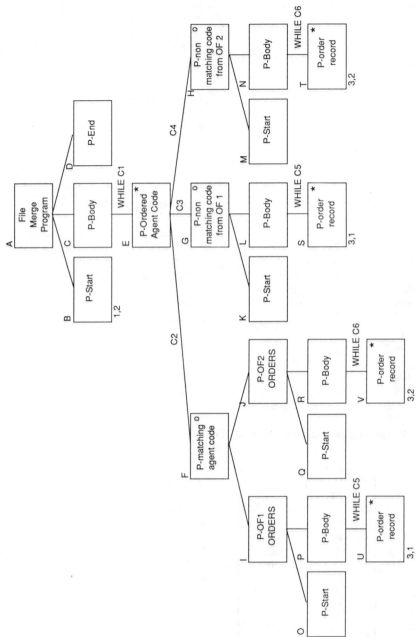

Figure 12.20

Condition List

CI OR-AGENT-CODE OF OF1 < HIGH-VALUES
     OR OR-AGENT-CODE OF OF2 < HIGH-VALUES
C2 OR-AGENT-CODE OF OF1 = OR-AGENT-CODE OF OF2
C3 OR-AGENT-CODE OF OF1 < OR-AGENT-CODE OF OF2
C4 OR-AGENT-CODE OF OF2 < OR-AGENT-CODE OF OF1
C5 OR-AGENT-CODE OF OF1 remains the same as that
     for the first record in the iteration
C6 OR-AGENT-CODE OF OF2 remains the same as that
     for the first record in the iteration

Function List (read/write functions only)

I Read record from file OF1 at end set
     OR-AGENT-CODE OF OF1 = HIGH-VALUES
2 Read record from file OF2 at end set
     OR-AGENT-CODE OF OF1 = HIGH-VALUES
3 Write record to file MF

Figure 12.20 Basic program structure and file operations for File Merge Program.

In the basic program structure (figure 12.20) the lowest level iterations represent repeated processing while the agent code remains the same. It is thus necessary to record the agent code before the iteration commences and compare it with that on each newly accessed order until there is a change. Thus START and BODY components must be included above each of these iterated components because an elementary START component will be needed for the "record agent code" operation. Also as in the previous example and in line with section 12.2.2(c) the literal value HIGH-VALUES has been used to represent a maximum key value signifying the end of each file.

12.5 Programs that Update Sequentially Organised Master Files

The process of updating a sequentially organised master file normally involves matching an ordered transaction file against a Brought Forward (B/F) version of the master file, bringing the information held on the master file up to date and generating a new Carried Forward (C/F) version of the master file. In addition various reports detailing the updating processes or the amended state of master file may be produced.

287

Update programs may conveniently be classed into two types in a similar way to merge programs. Simple updates or record updates may be considered to be those where the contents of individual records are changed, but the number of records on the file is not changed. They are generally similar in form to the record merges that we considered in the previous section. Complex updates or file updates may be considered to be those where the master file itself is much more volatile. Here transactions may not only cause the contents of existing master file records to be amended, but also complete records to be removed from the file (deleted) and/or new records to be added to the file (inserted). In this section we will consider simply the design of update programs of each type and then in the next chapter we will cover both design and implementation in much greater detail.

12.5.1 Simple Updates

The example we will consider here is based on the MOCO mail order operations and is typical of many update programs. A transaction file is used to update the data on a B/F master file producing an amended C/F master file and an error report which details the transactions which failed to match the B/F master. A system network diagram depicting the process is shown in figure 12.21. The specification is:

Each month the Monthly Orders File is used to update a yearly Value-of-Orders Master File which is used to record the total value of orders placed by each of the company's agents. The Value-of-Orders Master File is ordered on ascending agent code, as is the Monthly Orders File, and its records have the description:

```
01   VALUE-RECORD.
     03   VR-AGENT-CODE                PIC X(6).
     03   VR-TOTAL-VALUE-OF-ORDERS     PIC 9(5)V99.
```

The definition for records on the Monthly Orders File is as given in section 5.2. In addition to the updated Value-of-Orders Master File a Non-Matching Order Report is produced. This contains the heading: "Report on Non-Matching Monthly Orders" plus the date, followed by a print of each non-matching order record and finally a summary line detailing the number of non-matches that have occurred.

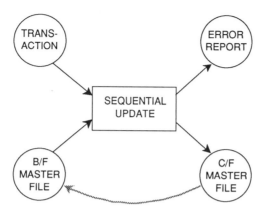

Figure 12.21 System Network Diagram for a simple update program. The dotted line indicates that on successive updates the C/F file from one run becomes the B/F file for the next.

Records will be matched by agent code and since we are only concerned with codes that are either on the B/F Value-of-Orders master file or on the Monthly Orders transaction file, the logical data structures will have the forms shown in figure 12.22. Note that the B/F Value of Orders file and the C/F Value of Orders file will each have the same logical structure, as no fundamental changes have been made during the update process and hence to save space only one common structure has been shown. The body of the Non-Matching Order Report (figure 12.22(c)) is simply shown as an iteration of non-matching orders; an alternative way of viewing this file will be covered in the next chapter.

The correspondences between the logical data structures are shown in figure 12.23 and the resultant basic program structure is detailed in figure 12.24. In figure 12.24 matched transactions are shown as being processed in the substructure below component F. Here records will be read from the Monthly Orders transaction file until there is a change of agent code. The value of each matching order will be used to increment the total value-of-orders field of the master record which will be written to the C/F file at the end of the substructure. At component G, non-matched B/F master file records are simply copied to the C/F master file and in the substructure below component H non matching transactions are copied to the Non-Matching Order Report.

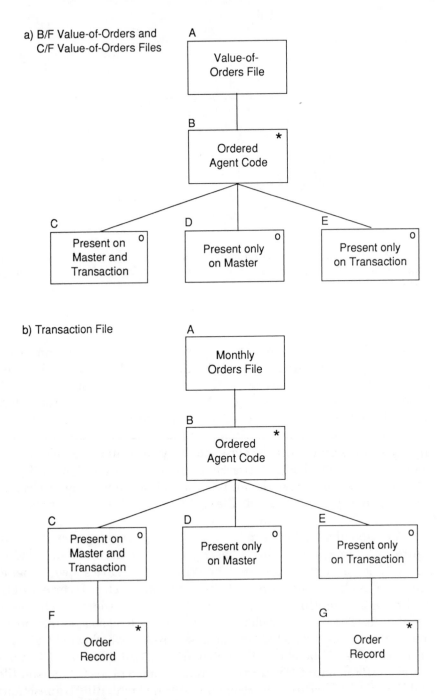

a) B/F Value-of-Orders and
   C/F Value-of-Orders Files

A Value-of-Orders File

B Ordered Agent Code *

C Present on Master and Transaction °

D Present only on Master °

E Present only on Transaction °

b) Transaction File

A Monthly Orders File

B Ordered Agent Code *

C Present on Master and Transaction °

D Present only on Master °

E Present only on Transaction °

F Order Record *

G Order Record *

Figure 12.22a and b

c) Error File

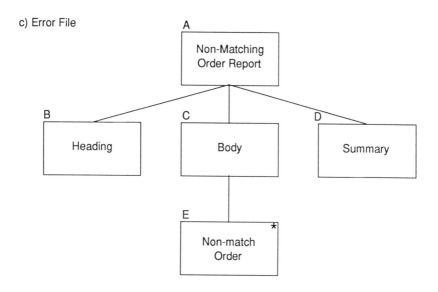

Figure 12.22c Logical data structures for Value-of-Orders Update Program.

B/F Value-of-Orders File	C/F Value-of-Orders File	Monthly Orders File	Non-Matching Orders File
A	A	A	A
–	–	–	B
–	–	–	C
–	–	–	D
B	B	B	–
C	C	C	–
D	D	D	–
E	E	E	–
–	–	F	–
–	–	G	E

Figure 12.23 Correspondence table for Update Value-of-Orders Program.

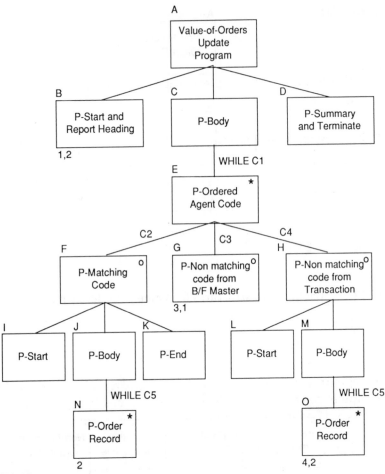

Condition List

CI VR-AGENT-CODE < HIGH-VALUES
    OR OR-AGENT-CODE < HIGH-VALUES
C2 VR-AGENT-CODE = OR-AGENT-CODE
C3 VR-AGENT-CODE < OR-AGENT-CODE
C4 OR-AGENT-CODE < VR-AGENT-CODE
C5 OR-AGENT-CODE remains the same as that
    for the first record in the iteration

Function List (read/write functions only)

1 Read record from B/F Value of Orders Master File at end set
       VR-AGENT-CODE = HIGH-VALUES
2 Read record from Monthly Orders File at end set
       OR-AGENT-CODE = HIGH-VALUES
3 Write record to C/F Value of Orders Master File
4 Write copy of Monthly Orders File record to Non-Matching Order Report

Figure 12.24 Basic program structure and file operations for Update Value-of-Orders Program.

292

The Value-of-Orders Update Program presented here represents a relatively straightforward design exercise. In the next chapter we will consider the design and implementation of an enhanced version of this program which not only involves the production of an updated master file but also a management information file giving details of agents orders.

12.5.2 Complex Updates

In the following example we are concerned not only with amending the contents of existing records on a master file but also with the addition of new records and the deletion of existing records. The specification is:-

> The MOCO mail order company maintains a sequential master file containing the names and addresses of all its agents. This Name-and-Address master file is held in ascending agent code order and its records have the description

```
01  NA-RECORD.
    03  NA-AGENT-CODE      PIC X(6).
    03  NA-DATA            PIC X(100).
```

At regular intervals this file is updated using information held on a sequential transaction file which is also held in agent code order. Its records have the description:

```
01  TRANSACTION-RECORD.
    03  TR-AGENT-CODE      PIC X(6).
    03  TR-TYPE            PIC X.
    03  TR-DATA            PIC X(100).
```

The field TR-TYPE specifies whether the transaction relates to the amendment of an existing record (value "A"), an insertion of a new record (value "I") or the deletion of an existing record (value "D"). Only one transaction type can occur on the file for any agent code. In addition to the production of a C/F master file, during the program run an error file is produced which details any errors that are encountered. For example, a deletion for a non-existent master record. The error file consists of a single line heading, followed by one-line reports detailing each error and finally a summary line detailing the number of non-matches that have occurred.

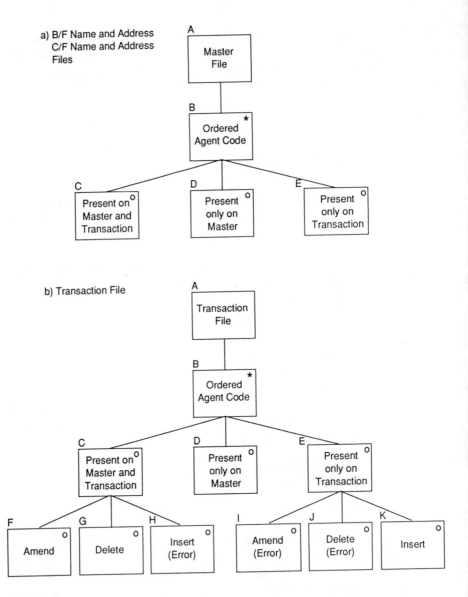

Figure 12.25

c) Error File

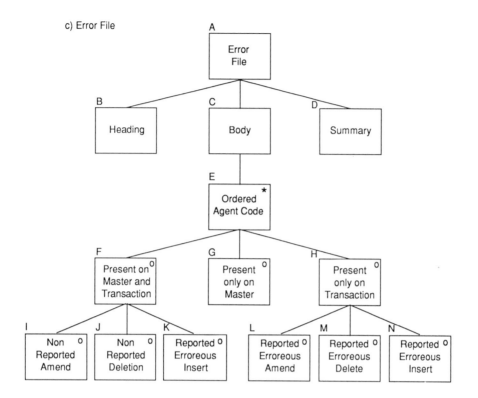

Figure 12.25 Logical data structures for Name and Address Update Program.

B/F Name and Address File	C/F Name and Address File	Transaction File	Error File
A	A	A	A
–	–	–	B
–	–	–	C
–	–	–	D
B	B	B	E
C	C	C	F
D	D	D	G
E	E	E	H
		F	I
		G	J
		H	K
		I	L
		J	M
		K	N

Figure 12.26 Correspondence table for Name and Address Update Program.

The system network diagram for the program again takes the form shown in figure 12.21 and the resultant logical data structures are detailed in figure 12.25. Those for the B/F Master, C/F Master and Transaction File are relatively straightforward, but that for the Error File needs careful consideration. The structure for this file is much more elaborate than the structure we had for the Error File depicted in figure 12.22. The more complex structure is needed because error reports can occur for three different situations:

(i)   Insertion when there is already a master record.

(ii) Amendment when there is no matching master record.

(iii) Deletion when there is no matching master record.

The structure for the error file given in figure 12.25c gives correct correspondences with the other structures (figure 12.26) and leads to a logically sound program structure (figure 12.27). The alternative structures shown in figure 12.28 do not and are therefore incorrect. The first of these alternative structures is incorrect as no single component in the transaction file will correspond with component E of figure 12.28(a). This is because the latter component represents three different types of report. The second alternative structure is incorrect because, even if we extend the structure to show the three different types of error report, correspondence checks with the program structure (figure 12.27) will fail. This failure occurs because no single component in the program structure will correspond with component E of figure 12.28(b). Thus we must adopt a structure as shown in figure 12.25. You should note that in figure 12.27 there is no file handling operation associated with component N. The B/F record is to be deleted and hence simply no C/F record is written.

12.5.3 More Complex Updates

In the specification for the previous example program it was stipulated that there could only be one transaction (an amendment, a deletion or an insertion) for any one agent code. If we allow more than one transaction per key the situation will become much more complex. For example, the following sequence of transactions for a single agent code which lies on the Name-and-Address master file may be perfectly valid if they represent various changes entered in time sequence order:

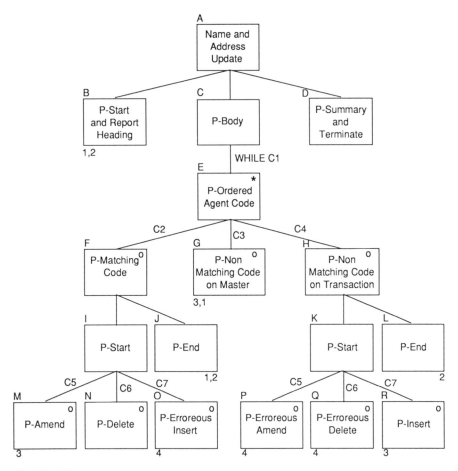

Condition List

CI NA-AGENT-CODE < HIGH-VALUES
    OR TR-AGENT-CODE < HIGH-VALUES
C2 NA-AGENT-CODE = TR-AGENT-CODE
C3 NA-AGENT-CODE < TR-AGENT-CODE
C4 TR-AGENT-CODE < NA-AGENT-CODE
C5 TR-TYPE = "A"
C6 TR-TYPE = "B"
C7 TR-TYPE = "C"

Function List (read/write functions only)

1 Read record from B/F Name and Address File at end set
    NA-AGENT-CODE = HIGH-VALUES
2 Read record from Transaction File at end set
    TR-AGENT-CODE = HIGH-VALUES
3 Write record to C/F Name and Address File
4 Write error line to Error File

Figure 12.27 Basic program structure and file operations for Name and Address Update Program

297

1. Amendment of details
2. Amendment of details
3. Deletion
4. Insertion
5. Amendment of details

However, the following is definitely erroneous for a single code:

1. Deletion
2. Deletion

Situations such as these need careful consideration and will often require the use of the Backtracking Technique which is covered in Chapter 20 (within Volume 2).

12.6 Summary

As we have seen in this chapter programs which involve the matching of sequentially organised files can be extremely varied and can become very complex. However, a common approach can be applied to their design which is to:

(i)   Identify the key used in the matching process.

(ii)   Identify all the match/non-match combinations for the key.

(iii) Produce logical data structures centred around the processing of the key and the identified match/non- match combinations. Elaborate these where necessary to cater for multiple records with the same key and/or for different record types.

(iv)   Identify correspondences and fuse the structures together.

During the final stage if any problems are encountered check carefully that the logical data structures really do represent the required processing.

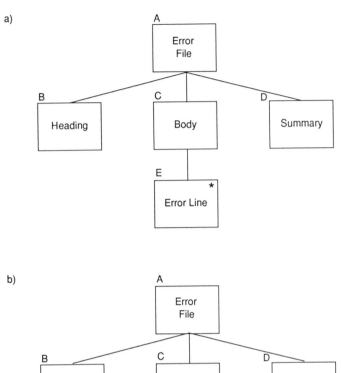

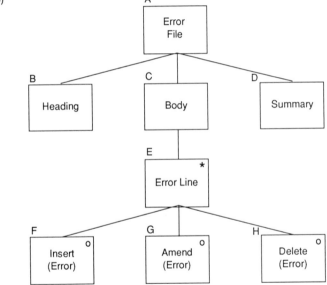

Figure 12.28 Incorrect logical structures for Error File in Name and Address Update Program.

TASKS - CHAPTER 12

1. Check the solution given in figure 12.9 and 12.10 for the file match program using the test data detailed below:

```
   Key on File F1              Key on File F2

           010                         015
           015                         020
           020                         030
   025                 045
           030                         050
           070                         055
           075                         060
           080                         080
           090                 end of file
           100
       end of file
```

2. (a) Amend the solution to the File Match Program (section 12.2.2) so that it uses boolean end of file indicators to implement the conditions. Check your answers with the test data given above.

    (b) What changes would have to be made to your solution and that given in section 12.2.2 if files F1 and F2 were held in descending key order?

3. Determine, for your version of COBOL, what are the contents of the record area associated with an input file after its end of file is detected. Hint - amend one of your earlier programs to display the contents just before the file is closed.

4. For each of the program detailed in sections 12.4 and 12.5 carry out the following

    (i)   from the specification draw up a complete function list,

    (ii) allocate your functions to the given basic program structure - adding any additional components if necessary,

    (iii) produce schematic logic,

    (iv) generate some test data and check your solution. Does it work?

CHAPTER 13

Master File Updates

13.1 Introduction

In the preceding chapter we considered the design of different types of programs which match together (collate) sequentially organised files. In this chapter we will cover both the design and implementation of an enhanced version of the mail order company's update program which was first introduced in section 12.5.1. This enhanced program is concerned not only with the production of a completely new master file and an error report but also with the production of a data file from which the commissions for agents and area operators can be calculated. Each of the JSP design stages for this program will be covered in detail so that you have the chance to experience full use of the method in the production of a realistically sized program. Following the implementation of this update program we will consider further COBOL's facilities for handling sequential files. Then finally the language's facilities for sequentially processing indexed sequential files will be explained.

13.2 Enhanced Value-of-Orders Update Program

The full specification for the enhanced program is as follows:

The MOCO mail order company maintains a sequential Value-of-Orders master file which is used to record details of the value of the orders placed by its agents during the year. At the start of each month each agent's commission for the previous month is calculated according to the value of orders placed by the agent during that month. Also, in addition to these monthly commissions, at the end of each year the agents receive an end-of-year bonus. The calculation of this bonus depends on the average value of the orders for the year and on the number of months for which orders were received. Agents are responsible to area operators whose commissions and bonuses are calculated on the monthly and yearly totals for orders placed by agents within their area.

The Value-of-Orders master file is ordered on ascending agent code and contains a record for each agent. In addition to holding the relevant agent's code each record contains fields which are used to hold the total value of orders for the year, the total number of orders for the year, the total value of orders for the previous month, the total number of orders for that month and a count of the number of months for which there has been an order. The COBOL description for these records is:

```
01   VALUE-RECORD.
     03   VR-AGENT-CODE.
          05   VR-AREA-CODE              PIC X(2).
          05   VR-AGENT-NUMBER           PIC 9(4).
     03   VR-TOTAL-VALUE-OF-ORDERS       PIC 9(5)V99.
     03   VR-TOTAL-NUMBER-OF-ORDERS      PIC 9(4).
     03   VR-LAST-MONTH-VALUE            PIC 9(4)V99.
     03   VR-LAST-MONTH-NUMBER           PIC 9(3).
     03   VR-COUNT-OF-MONTHS             PIC 99.
```

All of the value and counter fields in the master records are set to zero at the start of a new year by a program that extracts the data which is used to calculate the previous year's bonuses.

At the start of each month the sorted Monthly Orders file for the previous month is used as a transaction file to update the Value-of-Orders master file. As specified previously, the records on the Monthly Orders file have the following COBOL description

```
01   ORDER-RECORD.
     03   OR-AGENT-CODE.
          05   OR-AREA-CODE              PIC X(2).
          05   OR-AGENT-NUMBER           PIC 9(4).
     03   OR-CATALOGUE-REF               PIC X(6).
     03   OR-CATALOGUE-PRICE             PIC 9(3)V99.
     03   OR-NO-ORDERED                  PIC 9(2).
     03   OR-PAYMENT-TYPE                PIC X.
```

Each record provides details of an agent's order for a particular item and includes the quantity ordered and the item's catalogue price. The product of these two fields then gives the value of the order. The total value of all the orders from an agent that appear on the Monthly Orders file is used to update the relevant total value of orders for the year (VR-TOTAL-VALUE-OF-ORDERS) and gives the new total value of orders for the previous month (VR-LAST-MONTH-VALUE). When one or more orders from an agent occur on the Monthly-Orders file the counter fields (VR-TOTAL-NUMBER-OF-ORDERS, VR-LAST-MONTH-NUMBER and VR-COUNT-OF-MONTHS) are also incremented. If there are no orders from an agent on the Monthly Orders file the total value (VR-LAST-MONTH-VALUE) and the total number (VR-LAST-MONTH-NUMBER) of orders for the previous month are set to zero and the other fields are unaltered.

During each monthly update of the Value-of-Orders master file a Commission file and an Error-Report file are generated in addition to the updated C/F Value-of-Orders file. The Commission file, which is produced in agent code order, is comprised of records for agents and area operators that give the total value of orders placed during the past month and the number of these orders. The Commission file is processed by a subsequent program which calculates the final commission values and credits the agents accounts. Records on the Commission file have the COBOL description:

```
01  COMMISSION-RECORD.
    03  CR-AGENT-CODE.
        05  CR-AREA-CODE              PIC X(2).
        05  CR-AGENT-NUMBER           PIC 9(4).
    03  CR-LAST-MONTH-VALUE           PIC 9(5)V99.
    03  CR-LAST-MONTH-NUMBER          PIC 9(4).
```

Records which relate to area operators give the total value and total number of all orders placed within an area. They use the reserved agent number 9999 and follow the individual agent records for that area.

The Error Report file is a simple non paged printer file which, after headings at the start of the file, consists of reports for those records on the transaction file for which there is no current matching Value-of-Orders master record. The file is terminated with a summary line giving the total number of erroneous records and a line of Xs. An example of the report is shown in figure 13.1.

```
ERROR REPORT FROM VALUE OF ORDERS UPDATE PROGRAM

NON MATCHING TRANSACTION RECORDS ON xx/xx/xx

     RECORD NUMBER              RECORD CONTENT

          4                AA1235YW74320099902M

          19               DG1050WW86310099901M

          :                        :
          :                        :


TOTAL NUMBER OF NON MATCH RECORDS   15

XXXXXXXXXXXXXXXXXXXXXXXXXXXXXXXXXXXXXXXXXXXXXXXXXXXXX
```

Figure 13.1   Sample of the Error Report generated by the Value-of-Orders Update Program

13.3 Program Design

13.3.1 Stage 0 : Understand What is Required

The data streams on which the program operates are identified in the system network diagram shown in figure 13.2. The operation of the Value-of-Orders Update Program may be summarised from the specification as follows:

— records from the B/F Value-of-Orders master file and the Monthly Orders file are matched sequentially by agent code,

— each master file record has its value and counter fields updated and is then written to the new C/F Value-of-Orders master file,

— after each master record has been updated a Commission file record is generated for that agent,

— after all the master records for one area have been updated a Commission file record with the agent number 9999 and the relevant area code will be generated giving the total value of orders for that area,

304

– any non-matching transaction records are reported on the Error Report file.

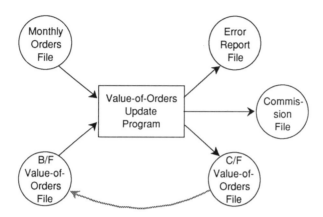

Figure 13.2 System Network Diagram for the Value-of-Orders Update Program.

13.3.2 Stage 1 : Produce Logical Data Structures

The logical data structures are shown in figures 13.3 a) to d). Here the underlying ordered structure of each of the files is emphasised by showing within each structure an iteration of ordered agent code values each of which may be either:

i)   present on the B/F Value-of-Orders master file and the Monthly Orders transaction file, and hence will be present on the C/F Value-of-Orders master file and the Commission file but will be absent from the Error Report file,

ii) present on the B/F Value-of-Orders master file but absent from the Monthly Orders transaction file and hence will be present on the C/F Value-of-Orders master file and the Commission file but will be absent from the Error Report file,

iii) absent from the B/F Value-of-Orders master file but present on the Monthly Orders transaction file and hence will be absent from the

C/F Value-of-Orders master file and the Commission file but will be present on the Error Report file.

As in chapter 12 a single diagram will suffice for both the B/F and C/F Value-of-Orders master file as the logical structure is not changed by the update process. In the structure for the Commission file it is necessary to introduce the iteration of areas to show the logical position of the commission records for area operators. The structure for the error file, figure 13.3 (d), could have been drawn as in figure 12.22 (c) i.e. components H, K, L and M could have been omitted. However, showing these components makes identifying correspondences easier and in my experience, including the iteration of keys and their logical presence or absence on every file involved in a collation program is helpful and avoids the types of errors detailed in section 12.5.2.

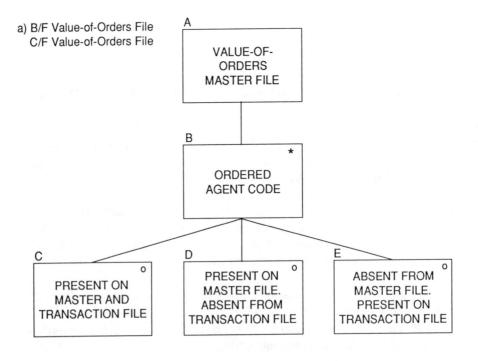

Figure 13.3a Logical data structures for the Value-of-Orders Update Program.

b) Monthly Orders File

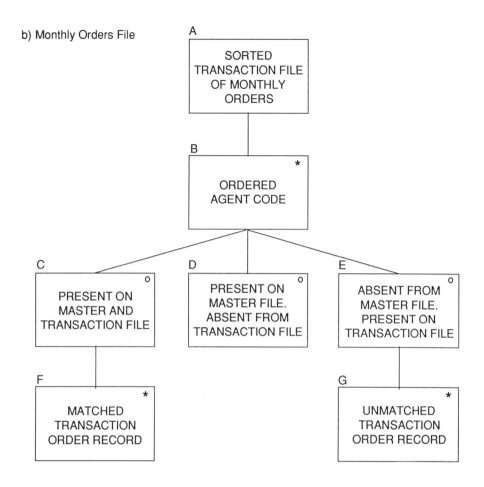

Figure 13.3b Logical data structures for the Value-of-Orders Update Program.

307

c) Commission File

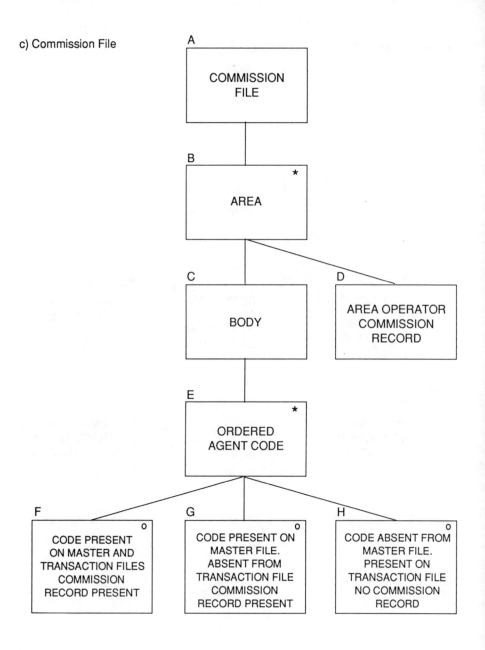

Figure 13.3c

d) Error Report File

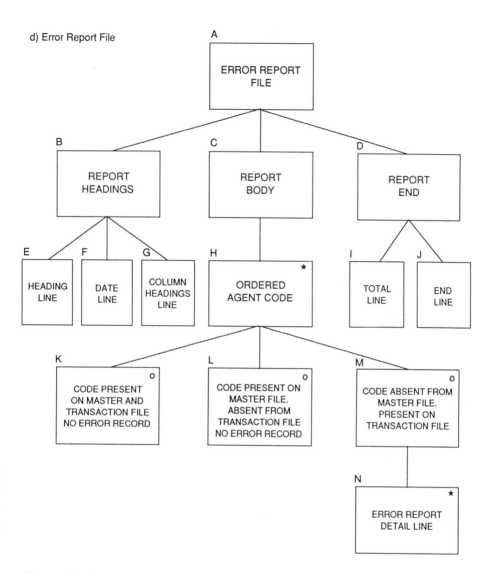

Figure 13.3d

309

Experienced JSP practitioners would probably omit levels E-G from the error report and treat them as one logical entity "Report Headings". This is acceptable as the processing that will be involved with them is basically a sequence of write statements which reference preset heading lines. Nevertheless, until you gain experience with the method it is best to take each file structure down to record level.

13.3.3 Stage 2 : Create a Basic Program Structure

Having constructed each of the logical data structures round the iteration of ordered agent codes correspondences can readily be identified (figure 13.4) and a fused data structure can be produced (figure 13.5) which then leads to the basic program structure as shown in figure 13.6.

B/F Value-of-Orders master file	C/F Value-of-Orders master file	Monthly Orders transaction file	Commission File	Error Report File	Fused Data Structure
A	A	A	A	A	A
–	–	–	–	B	B
–	–	–	–	C	C
–	–	–	–	D	D
–	–	–	–	E	E
–	–	–	–	F	F
–	–	–	–	G	G
–	–	–	B	–	H
–	–	–	–	I	I
–	–	–	–	J	J
–	–	–	C	–	K
–	–	–	D	–	L
B	B	B	E	H	M
C	C	C	F	K	N
D	D	D	G	L	O
E	E	E	H	M	P
–	–	F	–	–	Q
–	–	G	–	N	R

Figure 13.4 Correspondence table for Value-of-Orders Update Program.

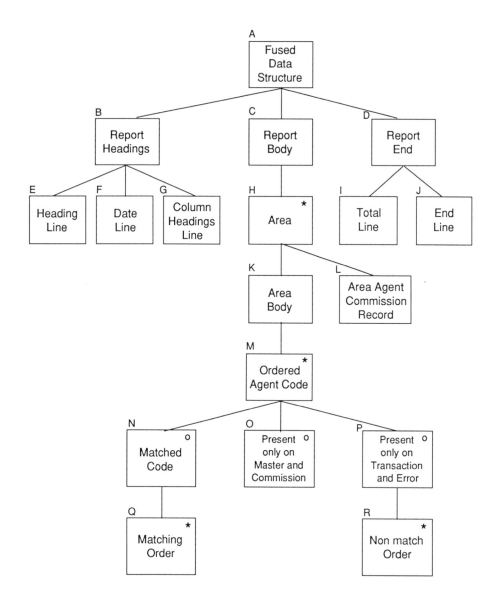

Figure 13.5 Fused Data Structure for Value-of-Orders Update Program.

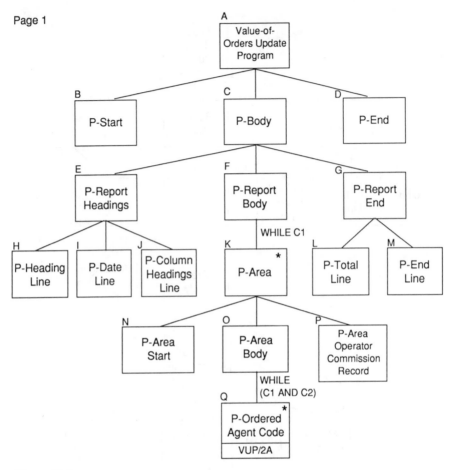

Figure 13.6

An additional start/body/end construct has been added in the basic program structure at the start of the program to cater for the housekeeping of five separate files rather than have all the functions allocated to the components that represent the heading line and the end line. This, and the other additional components, has resulted in the structure being extended onto a second page. The linking references are provided within the stripes at the top and bottom of the relevant components. The conditions which control the iterations and selections may be expressed in general terms as:

C1. there are records still to process from either input file,

312

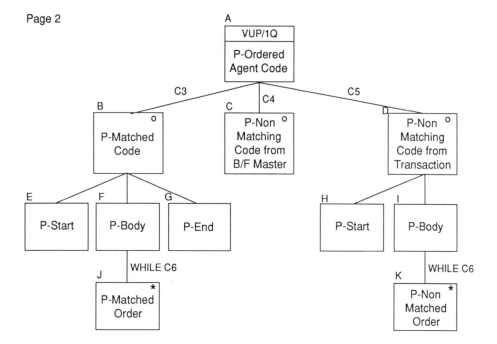

Figure 13.6 Basic Program Structure for Value of Orders Update Program. The conditions are detailed in the main text.

C2. VR-AREA-CODE for the current B/F Value-of-Orders record is the same as for the first record in the iteration,

You should note that both conditions C1 and C2 must remain true during the iteration that processes an area.

C3. there is a matching pair of input records to process,

C4. there is a non-matching record from the B/F Value-of-Orders file to process,

C5. there is a non-matching record from the Monthly Orders transaction file to process,

C6. OR-AGENT-CODE for the current Monthly Orders record is the same as for the first record in the iteration.

These conditions may be formalised by assuming that the literal HIGH-VALUES is moved to VR-AGENT-CODE or OR-AGENT-CODE when the relevant end of file is encountered. Also that on entering the iteration which processes an area, the area code is stored in a variable CURRENT-AREA-CODE and that on entering the iterations which deal with orders from the same agents, the agent code is stored in a variable CURRENT-AGENT-CODE. The conditions then become:

```
C1.   (VR-AGENT-CODE < HIGH-VALUES OR OR-AGENT-CODE < HIGH-VALUES)

C2.   (VR-AREA-CODE = CURRENT-AREA-CODE
             OR VR-AGENT-CODE = HIGH-VALUES)

C3.   VR-AGENT-CODE = OR-AGENT-CODE

C4.   VR-AGENT-CODE < OR-AGENT-CODE

C5.   OR-AGENT-CODE < VR-AGENT-CODE

C6.   OR-AGENT-CODE = CURRENT-AGENT-CODE
```

The second condition within C2 must be included to avoid problems caused by moving HIGH-VALUES to VR-AGENT-CODE when the end of file is encountered (see point (iii) in section 12.2.2 (c)). If the B/F Value-of-Orders file terminates before the Monthly Orders transaction file (which is actually an unlikely and erroneous situation) this condition will ensure that the HIGH-VALUES which have been set up in VR-AREA-CODE are not interpreted as a new valid area code. For if they were, they would cause the generation of an erroneous area operator's commission record with an area code equal to HIGH-VALUES.

13.3.4   Stage 3: Determine Functions and List Them

Following the guidelines given in section 6.1.2 the functions for the program may be determined. In the list given below functions have been grouped together leaving some function numbers free for possible future additions.

FILE HANDLING FUNCTIONS
1.   Open B/F Value-of-Orders master file for input
2.   Close B/F Value-of-Orders master file

3. Read record from B/F Value-of-Orders master file
   at end set VR-AGENT-CODE = HIGH-VALUES
6. Open Monthly Orders transaction file for input
7. Close Monthly Orders transaction file
8. Read record from Monthly Orders transaction file
   at end set OR-AGENT-CODE = HIGH-VALUES
11. Open C/F Value-of-Orders master file for output
12. Close C/F Value-of-Orders master file
13. Write updated Value record to C/F Value-of-Orders master
   file
16. Open Comission file for output
17. Close Comission file
18. Write Comission record to Comission file
21. Open Error Report file for output
22. Close Error Report file
23. Write Heading line to Error Report file
24. Write Date line to Error Report file
25. Write Column Headings line to Error Report file
26. Write Detail line to Error Report file
27. Write Total line to Error Report file
28. Write End line to Error Report file

DATA HANDLING FUNCTIONS
31. Calculate value of current order (VALUE-OF-ORDER)
   = quantity x price
32. Add value of current order (VALUE-OF-ORDER) to
   value of agent's orders (AGENT-VALUE-OF-ORDERS)
33. Add value of agent's orders (AGENT-VALUE-OF-ORDERS) to
   agent's yearly total (VR-TOTAL-VALUE-OF-ORDERS) and
   area operator's monthly total (AO-VALUE-OF-ORDERS)
34. Add 1 to number of agent's orders
   (AGENT-NUMBER-OF-ORDERS)
35. Add number of agent's orders (AGENT-NUMBER-OF-ORDERS)
   to agent's yearly count (VR-TOTAL-NUMBER-OF-ORDERS)
   and area operator's monthly count (AO-NUMBER-OF-ORDERS)
36. Replace values for previous month (VR-LAST-MONTH-VALUE
   and VR-LAST-MONTH-NUMBER) with newly accumulated
   totals (AGENT-VALUE-OF-ORDERS and AGENT-NUMBER-
   OF-ORDERS)
37. Zeroise value and number of agent's orders (AGENT-
   VALUE-OF-ORDERS and AGENT-NUMBER-OF-ORDERS)

38. Zeroise agent's monthly value and number of orders
    (VR-LAST-MONTH-VALUE and VR-LAST-MONTH-NUMBER)
41. Add 1 to count of months for which an order has been
    received (VR-COUNT-OF-MONTHS)
46. Create a Commission record for an agent from the
    updated Value-of-Orders record
47. Create a Commission record for area agent
51. Access current date and set up in Date line
52. Add 1 to count of transactions (TRANSACTION-COUNT)
53. Set up Detail line with count of transactions
    (TRANSACTION-COUNT) and copy of non-matching
    Monthly Orders record
55. Add 1 to count of non-match transactions
    (NON-MATCH-TRANSACTIONS)
56. Set up count of non-match transactions
    (NON-MATCH-TRANSACTIONS) in Total line

INITIAL AND TERMINAL FUNCTIONS
61. Set count of non-match transactions (NON-MATCH-
    TRANSACTIONS) = 0
62. Set count of transactions (TRANSACTION-COUNT) = 0
66. Stop program run
71. Copy area code from current Value-of-Orders record
    to CURRENT-AREA-CODE
72. Set value and counter fields for area operators
    (AA-VALUE-OF-ORDERS and AA-NUMBER-OF-ORDERS) = 0
73. Copy agent code from current Monthly Orders record
    to CURRENT-AGENT-CODE

In determining the conditions and the above functions the following
internal program variables have been identified:

Value of current order
```
      01   VALUE-OF-ORDER              PIC 9(4)V99   COMP.
```

Accumulated value of orders for agent for month
```
      01   AGENT-VALUE-OF-ORDERS       PIC 9(4)V99   COMP.
```

Accumulated number of orders for agent for month
```
      01   AGENT-NUMBER-OF-ORDERS      PIC 9(3)      COMP.
```

Accumulated value of orders for area operator for month
```
01   AO-VALUE-OF-ORDERS         PIC 9(5)V99  COMP.
```

Accumulated number of orders for area operator for month
```
01   AO-NUMBER-OF-ORDERS        PIC 9(4)     COMP.
```

Sequential transaction record count
```
01   TRANSACTION-COUNT          PIC 9(4)     COMP.
```

Count of non-match transactions
```
01   NON-MATCH-TRANSACTIONS     PIC 9(3)     COMP.
```

Area code for current group of of agents
```
01   CURRENT-AREA-CODE          PIC XX.
```

Agent code for current group of transactions
```
01   CURRENT-AGENT-CODE.
     03   CAA-AREA-CODE          PIC XX.
     03   CAA-AGENT-NUMBER       PIC 9(4).
```

Date in standard COBOL format
```
01   CURRENT-DATE.
     03   CD-YEAR                PIC 99.
     03   CD-MONTH               PIC 99.
     03   CD-DAY                 PIC 99.
```

13.3.5   Stage 4 : Finalise the Program Structure

The allocation of the functions listed above to the program structure is
shown in figures 13.7a and 13.7b. Remember that where several
functions are listed below one component they are given in the order
they are to be executed. (Note that figure 13.7 is presented in two parts
so that the relevant schematic logic lies opposite to it).

13.3.6   Stage 5 : Produce Schematic Logic

The schematic logic for the finalised program is given in figures 13.8 and
13.9. Note that a separate piece of schematic logic text is generated for
each page of the program structure. The second structure is referenced
from within the first by giving its name, preceded by the word DO. When
these are implemented in COBOL the code implementing the second
structure is simply encapsulated within the code for the first structure.

Page 1

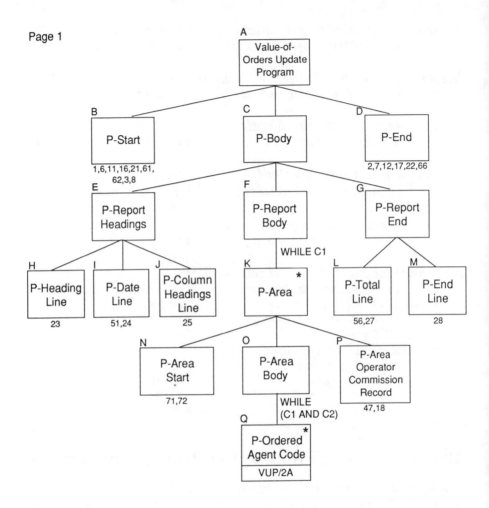

Figure 13.7a Program Structure for Value of Orders Update Program Page 1. The conditions are detailed in the main text

318

```
VUP1A-SEQ
   VUP1B
      Open B/F Value-of-Orders master file for input
      Open Monthly Orders transaction file for input
      Open C/F Value-of-Orders master file for output
      Open Comission file for output
      Open Error Report file for output
      Set count of non-match transactions (NON-MATCH-
         TRANSACTIONS) = 0
      Set count of transactions (TRANSACTION-COUNT) = 0
      Read record from B/F Value-of-Orders master file
                at end set VR-AGENT-CODE = HIGH-VALUES
      Read record from Monthly Orders transaction file
                at end set OR-AGENT-CODE = HIGH-VALUES
   VUP1C-SEQ
      VUP1E-SEQ
         VUP1H
            Write Heading line to Error Report file
         VUP1I
            Access current date and set up in Date line
            Write Date line to Error Report file
         VUP1J
            Write Column Headings line to Error Report file
      VUP1E-SEQ-END
      VUP1F-ITER while there are records still to process
         VUP1K-SEQ
            VUP1N
               Copy area code from current Value-of-Orders record
                  to CURRENT-AREA-CODE
               Set value and counter fields for area operators
                  (AA-VALUE-OF-ORDERS and AA-NUMBER-OF-ORDERS) = 0
            VUP1O-ITER while there are records still to process and
                        the area code of the current master file
                        record is the same as that of the first
                        in the iteration
               VUP1Q
                  DO VUP2A
            VUP1O-ITER-END
            VUP1P
               Create a Commission record for area agent
               Write Comission record to Comission file
         VUP1K-SEQ-END
      VUP1F-ITER-END
      VUP1G-SEQ
         VUP1L
            Set up count of non-match transactions
               (NON-MATCH-TRANSACTIONS) in Total line
            Write Total line to Error Report file
         VUP1M
            Write End line to Error Report file
      VUP1G-SEQ-END
   VUP1C-SEQ-END
```

```
VUP1D
    Close B/F Value-of-Orders master file
    Close Monthly Orders transaction file
    Close C/F Value-of-Orders master file
    Close Comission file
    Close Error Report file
    Stop program run
VUP1A-SEQ-END
```

Figure 13.8   Schematic Logic for the first page of the program structure for the Value-of-Orders Update Program

Page 2

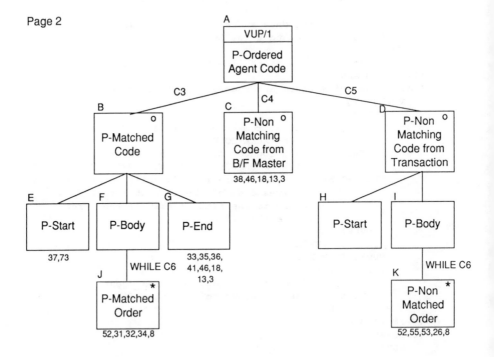

Figure 13.7b   Program Structure for Value of Orders Update Program Page 2. The conditions are detailed in the main text

VUP2A-SEL if B/F master record and transaction record match
   VUP2B-SEQ
      VUP2E
         Zeroise value and number of agent's orders (AGENT-
               VALUE-OF-ORDERS and AGENT-NUMBER-OF-ORDERS)
         Copy agent code from current Monthly Orders record
               to CURRENT-AGENT-CODE
      VUP2F-ITER while the agent code of the current transaction
               record is the same as that of the first in the
               iteration
         VUP2J
            Add 1 to count of transactions (TRANSACTION-COUNT)
            Calculate value of current order (VALUE-OF-ORDER)
                        = quantity x price
            Add value of current order (VALUE-OF-ORDER) to
               value of agent's orders (AGENT-VALUE-OF-ORDERS)
            Add 1 to number of agent's orders
                              (AGENT-NUMBER-OF-ORDERS)
            Read record from Monthly Orders transaction file
                  at end set OR-AGENT-CODE = HIGH-VALUES
      VUP2F-ITER-END
      VUP2G
         Add value of agent's orders (AGENT-VALUE-OF-ORDERS) to
               agent's yearly total (VR-TOTAL-VALUE-OF-ORDERS) and
               area operator's monthly total (AO-VALUE-OF-ORDERS)
         Add number of agent's orders (AGENT-NUMBER-OF-ORDERS) to
               agent's yearly count (VR-TOTAL-NUMBER-OF-ORDERS) and
               area operator's monthly count (AO-NUMBER-OF-ORDERS)
         Replace values for previous month (VR-LAST-MONTH-VALUE
               and VR-LAST-MONTH-NUMBER) with newly accumulated
               totals (AGENT-VALUE-OF-ORDERS and AGENT-NUMBER-
               OF-ORDERS)
         Add 1 to count of months for which an order has been
               received (VR-COUNT-OF-MONTHS)
         Create a Commission record for an agent from the
               updated Value-of-Orders record
         Write Comission record to Comission file
         Write updated Value record to C/F Value-of-Orders master
               file
         Read record from B/F Value-of-Orders master file
                  at end set VR-AGENT-CODE = HIGH-VALUES
   VUP2B-SEQ-END
VUP2A-OR1 if there is a non matching B/F master record to process
   VUP2C
      Zeroise agent's monthly value and number of orders
            (VR-LAST-MONTH-VALUE and VR-LAST-MONTH-NUMBER)
      Create a Commission record for an agent from the
            updated Value-of-Orders record
      Write Comission record to Comission file
      Write updated Value record to C/F Value-of-Orders master
            file
      Read record from B/F Value-of-Orders master file
            at end set VR-AGENT-CODE = HIGH-VALUES

```
VUP2A-OR2 if there is a non matching transaction record to process
  VUP2D-SEQ
    VUP2H
        Copy agent code from current Monthly Orders record
            to CURRENT-AGENT-CODE
    VUP2I-ITER while the agent code of the current transaction
               record is the same as that of the first in the
               iteration
      VUP2K
          Add 1 to count of transactions (TRANSACTION-COUNT)
          Add 1 to count of non-match transactions
            (NON-MATCH-TRANSACTIONS)
          Set up Detail line with count of transactions
            (TRANSACTION-COUNT) and copy of non matching
            Monthly Orders record
          Write Detail line to Error Report file
          Read record from Monthly Orders transaction file
                  at end set OR-AGENT-CODE = HIGH-VALUES
    VUP2I-ITER-END
  VUP2D-SEQ-END
VUP2A-SEL-END
```

Figure 13.9   Schematic Logic for the second page of the program structure for the Value-of-Orders Update Program

13.4 Program Implementation

The final stage of program production is to implement our design in the chosen target programming language. This gives the COBOL code for the Value-of-Orders Update Program (figure 13.10). Note that in the implementation in some cases several functions can be combined into one COBOL statement (e.g. the OPEN and CLOSE file statements) while other functions need to be expanded into several COBOL statements (e.g. functions 46 and 47). There does not need to be a one to one relationship between functions and COBOL statements. However, a function should always be straightforward to implement. If it is not it will probably indicate that the logical data structures and hence the program structure have not been developed sufficiently.

```
IDENTIFICATION DIVISION.
************************

PROGRAM-ID. VUP.

* A PROGRAM TO UPDATE THE VALUE-OF-ORDERS MASTER FILE WITH
* TRANSACTIONS FROM THE MONTHLY ORDERS FILE PRODUCING A C/F
* MASTER FILE, A COMMISION FILE AND AN ERROR FILE WHICH GIVES
* DETAILS OF ANY NON MATCHING TRANSACTIONS

ENVIRONMENT DIVISION.
*********************

CONFIGURATION SECTION.

SOURCE-COMPUTER. A-PC.
OBJECT-COMPUTER. A-PC.

INPUT-OUTPUT SECTION.

FILE-CONTROL.

    SELECT VALUE-FILE ASSIGN TO "VALUE.OLD".
    SELECT ORDERS-FILE ASSIGN TO "ORDERS.DAT".
    SELECT NEW-VALUE-FILE ASSIGN TO "VALUE.NEW".
    SELECT COMMISSION-FILE ASSIGN TO "COMMISS.DAT".
    SELECT ERROR-FILE ASSIGN TO "ERROR.REP".

DATA DIVISION.
**************

FILE SECTION.

FD  VALUE-FILE.
*   B/F VALUE OF ORDERS FILE
    01  VALUE-RECORD.
        03  VR-AGENT-CODE.
            05  VR-AREA-CODE              PIC X(2).
            05  VR-AGENT-NUMBER           PIC 9(4).
        03  VR-TOTAL-VALUE-OF-ORDERS      PIC 9(5)V99.
        03  VR-TOTAL-NUMBER-OF-ORDERS     PIC 9(4).
        03  VR-LAST-MONTH-VALUE           PIC 9(4)V99.
        03  VR-LAST-MONTH-NUMBER          PIC 9(3).
        03  VR-COUNT-OF-MONTHS            PIC 99.

FD  ORDERS-FILE.
    01  ORDER-RECORD.
        03  OR-AGENT-CODE.
            05  OR-AREA-CODE              PIC X(2).
            05  OR-AGENT-NUMBER           PIC 9(4).
```

```
      03   OR-CATALOGUE-REF                PIC X(6).
      03   OR-CATALOGUE-PRICE              PIC 9(3)V99.
      03   OR-NO-ORDERED                   PIC 9(2).
      03   OR-PAYMENT-TYPE                 PIC X.


 FD  NEW-VALUE-FILE.
 *   C/F VALUE OF ORDERS FILE
     01  NEW-VALUE-RECORD                  PIC X(28).


 FD  COMMISSION-FILE.
     01  COMMISSION-RECORD.
         03  CR-AGENT-CODE.
             05  CR-AREA-CODE              PIC X(2).
             05  CR-AGENT-NUMBER           PIC 9(4).
         03  CR-LAST-MONTH-VALUE           PIC 9(5)V99.
         03  CR-LAST-MONTH-NUMBER          PIC 9(4).


 FD  ERROR-FILE.
     01  ERROR-RECORD                      PIC X(50).


 WORKING-STORAGE SECTION.

     01  VALUE-OF-ORDER                    PIC 9(4)V99   COMP.
     01  AGENT-VALUE-OF-ORDERS             PIC 9(4)V99   COMP.
     01  AGENT-NUMBER-OF-ORDERS            PIC 9(3)      COMP.
     01  AO-VALUE-OF-ORDERS                PIC 9(5)V99   COMP.
     01  AO-NUMBER-OF-ORDERS               PIC 9(4)      COMP.
     01  TRANSACTION-COUNT                 PIC 9(4)      COMP.
     01  NON-MATCH-TRANSACTIONS            PIC 9(3)      COMP.


     01  CURRENT-AREA-CODE                 PIC XX.
     01  CURRENT-AGENT-CODE.
         03  CAA-AREA-CODE                 PIC XX.
         03  CAA-AGENT-NUMBER              PIC 9(4).


     01  CURRENT-DATE.
         03  CD-YEAR                       PIC 99.
         03  CD-MONTH                      PIC 99.
         03  CD-DAY                        PIC 99.


     01  HEADING-LINE                      PIC X(50)   VALUE
         " ERROR REPORT FROM VALUE OF ORDERS UPDATE PROGRAM ".

     01  DATE-LINE.
         03  FILLER                        PIC X(37)   VALUE
         " NON MATCHING TRANSACTION RECORDS ON ".
         03  CD-DAY                        PIC 99.
         03  FILLER                        PIC X       VALUE "/".
         03  CD-MONTH                      PIC 99.
         03  FILLER                        PIC X       VALUE "/".
         03  CD-YEAR                       PIC 99.
```

```
01  COLUMN-HEADINGS-LINE                PIC X(42)   VALUE
       "      RECORD NUMBER           RECORD CONTENT".

01  DETAIL-LINE.
    03  FILLER                          PIC X(9)  VALUE SPACES.
    03  DL-RECORD-NUMBER                PIC ZZ9.
    03  FILLER                          PIC X(13).
    03  DL-ORDER-RECORD                 PIC X(20).

01  TOTAL-LINE.
    03  FILLER                          PIC X(35)   VALUE
       " TOTAL NUMBER OF NON MATCH RECORDS ".
    03  TL-RECORD-COUNT                 PIC ZZ9.

01  END-LINE            PIC X(50)      VALUE ALL "X".

PROCEDURE DIVISION.
********************

VUP1A-SEQ.
VUP1B.
*    INITIAL OPERATIONS
     OPEN INPUT VALUE-FILE , ORDERS-FILE.
     OPEN OUTPUT NEW-VALUE-FILE , COMMISSION-FILE , ERROR-FILE.
     MOVE ZERO TO NON-MATCH-TRANSACTIONS , TRANSACTION-COUNT.
     READ VALUE-FILE AT END
         MOVE HIGH-VALUES TO VR-AGENT-CODE.
     READ ORDERS-FILE AT END
         MOVE HIGH-VALUES TO OR-AGENT-CODE.
VUP1C-SEQ.
VUP1E-SEQ.
VUP1H.
     WRITE ERROR-RECORD FROM HEADING-LINE AFTER ADVANCING PAGE.
VUP1I.
     ACCEPT CURRENT-DATE FROM DATE.
     MOVE CORRESPONDING CURRENT-DATE TO DATE-LINE.
     WRITE ERROR-RECORD FROM DATE-LINE AFTER ADVANCING 2 LINES.
VUP1J.
     WRITE ERROR-RECORD FROM COLUMN-HEADINGS-LINE
             AFTER ADVANCING 2 LINES.
VUP1E-SEQ-END.

VUP1F-ITER.
     IF VR-AGENT-CODE < HIGH-VALUES OR
             OR-AGENT-CODE < HIGH-VALUES NEXT SENTENCE
                 ELSE GO TO VUP1F-ITER-END.
VUP1K-SEQ.
*    PROCESS AREA
VUP1N.
     MOVE VR-AREA-CODE TO CURRENT-AREA-CODE.
     MOVE ZERO TO AO-VALUE-OF-ORDERS , AO-NUMBER-OF-ORDERS.
```

```
    VUP10-ITER.
        IF ( VR-AGENT-CODE < HIGH-VALUES OR
                OR-AGENT-CODE < HIGH-VALUES )   AND
            ( VR-AREA-CODE = CURRENT-AREA-CODE  OR
                VR-AGENT-CODE = HIGH-VALUES )   NEXT SENTENCE
                    ELSE GO TO VUP10-ITER-END.
    VUP1Q.
    VUP2A-SEL.
*       PROCESS AGENT CODE
        IF VR-AGENT-CODE = OR-AGENT-CODE NEXT SENTENCE
            ELSE GO TO VUP2A-OR1.
    VUP2B-SEQ.
*       PROCESS MATCHING AGENT CODE
    VUP2E.
        MOVE ZERO TO AGENT-VALUE-OF-ORDERS
                        AGENT-NUMBER-OF-ORDERS.
        MOVE OR-AGENT-CODE TO CURRENT-AGENT-CODE.


    VUP2F-ITER.
        IF OR-AGENT-CODE = CURRENT-AGENT-CODE
            NEXT SENTENCE ELSE GO TO VUP2F-ITER-END.
    VUP2J.
        ADD 1 TO TRANSACTION-COUNT.
        MULTIPLY OR-NO-ORDERED BY OR-CATALOGUE-PRICE
                GIVING VALUE-OF-ORDER.
        ADD VALUE-OF-ORDER TO AGENT-VALUE-OF-ORDERS.
        ADD 1 TO AGENT-NUMBER-OF-ORDERS.
        READ ORDERS-FILE AT END
            MOVE HIGH-VALUES TO OR-AGENT-CODE.
        GO TO VUP2F-ITER.
    VUP2F-ITER-END.


    VUP2G.
        ADD AGENT-VALUE-OF-ORDERS TO VR-TOTAL-VALUE-OF-ORDERS
                AO-VALUE-OF-ORDERS.
        ADD AGENT-NUMBER-OF-ORDERS TO VR-TOTAL-NUMBER-OF-ORDERS
                AO-NUMBER-OF-ORDERS.
        MOVE AGENT-VALUE-OF-ORDERS TO VR-LAST-MONTH-VALUE.
        MOVE AGENT-NUMBER-OF-ORDERS TO VR-LAST-MONTH-NUMBER.
        ADD 1 TO VR-COUNT-OF-MONTHS.
        MOVE VR-AGENT-CODE TO CR-AGENT-CODE.
        MOVE VR-LAST-MONTH-VALUE TO CR-LAST-MONTH-VALUE.
        MOVE VR-LAST-MONTH-NUMBER TO CR-LAST-MONTH-NUMBER.
        WRITE COMMISSION-RECORD.
        WRITE NEW-VALUE-RECORD FROM VALUE-RECORD.
        READ VALUE-FILE AT END
            MOVE HIGH-VALUES TO VR-AGENT-CODE.
    VUP2B-SEQ-END.
        GO TO VUP2A-SEL-END.


    VUP2A-OR1.
*       PROCESS NON MATCHING MASTER RECORD
        IF VR-AGENT-CODE < OR-AGENT-CODE NEXT SENTENCE
```

326

```
                ELSE GO TO VUP2A-OR2.
    VUP2C.
            MOVE ZERO TO VR-LAST-MONTH-VALUE , VR-LAST-MONTH-NUMBER.
            MOVE VR-AGENT-CODE TO CR-AGENT-CODE.
            MOVE VR-LAST-MONTH-VALUE TO CR-LAST-MONTH-VALUE.
            MOVE VR-LAST-MONTH-NUMBER TO CR-LAST-MONTH-NUMBER.
            WRITE COMMISSION-RECORD.
            WRITE NEW-VALUE-RECORD FROM VALUE-RECORD.
            READ VALUE-FILE AT END
                MOVE HIGH-VALUES TO VR-AGENT-CODE.
            GO TO VUP2A-SEL-END.


    VUP2A-OR2.
*       PROCESS NON MATCHING ORDER RECORD/GROUP
*       OR-AGENT-CODE < VR-AGENT-CODE
    VUP2D-SEQ.
    VUP2H.
            MOVE OR-AGENT-CODE TO CURRENT-AGENT-CODE.


    VUP2I-ITER.
            IF OR-AGENT-CODE = CURRENT-AGENT-CODE
                NEXT SENTENCE ELSE GO TO VUP2I-ITER-END.
    VUP2K.
            ADD 1 TO TRANSACTION-COUNT.
            ADD 1 TO NON-MATCH-TRANSACTIONS.
            MOVE TRANSACTION-COUNT TO DL-RECORD-NUMBER.
            MOVE ORDER-RECORD TO DL-ORDER-RECORD.
            WRITE ERROR-RECORD FROM DETAIL-LINE
                AFTER ADVANCING 2 LINES.
            READ ORDERS-FILE AT END
                MOVE HIGH-VALUES TO OR-AGENT-CODE.
            GO TO VUP2I-ITER.
    VUP2I-ITER-END.


    VUP2D-SEQ-END.
    VUP2A-SEL-END.
            GO TO VUP10-ITER.
    VUP10-ITER-END.


    VUP1P.
*       PRODUCE COMMISSION RECORD FOR AREA OPERATOR
            MOVE CURRENT-AREA-CODE TO CR-AREA-CODE.
            MOVE "9999" TO CR-AGENT-NUMBER.
            MOVE AO-VALUE-OF-ORDERS TO CR-LAST-MONTH-VALUE.
            MOVE AO-NUMBER-OF-ORDERS TO CR-LAST-MONTH-NUMBER.
            WRITE COMMISSION-RECORD.
    VUP1K-SEQ-END.
            GO TO VUP1F-ITER.
    VUP1F-ITER-END.


    VUP1G-SEQ.
*       TERMINATE ERROR REPORT
    VUP1L.
```

```
      MOVE NON-MATCH-TRANSACTIONS TO TL-RECORD-COUNT.
      WRITE ERROR-RECORD FROM TOTAL-LINE
          AFTER ADVANCING 2 LINES.
  VUP1M.
      WRITE ERROR-RECORD FROM END-LINE
          AFTER ADVANCING 2 LINES.
  VUP1G-SEQ-END.
  VUP1C-SEQ-END.
  VUP1D.
      CLOSE VALUE-FILE , ORDERS-FILE , NEW-VALUE-FILE
          COMMISSION-FILE , ERROR-FILE.
      STOP RUN.
  VUP1A-SEQ-END.
```

Figure 13.10   Code for Value-of-Orders Update Program

13.5 Updating Sequentially Organised Files in Situ

13.5.1 Sequential Files on Directly Processable Media

When we update a sequentially organised file which is held on a directly processable media such as magnetic disk we have a choice in the method of physically processing the file. We can either produce a completely new physical version of the file in addition to the original version, as has been described in the previous sections, or we can carry out the updates in situ. This means that we simply read, amend and then write back records to their original places in the file. A new logical version of the file is produced but it occupies the same physical position as the original. The first approach, producing a completely new physical version of the file, has the advantage that the previous version of the file can be kept as a backup for security purposes. While with the second approach, i.e. updating in situ, it is necessary to make periodic copies of the file if we require backups. However, the second approach will place smaller demands on file storage and can lead to faster processing during the update process as those records which do not need amending do not need to be explicitly written back to the file.

13.5.2 OPEN I-O

To update a file in situ it must be opened in I-O mode.

Format

```
OPEN I-O filename ...
```

Example

```
OPEN I-O VALUE-FILE.
```

13.5.3 REWRITE Statement

To write records back to a file we use a REWRITE statement. The file must have been opened in I-O mode and the last operation on the file must have been a successful read.

Format

```
REWRITE record-name [FROM identifier]
```

The REWRITE statement operates in the same way as a write statement, except that it replaces in the file the existing version of the record last read with the version currently in the record area. Obviously, the record that is being rewritten must not be larger than that which was read as it has to occupy the same space within the file.

Example

```
REWRITE VALUE-RECORD.
```

13.5.4 Amendments to the Value-of-Orders Update Program

To amend the design of the Value-of-Orders Update Program to allow for updating in situ all that is required is to make some minor modifications to the function list. Functions 11 and 12 are deleted and 1, 2, 3 and 13 become:

1. Open Value-of-Orders master file for input and output.

2. Close Value-of-Orders master file.

3. Read record from Value-of-Orders master file
   at end set VR-AGENT-CODE = HIGH-VALUES

13. Write updated Value record back to Value-of-Orders master file.

The COBOL implementations of functions 1 and 13 are as given in the examples in the previous two subsections and those for 2 and 3 are simply the same as in the original program. Also, in the coded program, all the Environment and Data Division entries which relate to NEW-VALUE-FILE can be deleted. These entries are no longer needed as the VALUE-FILE is now used for input and output. You should note that in this program every master record must be read and rewritten since each is updated. However, in many update programs not every master record is amended (see for example the simpler Value-of-Orders Update Program detailed in section 12.5.1) and hence it would be unnecessary to rewrite such records. But remember they must still be read for us to be able to progress sequentially through the file.

13.6 Sequential Processing of Indexed Sequential Files

As was explained in chapter 4 Indexed Sequential file organisations are extremely popular as they support both direct and sequential record processing. It is very common to find that such files are handled directly when the hit rate is low but that bulk updates involving high hit rates are carried out sequentially. COBOL supports Indexed Sequential files via its INDEXED organisation. Such files are always organised in ascending order according to the values held in the records' primary key field. Also you should note that within a COBOL indexed file these primary key values must be unique i.e. each record must have a different key value.

13.6.1 Select Entry for SequentiallyAccessed Indexed Sequential Files

In addition to assigning the file and giving the organisation and access mode the field that contains the primary key value which uniquely identifies each record on the file must be specified.

Format (Indexed Files)

```
SELECT file-name ASSIGN TO implementor-name

ORGANIZATION IS INDEXED

ACCESS MODE IS SEQUENTIAL

RECORD KEY IS data-name.
```

The RECORD KEY clause names the data item, within each record on the file, that contains the primary key value by which the records are indexed and ordered.

Example
```
SELECT INDEXED-FILE ASSIGN TO "INDEX.DAT"
       ORGANIZATION IS INDEXED
       ACCESS MODE IS SEQUENTIAL
       RECORD KEY IS KEY-FIELD.
```

The item identified by data-name (KEY-FIELD in the above example) must be defined within the file's FD and must have an alphanumeric picture. Even if the key is composed totally of numerics the description which is referenced by data-name must be alphanumeric. Often, as in the example given in the following section, a group name can be used as these are always classed as alphanumeric.

The file access statements (READ, WRITE etc) which are allowed with sequential access mode depend on the way in which the file is opened (INPUT, OUTPUT or I-O). They support the creation of new files, the referencing of files and the updating of existing files in situ.

13.6.2 Creating Indexed Sequential Files Sequentially

An indexed sequential file can be created by opening the file for OUTPUT and then transferring the records to it in sequence using the following extended form of the WRITE statement.

Format (Indexed Files)

```
WRITE record-name [FROM-identifier]

     INVALID KEY imperative-statement
```

For a file in sequential access mode the imperative-statement(s) associated with the INVALID KEY phase will be executed if the key value of the record being written is not higher than all the keys presently on the file. Thus if records are being transferred from an input file to the indexed sequential file the records must already be sorted into ascending key value order.

The following program extract illustrates how the Value-of-Orders master file defined in section 13.2 may be recreated as an indexed sequential file. In this simple example any error encountered when writing a record will simply cause an error message to be displayed and processing will then continue.

```
                        :
                        :
        FILE-CONTROL.

            SELECT IN-FILE ASSIGN TO "VALUE.NEW".
            SELECT INDEXED-VALUE-FILE ASSIGN TO "VALUE.ISF"
                ORGANIZATION IS INDEXED
                ACCESS MODE IS SEQUENTIAL
                RECORD KEY IS VR-AGENT-CODE.

        DATA DIVISION.

        FILE SECTION.

        FD  IN-FILE.
            01  IN-RECORD                   PIC X(28).

        FD  INDEXED-VALUE-FILE.
            01  VALUE-RECORD.
                03  VR-AGENT-CODE.
                    05  VR-AREA-CODE         PIC X(2).
                    05  VR-AGENT-NUMBER      PIC 9(4).
                03  VR-TOTAL-VALUE-OF-ORDERS PIC 9(5)V99.
                03  VR-TOTAL-NUMBER-OF-ORDERS PIC 9(4).
                03  VR-LAST-MONTH-VALUE      PIC 9(4)V99.
                03  VR-LAST-MONTH-NUMBER     PIC 9(3).
                03  VR-COUNT-OF-MONTHS       PIC 99.

        WORKING-STORAGE SECTION.

            01  EOF-IN-FILE                  PIC 9.
            01  RECORD-COUNT                 PIC 9(3) COMP.
```

```
PROCEDURE DIVISION.

CIS1A-SEQ.
CIS1B.
     OPEN INPUT IN-FILE.
     OPEN OUTPUT INDEXED-VALUE-FILE.
     MOVE ZERO TO EOF-IN-FILE, RECORD-COUNT.
     READ IN-FILE AT END
          MOVE 1 TO EOF-IN-FILE.
CIS1C-ITER.
     IF EOF-IN-FILE = 0 NEXT SENTENCE
                    ELSE GO TO CIS1C-ITER-END.
CIS1E.
     ADD 1 TO RECORD-COUNT.
     WRITE VALUE-RECORD FROM IN-RECORD
          INVALID KEY
          DISPLAY "SEQUENCE ERROR ON RECORD ", RECORD-COUNT.
     READ IN-FILE AT END
          MOVE 1 TO EOF-IN-FILE.
     GO TO CIS1C-ITER.
CIS1C-ITER-END.
CIS1D.
     CLOSE IN-FILE, INDEXED-VALUE-FILE.
     STOP RUN.
CIS1A-SEQ-END.
```

An indexed sequential file which is very volatile (i.e. suffers many insertions and deletions of records) will have to be reorganised at regular intervals. This operation is needed to recover the space where deleted records resided and to also insert records, which have been placed in overflow areas, back into the main body of the file. To achieve this a program analogous to that given above can be used to sequentially read each record in turn and then write it to a new indexed sequential file. Often a utility program will be available on your system which will carry out this type of processing as well as file creation.

13.6.3 Referencing and Updating Indexed Sequential Files Sequentially

If an Indexed Sequential file is opened for INPUT records can be read from it sequentially in exactly the same manner as for a normal sequential file. If it is opened for I-O then the file can be updated in situ using READ and REWRITE statements in a similar manner to that detailed in section 13.5. The only difference is that the REWRITE statement can have the extended form:

<u>REWRITE</u> record-name [<u>FROM</u> identifier]

[<u>INVALID</u> KEY imperative-statement]

For a file in sequential access mode the imperative-statement(s) associated with the INVALID KEY phrase, if given, will be executed if the key of the record being written to the file is different from that which was last read i.e. if somehow between the READ and the REWRITE the record key has been corrupted. The process of updating an indexed sequential file in situ is illustrated by the following extracts of code which are taken from a program that updates the Value-of-Orders master file which is now defined to be indexed sequentially organised. The program has the same structure as that given in Figure 13.6 for the original version. The only addition to the specification is that if an error is detected on a rewrite statement then an error message is to be displayed and the process is to continue.

The File-Control and File-Section code now becomes:

```
FILE-CONTROL.
    SELECT VALUE-FILE ASSIGN TO "VALUE.ISF"
        ORGANIZATION IS INDEXED
        ACCESS MODE IS SEQUENTIAL
        RECORD KEY IS VR-AGENT-CODE.
    SELECT ORDERS-FILE ASSIGN TO "ORDERS.DAT"
        ORGANIZATION IS LINE SEQUENTIAL.
    SELECT COMMISSION-FILE ASSIGN TO "COMMISS.DAT"
        ORGANIZATION IS LINE SEQUENTIAL.
    SELECT ERROR-FILE ASSIGN TO "ERROR.REP".

        :
        :

FILE SECTION.

FD  VALUE-FILE.
    01  VALUE-RECORD.
        03  VR-AGENT-CODE.
            05  VR-AREA-CODE              PIC X(2).
            05  VR-AGENT-NUMBER           PIC 9(4).
        03  VR-TOTAL-VALUE-OF-ORDERS      PIC 9(5)V99.
        03  VR-TOTAL-NUMBER-OF-ORDERS     PIC 9(4).
        03  VR-LAST-MONTH-VALUE           PIC 9(4)V99.
```

```
        03   VR-LAST-MONTH-NUMBER              PIC 9(3).
        03   VR-COUNT-OF-MONTHS               PIC 99.

   FD  ORDERS-FILE.
       01  ORDER-RECORD.
           03  OR-AGENT-CODE.
               05  OR-AREA-CODE               PIC X(2).
               05  OR-AGENT-NUMBER            PIC 9(4).
           03  OR-CATALOGUE-REF               PIC X(6).
           03  OR-CATALOGUE-PRICE             PIC 9(3)V99.
           03  OR-NO-ORDERED                  PIC 9(2).
           03  OR-PAYMENT-TYPE                PIC X.

   FD  COMMISSION-FILE.
       01  COMMISSION-RECORD.
           03  CR-AGENT-CODE.
               05  CR-AREA-CODE               PIC X(2).
               05  CR-AGENT-NUMBER            PIC 9(4).
           03  CR-LAST-MONTH-VALUE            PIC 9(5)V99.
           03  CR-LAST-MONTH-NUMBER           PIC 9(4).

   FD  ERROR-FILE.
       01  ERROR-RECORD                       PIC X(50).
```

the files are opened as follows:

```
        OPEN I-O VALUE-FILE.
        OPEN INPUT ORDERS-FILE.
        OPEN OUTPUT COMMISSION-FILE , ERROR-FILE.
```

and the transfers back to the master file in paragraphs VUP2G and VUP2C become:

```
        REWRITE VALUE-RECORD
        INVALID KEY DISPLAY "REWRITE ERROR ON MASTER FILE"
        DISPLAY "AGENT CODE FOR REWRITE ", VR-AGENT-CODE.
```

Two additional file handling statements may also be used to process an Indexed Sequential file whose access mode is sequential and which has been opened for I-O. These are the START and DELETE statements. The former allows processing to start (or continue) from a particular logical position in the file and the latter causes records to be marked for deletion from the file. The DELETE statement operates as the RE-WRITE statement on the record last accessed from the file. Details of the format of these statements and their operation will be found in your COBOL Reference Manual.

TASKS - CHAPTER 13

1. Implement on your computer the Value-of-Orders Update Program as described in section 13.4. Set up a test Value-of-Orders master file and update it with a test Monthly Orders file - check the results. Generate new Monthly Orders files for the next two months and repeat the updates - check the results. Has the master file been correctly updated? Are commission records generated for both agents and area operators? Are the values on these records correct? Are errors being correctly reported? Test data files of about 10-20 records should prove to be sufficient for your testing but ensure you include examples of match and non match situations and that you check for either file terminating before the other.

2. Modify your update program as detailed in section 13.5 so that it carries out updates in situ. Repeat your test runs and check the results.

3. Implement and run a program that will read your current Value-of-Orders Master File and produce a copy which is indexed sequentially organised (see section 13.6.2). Check whether there is also a utility program on your system which will perform the same task. If there is such a program become familiar with its operation.

4. Modify your update program so that it now carries out updates in situ on your new indexed sequentially organised master file. Repeat your test runs and check the results. If you use the invalid key clause with the REWRITE statement check whether it is accepted by your compiler. Since it is an optional clause you may find that it is not.

APPENDIX A

ANS COBOL 74 RESERVED WORDS

ACCEPT	ACCESS	ADD
ADVANCING	AFTER	ALL
ALPHABETIC	ALSO	ALTER
ALTERNATE	AND	ARE
AREA	AREAS	ASCENDING
ASSIGN	AT	AUTHOR
BEFORE	BLANK	BLOCK
BOTTOM	BY	
CALL	CANCEL	CD
CF	CH	CHARACTER
CHARACTERS	CLOCK-UNITS	CLOSE
COBOL	CODE	CODE-SET
COLLATING	COLUMN	COMMA
COMMUNICATION	COMP	COMPUTATIONAL
COMPUTE	CONFIGURATION	CONTAINS
CONTROL	CONTROLS	COPY
CORR	CORRESPONDING	COUNT
CURRENCY		
DATA	DATE	DATE-COMPILED
DATE-WRITTEN	DAY	DE
DEBUG-CONTENTS	DEBUG-ITEM	DEBUG-LINE
DEBUG-NAME	DEBUG-SUB-1	DEBUG-SUB-2
DEBUG-SUB-3	DEBUGGING	DECIMAL-POINT
DECLARATIVES	DELETE	DELIMITED
DELIMITER	DEPENDING	DESCENDING
DESTINATION	DETAIL	DISABLE
DISPLAY	DIVIDE	DIVISION
DOWN	DUPLICATES	DYNAMIC
EGI	ELSE	EMI
ENABLE	END	END-OF-PAGE
ENTER	ENVIRONMENT	EOP
EQUAL	ERROR	ESI
EVERY	EXCEPTION	EXIT
EXTEND		

FD	FILE	FILE-CONTROL
FILLER	FINAL	FIRST
FOOTING	FOR	FROM
GENERATE	GIVING	GO
GREATER	GROUP	
HEADING	HIGH-VALUE	HIGH-VALUES
I-O	I-O-CONTROL	IDENTIFICATION
IF	IN	INDEX
INDEXED	INDICATE	INITIAL
INITIATE	INPUT	INPUT-OUTPUT
INSPECT	INSTALLATION	INTO
INVALID	IS	
JUST	JUSTIFIED	
KEY		
LABEL	LAST	LEADING
LEFT	LENGTH	LESS
LIMIT	LIMITS	LINAGE
LINAGE-COUNTER	LINE	LINE-COUNTER
LINES	LINKAGE	LOCK
LOW-VALUE	LOW-VALUES	
MEMORY	MERGE	MESSAGE
MODE	MODULES	MOVE
MULTIPLE	MULTIPLY	
NATIVE	NEGATIVE	NEXT
NO	NOT	NUMBER
NUMERIC		
OBJECT-COMPUTER	OCCURS	OF
OFF	OMITTED	ON
OPEN	OPTIONAL	OR
ORGANIZATION	OUTPUT	OVERFLOW
PAGE	PAGE-COUNTER	PERFORM
PF	PH	PIC
PICTURE	PLUS	POINTER
POSITION	POSITIVE	PRINTING
PROCEDURE	PROCEDURES	PROCEED
PROGRAM	PROGRAM-ID	
QUEUE	QUOTE	QUOTES

RANDOM	RD	READ
RECEIVE	RECORD	RECORDS
REDEFINES	REEL	REFERENCES
RELATIVE	RELEASE	REMAINDER
REMOVAL	RENAMES	REPLACING
REPORT	REPORTING	REPORTS
RERUN	RESERVE	RESET
RETURN	REVERSED	REWIND
REWRITE	RF	RH
RIGHT	ROUNDED	RUN
SAME	SD	SEARCH
SECTION	SECURITY	SEGMENT
SEGMENT-LIMIT	SELECT	SEND
SENTENCE	SEPARATE	SEQUENCE
SEQUENTIAL	SET	SIGN
SIZE	SORT	SORT-MERGE
SOURCE	SOURCE-COMPUTER	SPACE
SPACES	SPECIAL-NAMES	STANDARD
STANDARD-1	START	STATUS
STOP	STRING	SUB-QUEUE-1
SUB-QUEUE-2	SUB-QUEUE-3	SUBTRACT
SUM	SUPPRESS	SYMBOLIC
SYNC	SYNCHRONIZED	
TABLE	TALLYING	TAPE
TERMINAL	TERMINATE	TEXT
THAN	THROUGH	THRU
TIME	TIMES	TO
TOP	TRAILING	TYPE
UNIT	UNSTRING	UNTIL
UP	UPON	USAGE
USE	USING	
VALUE	VALUES	VARYING
WHEN	WITH	WORDS
WORKING-STORAGE	WRITE	
ZERO	ZEROES	ZEROS
+	−	*
/	**	>
<	=	

APPENDIX B

ANS COBOL 85 RESERVED WORDS

ACCEPT	ACCESS	ADD
ADVANCING	AFTER	ALL
ALPHABET	ALPHABETIC	ALPHABETIC-LOWER
ALPHABETIC-UPPER	ALPHANUMERIC	ALPHANUMERIC-EDITED
ALSO	ALTER	ALTERNATE
AND	ANY	ARE
AREA	AREAS	ASCENDING
ASSIGN	AT	AUTHOR
BEFORE	BINARY	BLANK
BLOCK	BOTTOM	BY
CALL	CANCEL	CD
CF	CH	CHARACTER
CHARACTERS	CLASS	CLOCK-UNITS
CLOSE	COBOL	CODE
CODE-SET	COLLATING	COLUMN
COMMA	COMMON	COMMUNICATION
COMP	COMPUTATIONAL	COMPUTE
CONFIGURATION	CONTAINS	CONTENT
CONTINUE	CONTROL	CONTROLS
CONVERTING	COPY	CORR
CORRESPONDING	COUNT	CURRENCY
DATA	DATE	DATE-COMPILED
DATE-WRITTEN	DAY	DAY-OF-WEEK
DE	DEBUG-CONTENTS	DEBUG-ITEM
DEBUG-LINE	DEBUG-NAME	DEBUG-SUB-1
DEBUG-SUB-2	DEBUG-SUB-3	DEBUGGING
DECIMAL-POINT	DECLARATIVES	DELETE
DELIMITED	DELIMITER	DEPENDING
DESCENDING	DESTINATION	DETAIL
DISABLE	DISPLAY	DIVIDE
DIVISION	DOWN	DUPLICATES
DYNAMIC		
EGI	ELSE	EMI
ENABLE	END	END-ADD

A5

END-CALL	END-COMPUTE	END-DELETE
END-DIVIDE	END-EVALUATE	END-IF
END-MULTIPLY	END-OF-PAGE	END-PERFORM
END-READ	END-RECEIVE	END-RETURN
END-REWRITE	END-SEARCH	END-START
END-STRING	END-SUBTRACT	END-UNSTRING
END-WRITE	ENTER	ENVIRONMENT
EOP	EQUAL	ERROR
ESI	EVALUATE	EVERY
EXCEPTION	EXIT	EXTEND
EXTERNAL		
FALSE	FD	FILE
FILE-CONTROL	FILLER	FINAL
FIRST	FOOTING	FOR
FROM		
GENERATE	GIVING	GLOBAL
GO	GREATER	GROUP
HEADING	HIGH-VALUE	HIGH-VALUES
I-O	I-O-CONTROL	IDENTIFICATION
IF	IN	INDEX
INDEXED	INDICATE	INITIAL
INITIALIZE	INITIATE	INPUT
INPUT-OUTPUT	INSPECT	INSTALLATION
INTO	INVALID	IS
JUST	JUSTIFIED	
KEY		
LABEL	LAST	LEADING
LEFT	LENGTH	LESS
LIMIT	LIMITS	LINAGE
LINAGE-COUNTER	LINE	LINE-COUNTER
LINES	LINKAGE	LOCK
LOW-VALUE	LOW-VALUES	
MEMORY	MERGE	MESSAGE
MODE	MODULES	MOVE
MULTIPLE	MULTIPLY	
NATIVE	NEGATIVE	NEXT
NO	NOT	NUMBER
NUMERIC	NUMERIC-EDITED	

OBJECT-COMPUTER	OCCURS	OF
OFF	OMITTED	ON
OPEN	OPTIONAL	OR
ORDER	ORGANIZATION	OTHER
OUTPUT	OVERFLOW	
PACKED-DECIMAL	PADDING	PAGE
PAGE-COUNTER	PERFORM	PF
PH	PIC	PICTURE
PLUS	POINTER	POSITION
POSITIVE	PRINTING	PROCEDURE
PROCEDURES	PROCEED	PROGRAM
PROGRAM-ID	PURGE	
QUEUE	QUOTE	QUOTES
RANDOM	RD	READ
RECEIVE	RECORD	RECORDS
REDEFINES	REEL	REFERENCE
REFERENCES	RELATIVE	RELEASE
REMAINDER	REMOVAL	RENAMES
REPLACE	REPLACING	REPORT
REPORTING	REPORTS	RERUN
RESERVE	RESET	RETURN
REVERSED	REWIND	REWRITE
RF	RH	RIGHT
ROUNDED	RUN	
SAME	SD	SEARCH
SECTION	SECURITY	SEGMENT
SEGMENT-LIMIT	SELECT	SEND
SENTENCE	SEPARATE	SEQUENCE
SEQUENTIAL	SET	SIGN
SIZE	SORT	SORT-MERGE
SOURCE	SOURCE-COMPUTER	SPACE
SPACES	SPECIAL-NAMES	STANDARD
STANDARD-1	STANDARD-2	START
STATUS	STOP	STRING
SUB-QUEUE-1	SUB-QUEUE-2	SUB-QUEUE-3
SUBTRACT	SUM	SUPPRESS
SYMBOLIC	SYNC	SYNCHRONIZED
TABLE	TALLYING	TAPE
TERMINAL	TERMINATE	TEST
TEXT	THAN	THEN
THROUGH	THRU	TIME
TIMES	TO	TOP
TRAILING	TRUE	TYPE

A7

```
UNIT               UNSTRING           UNTIL
UP                 UPON               USAGE
USE                USING

VALUE              VALUES             VARYING

WHEN               WITH               WORDS
WORKING-STORAGE    WRITE

ZERO               ZEROES             ZEROS

+                  -                  *
/                  **                 >
<                  =                  >=
<=
.PA
```

APPENDIX C

COBOL Statement Formats

These formats represent the statements covered in this text book. The formats for a particular COBOL implementation will be given in the COBOL Reference Manual for that implementation.

The conventions used within the formats given in this appendix are as follows:

(i)   Underlined, upper case words are used to indicate mandatory reserved words. They must be written in the position shown in the format.

(ii) Non-underlined, upper case words are used to indicate optional reserved words. Such words may be included, in the positions shown in the format, to improve the readability of the code but their omission would not affect the execution of the element being described.

(iii) Lower case words represent a word or an entry which must be specified by the programmer. The lower case word indicates the type of word or entry which the programmer has to supply.

(iv) Brackets, [and], indicate an optional feature which can be omitted.

(v)   Braces, { }, show that a choice has to be made. Where alternatives are given within the braces one of these must be selected. If there is only one entry within the braces, it will be found that the braces are followed by ellipsis indicating repetition (see below) in this case the programmer must choose how many times the entry is used, but the entry must be written at least once.

(vi) Ellipsis, ... , indicates that the item immediately preceeding the ellipsis may be repeated as many times as required. If the ellipsis follows a closing bracket or brace the whole entry in the brackets or braces is repeated. Otherwise the word immediately preceeding the ellipsis is repeated.

(vii) Full Stop, . , shows where a full stop is required.

```
IDENTIFICATION DIVISION.

PROGRAM-ID.   program-name.


ENVIRONMENT DIVISION.

CONFIGURATION SECTION.

SOURCE-COMPUTER.      computer-name-1.

OBJECT-COMPUTER.      computer-name-2.

[ SPECIAL-NAMES. [implementor-name IS mnemonic-name] ...

               [CURRENCY SIGN IS literal]

               [DECIMAL-POINT IS COMMA]. ]


[ INPUT-OUTPUT SECTION.

FILE-CONTROL.

    [select entry] ... ]
```

Format 1 (Sequential Files)

```
SELECT file-name ASSIGN TO implementor-name

[ ORGANIZATION IS SEQUENTIAL ]

[ ACCESS MODE IS SEQUENTIAL ].
```

Format 2 (Indexed Files)

```
SELECT file-name ASSIGN TO implementor-name

ORGANIZATION IS INDEXED

⎡                      ⎧ SEQUENTIAL ⎫ ⎤
⎢ ACCESS MODE IS       ⎨ RANDOM     ⎬ ⎥
⎣                      ⎩ DYNAMIC    ⎭ ⎦

RECORD KEY IS data-name

[ ALTERNATE RECORD KEY IS data-name-2

                    [WITH DUPLICATES ] ] ... .
```

Format 3 (Relative Files)

```
SELECT file-name ASSIGN TO implementor-name

ORGANIZATION IS RELATIVE

⎡                      ⎧ SEQUENTIAL ⎫ ⎤
⎢ ACCESS MODE IS       ⎨ RANDOM     ⎬ ⎥
⎣                      ⎩ DYNAMIC    ⎭ ⎦

[ RELATIVE KEY IS data-name].
```

Format 4 (Sort-Merge Files)

```
SELECT file-name ASSIGN TO implementor-name.
```

DATA DIVISION.

[FILE SECTION.

[{file description entry
sort-merge description entry}

   [record description entry] ...] ...]

[WORKING-STORAGE SECTION.

   [record description entry] ...]

[LINKAGE SECTION.

   [record description entry] ...]

File Description Entry

   FD   file-name

$$\text{LABEL} \begin{Bmatrix} \underline{RECORD} & IS \\ \underline{RECORDS} & ARE \end{Bmatrix} \begin{Bmatrix} \underline{STANDARD} \\ \underline{OMITTED} \end{Bmatrix}$$

$$[\underline{VALUE} \ \underline{OF} \ \{ \text{implementor-name IS} \begin{Bmatrix} \text{literal} \\ \text{data-name} \end{Bmatrix} \} \ ... \ ] \ .$$

Sort-Merge Description Entry

   SD filename.

Record Description Entry

   data-description-entry-1
   [data-description-entry-2] ...

Data Description Entry

Format 1

```
level-number ⎰ data-name-1 ⎱
             ⎱ FILLER      ⎰

   [ REDEFINES  data-name-2 ]

   [ ⎰ PICTURE ⎱ IS picture-string ]
     ⎱ PIC     ⎰

                ⎧ COMPUTATIONAL ⎫
   [[ USAGE IS] ⎨ COMP          ⎬ ]
                ⎩ DISPLAY       ⎭

   [[ SIGN IS] ⎰ LEADING  ⎱ [ SEPARATE CHARACTER] ]
               ⎱ TRAILING ⎰

   [ OCCURS integer-1

          ⎰ TIMES                                           ⎱
          ⎱ TO integer-2 TIMES DEPENDING ON data-name       ⎰

       [ [ ⎰ ASCENDING  ⎱ KEY IS data-name-1 ... ] ...
           ⎱ DESCENDING ⎰

          [ INDEXED BY index-name ... ]  ]   ]

   [ VALUE IS literal ].
```

Format 2

```
88  condition-name ⎰ VALUE IS  ⎱ literal-1
                   ⎱ VALUES ARE ⎰

                          ⎡ ⎰ THROUGH ⎱ literal-2 ⎤
                          ⎢ ⎱ THRU    ⎰           ⎥
          ⎡ literal-3 ⎡ ⎰ THROUGH ⎱ literal-4 ⎤ ⎤ ...  .
          ⎣           ⎣ ⎱ THRU    ⎰           ⎦ ⎦
```

A13

    PROCEDURE DIVISION [USING data-name ...].

Format 1

    {section-name SECTION.

    {paragraph-name.

        [sentence] ... } ... } ...

Format 2

    {paragraph-name.

        [sentence] ... } ...

Sentence

    {statement} ... .

    ACCEPT   identifier [FROM mnemonic-name]

    ACCEPT identifier FROM $\left\{ \begin{array}{l} \text{DATE} \\ \text{DAY} \\ \text{TIME} \end{array} \right\}$

    ADD $\left\{ \begin{array}{l} \text{identifier-1} \\ \text{numeric-literal-1} \end{array} \right\}$ ... TO {identifier-2 [ROUNDED]} ...

        [ON SIZE ERROR imperative-statement]

    ADD $\left\{ \begin{array}{l} \text{CORRESPONDING} \\ \text{CORR} \end{array} \right\}$ identifier-1 TO identifier-2

        [ROUNDED]   [ON SIZE ERROR imperative-statement]

    ADD $\left\{ \begin{array}{l} \text{identifier-1} \\ \text{numeric-literal-1} \end{array} \right\} \left\{ \begin{array}{l} \text{identifier-2} \\ \text{numeric-literal-2} \end{array} \right\}$ ...

        GIVING {identifier-3 [ROUNDED]} ...

        [ON SIZE ERROR imperative-statement]

A14

CALL $\begin{Bmatrix} \text{literal} \\ \text{identifier} \end{Bmatrix}$ [USING data-name ...]

CLOSE file-name ...

COMPUTE {identifier-1 [ROUNDED]} ...

= arithmetic expression.

[ON SIZE ERROR imperative-statement]

DELETE file-name RECORD

[INVALID KEY imperative-statement]

DISPLAY $\begin{Bmatrix} \text{identifier} \\ \text{literal} \end{Bmatrix}$ ... [UPON mnemonic-name]

DIVIDE $\begin{Bmatrix} \text{identifier-1} \\ \text{numeric-literal-1} \end{Bmatrix}$ INTO {identifier-2 [ROUNDED]} ...

[ON SIZE ERROR imperative-statement]

DIVIDE $\begin{Bmatrix} \text{identifier-1} \\ \text{numeric-literal-1} \end{Bmatrix}$ $\begin{Bmatrix} \text{INTO} \\ \text{BY} \end{Bmatrix}$ $\begin{Bmatrix} \text{identifier-2} \\ \text{numeric-literal-2} \end{Bmatrix}$

GIVING {identifier-3 [ROUNDED]} ...

[ON SIZE ERROR imperative-statement]

DIVIDE $\begin{Bmatrix} \text{identifier-1} \\ \text{numeric-literal-1} \end{Bmatrix}$ $\begin{Bmatrix} \text{INTO} \\ \text{BY} \end{Bmatrix}$ $\begin{Bmatrix} \text{identifier-2} \\ \text{numeric-literal-2} \end{Bmatrix}$

GIVING {identifier-3 [ROUNDED]} ...

REMAINDER identifier-4

[ON SIZE ERROR imperative-statement]

EXIT

A15

EXIT PROGRAM

GO TO procedure-name

GO TO procedure-name ... DEPENDING ON identifier

IF condition $\left\{ \begin{array}{l} \{\text{statement-1}\} \ ... \\ \underline{\text{NEXT}} \ \underline{\text{SENTENCE}} \end{array} \right\}$

$\left[\underline{\text{ELSE}} \left\{ \begin{array}{l} \{\text{statement-2}\} \ ... \\ \underline{\text{NEXT}} \ \underline{\text{SENTENCE}} \end{array} \right\} \right]$

INITIALIZE identifier ...

INSPECT identifier-1

TALLYING $\left\{ \text{identifier-2} \ \underline{\text{FOR}} \left\{ \left\{ \begin{array}{l} \underline{\text{ALL}} \\ \underline{\text{LEADING}} \\ \underline{\text{CHARACTERS}} \end{array} \right\} \left\{ \begin{array}{l} \text{identifier-3} \\ \text{literal-3} \end{array} \right\} \right\} \right.$

$\left. \left[\left\{ \begin{array}{l} \underline{\text{BEFORE}} \\ \underline{\text{AFTER}} \end{array} \right\} \text{INITIAL} \left\{ \begin{array}{l} \text{identifier-4} \\ \text{literal-4} \end{array} \right\} \right] \right\} ... \right\} \ ...$

INSPECT identifier-1

REPLACING

$\left\{ \left\{ \begin{array}{l} \underline{\text{ALL}} \\ \underline{\text{LEADING}} \\ \underline{\text{FIRST}} \end{array} \right\} \left\{ \left\{ \begin{array}{l} \text{identifier-5} \\ \text{literal-5} \end{array} \right\} \underline{\text{BY}} \left\{ \begin{array}{l} \text{identifier-6} \\ \text{literal-6} \end{array} \right\} [\ A \ ] \right\} ... \right\} ... \right.$

$\left. \underline{\text{CHARACTERS}} \ \underline{\text{BY}} \left\{ \begin{array}{l} \text{identifier-7} \\ \text{literal-7} \end{array} \right\} [\ A \ ] \right\}$

where A represents

$\left\{ \begin{array}{l} \underline{\text{BEFORE}} \\ \underline{\text{AFTER}} \end{array} \right\} \text{INITIAL} \left\{ \begin{array}{l} \text{identifier-4} \\ \text{literal-4} \end{array} \right\}$

A16

INSPECT identifier-1

TALLYING $\left\{ \text{identifier-2 } \underline{\text{FOR}} \left\{ \left\{ \begin{array}{l} \underline{\text{ALL}} \\ \underline{\text{LEADING}} \\ \underline{\text{CHARACTERS}} \end{array} \right\} \left\{ \begin{array}{l} \text{identifier-3} \\ \text{literal-3} \end{array} \right\} \right. \right.$

$\left. \left. \left[\left\{ \begin{array}{l} \underline{\text{BEFORE}} \\ \underline{\text{AFTER}} \end{array} \right\} \text{INITIAL} \left\{ \begin{array}{l} \text{identifier-4} \\ \text{literal-4} \end{array} \right\} \right] \right\} \dots \right\} \dots$

REPLACING

$\left\{ \left\{ \begin{array}{l} \underline{\text{ALL}} \\ \underline{\text{LEADING}} \\ \underline{\text{FIRST}} \end{array} \right\} \left\{ \left\{ \begin{array}{l} \text{identifier-5} \\ \text{literal-5} \end{array} \right\} \underline{\text{BY}} \left\{ \begin{array}{l} \text{identifier-6} \\ \text{literal-6} \end{array} \right\} [\text{ A }] \right\} \dots \right\} \dots \right.$

$\left. \underline{\text{CHARACTERS}} \underline{\text{BY}} \left\{ \begin{array}{l} \text{identifier-7} \\ \text{literal-7} \end{array} \right\} [\text{ A }] \right\}$

where A represents

$\left\{ \begin{array}{l} \underline{\text{BEFORE}} \\ \underline{\text{AFTER}} \end{array} \right\}$ INITIAL $\left\{ \begin{array}{l} \text{identifier-4} \\ \text{literal-4} \end{array} \right\}$

MERGE file-name-1

$\{$ ON $\left\{ \begin{array}{l} \underline{\text{ASCENDING}} \\ \underline{\text{DESCENDING}} \end{array} \right\}$ KEY data-name ... $\}$ ...

USING file-name-2 ...

$\left\{ \begin{array}{l} \underline{\text{GIVING}} \text{ file-name-3} \\ \underline{\text{OUTPUT}} \underline{\text{PROCEDURE}} \text{ IS section-name-1} \left[\left\{ \begin{array}{l} \underline{\text{THRU}} \\ \underline{\text{THROUGH}} \end{array} \right\} \text{section-name-2} \right] \end{array} \right\}$

MOVE $\left\{ \begin{array}{l} \text{identifer-1} \\ \text{literal} \end{array} \right\}$ TO identifier-2 ...

MOVE $\left\{ \begin{array}{l} \underline{\text{CORRESPONDING}} \\ \underline{\text{CORR}} \end{array} \right\}$ identifer-1 TO identifier-2

A17

MULTIPLY $\left\{\begin{array}{l}\text{identifier-1} \\ \text{numeric-literal-1}\end{array}\right\}$ BY {identifier-2 [ROUNDED]} ...

      [ON SIZE ERROR imperative-statement]

MULTIPLY $\left\{\begin{array}{l}\text{identifier-1} \\ \text{numeric-literal-1}\end{array}\right\}$ BY $\left\{\begin{array}{l}\text{identifier-2} \\ \text{numeric-literal-1}\end{array}\right\}$

    GIVING {identifier-3 [ROUNDED]} ...

      [ON SIZE ERROR imperative-statement]

OPEN $\left\{\begin{array}{l}\underline{\text{INPUT}} \ \text{file-name-1} \ ... \\ \underline{\text{OUTPUT}} \ \text{file-name-2} \ ... \\ \underline{\text{I-O}} \ \text{filename-3} \ ...\end{array}\right\}$ ...

PERFORM procedure-name-1

PERFORM procedure-name-1 $\left\{\begin{array}{l}\underline{\text{THROUGH}} \\ \underline{\text{THRU}}\end{array}\right\}$ procedure-name-2

PERFORM procedure-name-1 $\left[\begin{array}{l}\left\{\begin{array}{l}\underline{\text{THROUGH}} \\ \underline{\text{THRU}}\end{array}\right\} \text{procedure-name-2}\end{array}\right]$

        $\left\{\begin{array}{l}\text{identifier} \\ \text{literal}\end{array}\right\}$ TIMES

PERFORM procedure-name-1 $\left[\begin{array}{l}\left\{\begin{array}{l}\underline{\text{THROUGH}} \\ \underline{\text{THRU}}\end{array}\right\} \text{procedure-name-2}\end{array}\right]$

      UNTIL condition

A18

```
PERFORM procedure-name-1 ⎡ ⎧ THROUGH ⎫ procedure-name-2 ⎤
                         ⎢ ⎩ THRU    ⎭                   ⎥
                         ⎣                               ⎦

  VARYING ⎧ identifier-1 ⎫ FROM ⎧ identifier-2 ⎫
          ⎩ index-name-1 ⎭      ⎨ index-name-2 ⎬
                                ⎩ literal-2    ⎭

  BY ⎧ identifier-3 ⎫ UNTIL condition-1
     ⎩ literal-3    ⎭

  ⎡ AFTER ⎧ identifier-4 ⎫ FROM ⎧ identifier-5 ⎫
  ⎢       ⎩ index-name-4 ⎭      ⎨ index-name-5 ⎬
  ⎣                            ⎩ literal-5    ⎭

  BY ⎧ identifier-6 ⎫ UNTIL condition-2
     ⎩ literal-6    ⎭

  ⎡ AFTER ⎧ identifier-7 ⎫ FROM ⎧ identifier-8 ⎫
  ⎢       ⎩ index-name-7 ⎭      ⎨ index-name-8 ⎬
  ⎣                            ⎩ literal-8    ⎭

  BY ⎧ identifier-9 ⎫ UNTIL  condition-3 ⎤⎤
     ⎩ literal-9    ⎭                    ⎦⎦
```

Read Statement - Sequential Files

```
READ file-name RECORD  [ INTO identifier]
     AT END imperative-statement
```

Read Statements - Indexed Files

```
READ filename [ NEXT] RECORD  [ INTO identifier]
     AT END imperative-statement

READ file-name RECORD [ INTO identifier]

     [ KEY IS data-name]

     INVALID KEY imperative-statement
```

Read Statements - Relative Files

```
READ filename [ NEXT] RECORD  [ INTO identifier]
     AT END imperative-statement

READ filename RECORD [ INTO identifier]
     INVALID KEY imperative-statement
```

A19

```
RELEASE record-name [ FROM identifier]


RETURN file-name RECORD [ INTO identifier]
       AT END imperative statement


REWRITE record-name [ FROM identifier]

[ INVALID KEY imperative-statement]


SEARCH data-name

   [ VARYING { identifier } ]
             { index-name }

    [AT END imperative-statement-1]

    { WHEN condition { imperative-statement-2 } } ...
    {                { NEXT SENTENCE          } }


SEARCH ALL data-name

   [AT END imperative-statement-1]

   WHEN  test [ AND  test ] ... { imperative-statement-2 }
                                { NEXT SENTENCE          }
```

Data-name must identify a data item that has OCCURS, INDEXED and
KEY clauses in its definition and test must have the form

$$
\left\{
\begin{array}{l}
\text{identifier-1}
\left\{
\begin{array}{l}
\text{IS EQUAL TO} \\
\text{IS =}
\end{array}
\right\}
\left\{
\begin{array}{l}
\text{identifier-2} \\
\text{literal} \\
\text{arithmetic-expression}
\end{array}
\right\} \\
\text{condition-name condition}
\end{array}
\right\}
$$

```
   SET index-name-1 ... TO { identifier-1 }
                           { integer-1    }
                           { index-name-2 }


   SET index-name-3 ... { UP BY   } { identifier-3 }
                        { DOWN BY } { integer-2    }

   SET identifier ... TO index-name
```

A20

<u>SORT</u> file-name-1

    { ON $\left\{\begin{array}{l}\underline{\text{ASCENDING}}\\\underline{\text{DESCENDING}}\end{array}\right\}$ KEY data-name ... } ...

$$\left\{\begin{array}{l}\underline{\text{USING}} \text{ file-name-2...}\\[1em]\underline{\text{INPUT}}\ \underline{\text{PROCEDURE}}\ \text{IS section-name-1}\left[\left\{\begin{array}{l}\underline{\text{THRU}}\\\underline{\text{THROUGH}}\end{array}\right\}\text{section-name-2}\right]\end{array}\right\}$$

$$\left\{\begin{array}{l}\underline{\text{GIVING}} \text{ file-name-3}\\[1em]\underline{\text{OUTPUT}}\ \underline{\text{PROCEDURE}}\ \text{IS section-name-3}\left[\left\{\begin{array}{l}\underline{\text{THRU}}\\\underline{\text{THROUGH}}\end{array}\right\}\text{section-name-3}\right]\end{array}\right\}$$

$$\underline{\text{START}} \text{ file-name} \left[\underline{\text{KEY}}\left\{\begin{array}{l}\text{IS}\quad\underline{\text{EQUAL}}\ \text{TO}\\\text{IS}\quad =\\\text{IS}\quad\underline{\text{GREATER}}\ \text{THAN}\\\text{IS}\quad >\\\text{IS}\quad\underline{\text{NOT}}\ \underline{\text{LESS}}\ \text{THAN}\\\text{IS}\quad\underline{\text{NOT}}\ <\end{array}\right\}\text{data-name}\right]$$

    <u>INVALID</u> KEY imperative-statement

<u>STOP</u> <u>RUN</u>

<u>STRING</u> { $\left\{\begin{array}{l}\text{identifier-1}\\\text{literal-1}\end{array}\right\}$ ... <u>DELIMITED</u> BY $\left\{\begin{array}{l}\text{identifier-2}\\\text{literal-2}\\\text{SIZE}\end{array}\right\}$ } ...

    <u>INTO</u>   identifier-3

    [WITH <u>POINTER</u> identifier-4]

    [ON <u>OVERFLOW</u> imperative-statement]

<u>SUBTRACT</u> $\left\{\begin{array}{l}\text{identifier-1}\\\text{numeric-literal-1}\end{array}\right\}$ ...

        <u>FROM</u> {identifier-2 [<u>ROUNDED</u>]} ...

          [ON <u>SIZE</u> <u>ERROR</u> imperative-statement]

<u>SUBTRACT</u> $\left\{\begin{array}{l}\underline{\text{CORRESPONDING}}\\\underline{\text{CORR}}\end{array}\right\}$ identifier-1 <u>FROM</u>   identifier-2

        [<u>ROUNDED</u>]   [ON <u>SIZE</u> <u>ERROR</u> imperative-statement]

A21

```
SUBTRACT  ⎰identifier-1        ⎱ ... FROM  ⎰identifier-2       ⎱
          ⎱numeric-literal-1   ⎰           ⎱numeric-literal-2  ⎰

          GIVING {identifier-3 [ ROUNDED]} ...

          [ON SIZE ERROR imperative-statement]


UNSTRING  identifier-1

    [ DELIMITED BY [ ALL]  ⎰identifier-2⎱
                           ⎱literal-2   ⎰

        [ OR [ ALL]  ⎰identifier-3⎱ ] ... ]
                     ⎱literal-3   ⎰

    INTO  ⎰identifier-4 [ DELIMITER IN identifier-5]
          ⎱
                        [ COUNT IN identifier-6] ⎱ ...

    [WITH POINTER identifier-7] [ TALLYING IN identifier-8]

    [ON OVERFLOW imperative-statement]
```

Write Statement - Sequential Non-Print Files

```
WRITE record-name [ FROM identifier]
```

Write Statement - Sequential Print Files

```
WRITE record-name [ FROM identifier-1]

  ⎡ ⎰BEFORE⎱  ADVANCING                      ⎤
  ⎢ ⎱AFTER ⎰                                 ⎥
  ⎢                                          ⎥
  ⎢ ⎰identifier-2⎱  ⎡ LINE  ⎤      ⎫         ⎥
  ⎢ ⎱integer     ⎰  ⎣ LINES ⎦      ⎬         ⎥
  ⎢                               ⎭         ⎥
  ⎢         PAGE                             ⎥
  ⎣         mneumonic-name                   ⎦
```

Write Statement - Indexed Files

```
WRITE record-name [ FROM identifier]

    INVALID KEY imperative-statement
```

A22

Write Statement - Relative Files

```
WRITE record-name [ FROM identifier]

INVALID KEY imperative-statement
```

Conditions

Relation Condition

```
                       ⎧ GREATER THAN ⎫
                       ⎪ LESS THAN    ⎪
operand-1 IS [ NOT]    ⎨ EQUAL TO     ⎬    operand-2
                       ⎪ >            ⎪
                       ⎪ <            ⎪
                       ⎩ =            ⎭
```

Class Condition

```
                       ⎧ NUMERIC    ⎫
identifier IS [ NOT]   ⎨ ALPHABETIC ⎬
                       ⎩            ⎭
```

Condition-Name Conditions

```
[ NOT] condition-name
```

Sign Condition

```
⎧ identifier           ⎫              ⎧ POSITIVE ⎫
⎨ arithmetic-expression ⎬  IS  [ NOT] ⎨ ZERO     ⎬
⎩                      ⎭              ⎩ NEGATIVE ⎭
```

Compound Conditions

```
                        ⎧ AND ⎫
simple-condition-1  {   ⎨ OR  ⎬  simple-condition-2}  ...
                        ⎩     ⎭
```

REFERENCES

1. G. B. Bleazard, Program Design Methods, NCC Publications, Manchester 1976.
2. R. Fairley, Software Engineering Concepts, McGraw-Hill Inc., New York, 1985.
3. G. Longworth, Standards in Programming, NCC Publications, Manchester, 1981.
4. E. Yourdon, Techniques of Program Structure and Design, Prentice Hall, Englewood Cliffs, 1975.
5. O.-J. Dahl, E. W. Dijkstra and C. A. R. Hoare, Structured Programming, Academic Press, London, 1972.
6. C. Bohm and G. Jacopini, Flow Diagrams, Turing Machines and Languages with Only Two Formation Rules, Communication of the ACM, Vol. 9, No. 5, May 1966, pp366-371. Reprinted in reference 7.
7. E. N. Yourdon (Ed.), Classics in Software Engineering, Yourdon Press, New York, 1979.
8. E. N. Yourdon (Ed.), Writings of the Revolution, Yourdon Press, New York, 1982.
9. M. A. Jackson, Principles of Program Design, Academic Press, London, 1975.
10. Central Computer and Telecommunications Agency, Central Government Mandatory Standard No. 18, Parts 1-6, Central Computer and Telecommunications Agency, London, 1983.
11. T. W. Pratt, Programming Languages : Design and Implementation, Prentice-Hall, Englewood Cliffs, 1984.
12. C. Ghezzi and M. Jazayeri, Programming Language Concepts, John Wiley and Sons Inc., New York, 1982.
13. Reference No. 10 Part 2.
14. E. W. Dykstra, Go To Statement Considered Harmful, Communications of the A.C.M., Vol. 11, No. 3, March 1968, pp147-148. Reprinted in reference 7.
15. Datapro Research Corporation, British User Ratings of Computer Systems, Datapro Services S.A., Buchillon, Switzerland, published annually.

16. J. A. N. Lee (Ed), COBOL : 25th Anniversary, Annals of the History of Computing, Volume 7, No. 4, October 1965, pp286-352. (Contains 8 papers on the development of COBOL).

17. J. E. Sammet, The Early History of COBOL. In R. L. Wexelblat (Ed) History of Programming Languages, Academic Press, New York, 1981.

18. J. M. Triance, COBOL. In I. D. Hill and B. L. Meek (Eds), Programming Language Standardisation, Ellis Horwood, Chichester, 1982.

19. P. R. Brown, The Impact of COBOL 85, Computer Bulletin, June 1985, pp28-31 and 35.

20. P. Brown and V. Gwillum, User Guide to COBOL 85, NCC Publications, Manchester, 1985.

21. National Computing Centre, COBOL 85 Reference Summary, NCC Publications, Manchester, 1986.

22. M. Cunningham, File Structure and Design, Chartwell-Bratt, Bromley, 1985.

23. O. Hanson, Design of Computer Data Files, Pitman, London, 1982.

24. B. Lee, Introducing Systems Analysis and Design, Volume 2, Chapters 10 and 11, NCC Publications, Manchester, 1979.

25. National Computing Centre, Data Processing Documentation Standards, NCC Publications, Manchester, 1977.

26. National Computing Centre, Student Notes on NCC Data Processing Documentation Standards, NCC Publications, Manchester, 1978.

27. International Computers Ltd., COBOL Techniques, Technical Publication 6739, International Computers Limited, London, 1982.

28. School of Computer Studies and Mathematics, Documentation Standards, Sunderland Polytechnic, Sunderland, 1984.

29. National Computing Centre, COBOL Reference Summary, NCC Publications, Manchester, 1981.

30. Reference No. 9, pages 70-74.

INDEX

Computing Books from Chartwell-Bratt

GENERAL COMPUTING BOOKS

Compiler Physiology for Beginners, M Farmer, 279pp, ISBN 0-86238-064-2
Dictionary of Computer and Information Technology, D Lynch, 225 pages,
ISBN 0-86238-128-2
File Structure and Design, M Cunningham, 211pp, ISBN 0-86238-065-0
Information Technology Dictionary of Acronyms and Abbreviations, D
Lynch, 270pp, ISBN 0-86238-153-3
The IBM Personal Computer with BASIC and PC-DOS, B Kynning, 320pp,
ISBN 0-86238-080-4

PROGRAMMING LANGUAGES

An Intro to LISP, P Smith, 130pp, ISBN 0-86238-187-8
An Intro to OCCAM 2 Programming, Bowler, *et al,* 109pp,
ISBN 0-86238-137-1
Cobol for Mainframe and Micro: 2nd Ed, D Watson, 177pp,
ISBN 0-86238-211-4
Comparative Languages: 2nd Ed, J R Malone, 125pp, ISBN 0-86238-123-1
Fortran 77 for Non-Scientists, P Adman, 109pp, ISBN 0-86238-074-X
Fortran 77 Solutions to Non-Scientific Problems, P Adman, 150pp,
ISBN 0-86238-087-1
Fortran Lectures at Oxford, F Pettit, 135pp, ISBN 0-86238-122-3
LISP: From Foundations to Applications, G Doukidis *et al,* 228pp,
ISBN 0-86238-191-6
Prolog versus You, A-L Johansson, 296pp, ISBN 0-86238-174-6
Simula Begin, G M Birtwistle *et al,* 391pp, ISBN 0-86238-009-X
The Intensive C Course, M Farmer, 167pp, ISBN 0-86238-114-2
The Intensive Pascal Course, M Farmer, 111pp, ISBN 0-86238-063-4

ASSEMBLY LANGUAGE PROGRAMMING

Coding the 68000, N Hellawell, 214pp, ISBN 0-86238-180-0
Computer Organisation and Assembly Language Programming, L
Ohlsson & P Stenstrom, 128pp, ISBN 0-86238-129-0
What is machine code and what can you do with it? N Hellawell, 104pp,
ISBN 0-86238-132-0

PROGRAMMING TECHNIQUES

**Discrete-events simulations models in PASCAL/MT+ on a
microcomputer,** L P Jennergren, 135pp, ISBN 0-86238-053-7
Information and Coding, J A Llewellyn, 152pp, ISBN 0-86238-099-5
JSP - A Practical Method of Program Design: 2nd Ed, L Ingevaldsson,
204pp, ISBN 0-86238-107-X
JSD - Method for System Development, L Ingevaldsson, 248pp,
ISBN 0-86238-103-7

Programming for Beginners: the structured way, D Bell & P Scott, 178pp, ISBN 0-86238-130-4

Software Engineering for Students, M Coleman & S Pratt, 195pp, ISBN 0-86238-115-0

Software Taming with Dimensional Design, M Coleman & S Pratt, 164pp, ISBN 0-86238-142-8

Systems Programming with JSP, B Sanden, 186pp, ISBN 0-86238-054-5

MATHEMATICS AND COMPUTING

Fourier Transforms in Action, F Pettit, 133pp, ISBN 0-86238-088-X

Generalised Coordinates, L G Chambers, 90pp, ISBN 0-86238-079-0

Linear Programming: A Computational Approach: 2nd Ed, K K Lau, 150pp, ISBN 0-86238-182-7

Statistics and Operations Research, I Schagen, 300pp, ISBN 0-86238-077-4

Teaching of Modern Engineering Mathematics, L Rade (ed), 225pp, ISBN 0-86238-173-8

Teaching of Statistics in the Computer Age, L Rade (ed), 248pp, ISBN 0-86238-090-1

The Essentials of Numerical Computation, M Bartholomew-Biggs, 241pp, ISBN 0-86238-029-4

DATABASES AND MODELLING

Computer Systems Modelling & Development, D Cornwell, 200pp, ISBN 0-86238-220-3

Database Analysis and Design, H Robinson, 378pp, ISBN 0-86238-018-9

Databases and Database Systems, E Oxborrow, 256pp, ISBN 0-86238-091-X

Data Bases and Data Models, B Sundgren, 134pp, ISBN 0-86238-031-6

Text Retrieval and Document Databases, J Ashford/P Willett, 125pp, ISBN 0-86238-204-1

Information Modelling, J Bubenko (ed), 687pp, ISBN 0-86238-006-5

UNIX

An Intro to the Unix Operating System, C Duffy, 152p, ISBN 0-86238-143-6

Operating Systems through Unix, G Emery, 96pp, ISBN 0-86238-086-3

SYSTEMS ANALYSIS AND DEVELOPMENT

Systems Analysis and Development: 3rd Ed, P Layzell & P Loucopoulos, 272pp, ISBN 0-86238-215-7

SYSTEMS DESIGN

Computer Systems: Where Hardware meets Software, C Machin, 200pp, ISBN 0-86238-075-8

Distributed Applications and Online Dialogues: a design method for application systems, A Rasmussen, 271pp, ISBN 0-86238-105-3

Microcomputer Systems: hardware and software, J Tierney, 168pp, ISBN 0-86238-218-1

SSADM Techniques, M Leijk, *et al,* 350pp, ISBN 0-86238-224-6

HARDWARE

Computers from First Principles, M Brown, 128pp, ISBN 0-86238-027-8
Fundamentals of Microprocessor Systems, P Witting, 525pp,
ISBN 0-86238-030-8

ELECTRICAL & ELECTRONIC ENGINEERING

Analogue and Digital Signal Processing and Coding, P M Grant, *et al,*
450pp, ISBN 0-86238-206-8
Handbook of Electronics, J de Sousa Pires, 800pp, ISBN 0-86238-061-8

NETWORKS

Communication Network Protocols: 2nd Ed, B Marsden, 345pp,
ISBN 0-86238-106-1
Computer Networks: Fundamentals and Practice, M D Bacon *et al,* 109pp,
ISBN 0-86238-028-6
Datacommunication: Data Networks, Protocols and Design, L Ewald &
E Westman, 343pp, ISBN 0-86238-092-8
Data Networks 1, Ericsson & Televerket, ISBN 0-86238-193-2
Telecommunications: Telephone Networks 1, Ericsson & Televerket, 147pp,
ISBN 0-86238-093-6
Telecommunications: Telephone Networks 2, Ericsson & Televerket, 176pp,
ISBN 0-86238-113-4

GRAPHICS

An Introductory Course in Computer Graphics, R Kingslake, 146pp,
ISBN 0-86238-073-1
Techniques of Interactive Computer Graphics, A Boyd, 242pp,
ISBN 0-86238-024-3
Two-dimensional Computer Graphics, S Laflin, 85pp, ISBN 0-86238-127-4

APPLICATIONS

Computers in Health and Fitness, J Abas, 106pp, ISBN 0-86238-155-X
Developing Expert Systems, G Doukidis, E Whitley, ISBN 0-86238-196-7
Expert Systems Introduced, D Daly, 180pp, ISBN 0-86238-185-1
Handbook of Finite Element Software, J Mackerle & B Fredriksson, approx
1000pp, ISBN 0-86238-135-5
Inside Data Processing: computers and their effective use in business,
A deWatteville, 150pp, ISBN 0-86238-181-9
Proceedings of the Third Scandinavian Conference on Image Analysis,
P Johansen & P Becker (eds) 426pp, ISBN 0-86238-039-1
Programmable Control Systems, G Johannesson, 136pp, ISBN 0-86238-046-4
Project Skills Handbook, S Rogerson, approx 100pp, ISBN 0-86238-146-0
Risk and Reliability Appraisal on Microcomputers, G Singh, + G Kiangi,

142pp, ISBN 0-86238-159-2
Statistics with Lotus 1-2-3, M Lee & J Soper, 207pp, ISBN 0-86238-131-2

HCI

Human/Computer Interaction: from voltage to knowledge, J Kirakowski, 250pp, ISBN 0-86238-179-7
Information Ergonomics, T Ivegard, 228pp, ISBN 0-86238-032-4
Computer Display Designer's Handbook, E Wagner, approx 300pp, ISBN 0-86238-171-1

INFORMATION AND SOCIETY

Access to Government Records: International Perspectives and Trends, T Riley, 112pp, ISBN 0-86238-119-3
CAL/CBT - the great debate, D Marshall, 300pp, ISBN 0-86238-144-4
Economic and Trade-Related Aspects of Transborder Dataflow, R Wellington-Brown, 93pp, ISBN 0-86238-110-X
Information Technology and a New International Order, J Becker, 141pp, ISBN 0-86238-043-X
People or Computers: 3 ways of looking at information systems, M Nurminen, 1218pp, ISBN 0-86238-184-3
Transnational Data Flows in the Information Age, C Hamelink, 115pp, ISBN 0-86238-042-1

MATHS & SCIENCE HANDBOOKS

Alpha Maths Handbook, L Rade, 199pp, ISBN 0-86238-036-7
Beta Maths Handbook, L Rade, 425pp, ISBN 0-86238-140-1
Nuclear Analytical Chemistry, D Brune *et al,* 557pp, ISBN 0-86238-047-2
Physics Handbook, C Nordling & J Osterman, 430pp, ISBN 0-86238-037-5
The V-Belt Handbook, H Palmgren, 287pp, ISBN 0-86238-111-8

Chartwell-Bratt specialise in excellent books at affordable prices.

For further details contact your local bookshop, or ring Chartwell-Bratt direct on **01-467 1956**(Access/Visa welcome.)

Ring or write for our *free* catalogue.

Chartwell-Bratt (Publishing & Training) Ltd, Old Orchard, Bickley Road, Bromley, Kent, BR1 2NE, United Kingdom.
Tel 01-467 1956, Fax 01-467 1754, Telecom Gold 84:KJM001, Telex 9312100451(CB)